Paper Crafts & STAMP IT!
MAGAZINE®

treasury of tips & tricks

Presenting over 650 unique projects and ideas from *Paper Crafts* magazine and its *Stamp It!* special editions, with expert advice on lots of stamping and paper crafting techniques for beginner and advanced levels.

A TREASURY OF FAVORITES PRODUCED EXCLUSIVELY FOR LEISURE ARTS

Editorial

Editor-in-Chief Stacy Croninger
Managing Editor Vee Kelsey-McKee
Special Issues Editor Jennafer Martin
Sr. Special Issues Editor Marissa Dorny
Creative Editor Catherine Edvalson
Assistant Editors Natalie Jackman, Melinda Frewin
Contributing Editor Valerie Pingree
Copy Editor Erin Poulson
Editorial Assistant Brenda Peterson
Web Site Manager Emily Johnson
Web Site Editor April Tarter

Design

Art Director Stace Hasegawa
Designer Junko Barker
Photographer Skylar Nielsen, Mark Newton, Matthew Reier

Events

Events Director Paula Kraemer
Events Coordinator David Ray

Advertising

Publisher Tony Golden
Advertising Manager Becky Lowder
Advertising Assistant Kristi Larsen
Advertising Sales U.S. & International Donna Summers, 815/389-3289
Advertising Sales AZ, CO, NM, UT Barbara Tanner, 801/942-6080

Operations

VP, Group Publisher Dave O'Neil
Circulation Marketing Director Kristy LoRusso
Promotions Director Dana Smith
Finance Director Brad Bushlack
Director, Sales and Marketing Tara Green
Senior Production Director Terry Boyer
Production Manager Gary Whitehead

Subscriptions/address change/product customer service

Subscriptions and customer service PO Box 420235, Palm Coast, FL 32142
Phone 800/727-2387
E-mail papercrafts@palmcoastd.com
Back issues and special issues www.PaperCraftsMag.com or 800/727-2387

Offices

Editorial Paper Crafts Magazine, 14850 Pony Express Road, Bluffdale, UT 84065-4801
Phone 801/984-2070
Fax 801/984-2080
E-mail editor@PaperCraftsMag.com
Web site www.PaperCraftsMag.com

Projects listed as courtesy of were used with permission from Stampin' Up! and Anna Griffin.

Treasury of Tips & Tricks
Softcover ISBN 1-57486-572-2
Library of Congress Control Number 2005932028
Printed in the United States of America.

Published by Leisure Arts, Inc., 5701 Ranch Drive, Little Rock, Arkansas 72223-9633. 501-868-8800. *www.leisurearts.com*.

Technique heaven

The list of things I love could take up pages, but there are a few items that top the list:

chocolate

dogs

friends

learning new things

(This is in no particular order, by the way). I'm not the only one that lists learning as one of their favorites. Our readers have told us they like trying new techniques and unique ways to paper craft.

Part of learning is easily locating the information, which is even easier with this book. We've compiled some of our favorite techniques and projects from past *Paper Crafts* magazines and special issues such as *Stamp It!*. So, now you have a wonderful reference that is organized by technique and shows creative ways to apply what you learn.

So, if learning is one of your favorite things, this book will give you hours of inspiration and enjoyment.

Have fun paper crafting!

StacyC

Note: Because these projects are from past issues, some products may not be available. Luckily, the Internet provides a wonderful way to search for similar items so you can still create a beautiful project using these inspiring techniques. So, if you can't find a product, use your creativity to adapt the project or find a replacement.

116

141

164

246

176

A Guided Tour

Often when you go to a museum or exhibit, you have the option to browse on your own or rent a guided tour. The advantage of the guided tour is additional information that you may not discover while browsing on your own.

In this book, you have the same options: start browsing on your own or take the guided tour. The nice part is you can choose either option at any time. The guided tour will always be here and you can browse whenever the desire strikes.

Let the tour begin!

STAMPING

Stamping is a versatile tool that can add variety and depth to your projects. You can change a project's look by stamping with a different color or fill in the stamped image with a variety of techniques, such as watercolor, chalk, or multi-color stamping. You can create your own backgrounds or patterned paper by stamping a pattern. And best of all, you can stamp on almost any surface, including paper, fabric, glass, metal, or walls.

Stamps come in all sizes, shapes, and designs. They can be rubber-mounted, acrylic, or foam. Need a quote? Quote and alphabet stamps can be found in abundance in a variety of styles.

Once you've selected the stamp, you'll need to choose the color medium. There are several types of inks, as well as paints you can use. The surface you are stamping on often determines the ink type you'll use, for example, fabric inks or paint for fabric.

ADDITIONAL TIPS:

● Regardless of the ink type you use, save yourself some time in clean-up by keeping your cleaning supplies close by while stamping. Whether you use a scrubber or wet wipes, if your cleaning tools are within easy reach, you can quickly clean the ink from your stamp after you use it.

● Water coloring is one of my favorite color techniques. I love the soft look. I like to use watercolor pencils. They are easy to use and portable. All you need is a set of watercolor pencils, several watercolor brushes of various sizes, and a cup of water.

■ Sometimes I like the pattern I stamp to play a major role in the project, and at other times I want it to hold a supporting role. To create a subtle background, I stamp with a watermark or embossing ink to create a tone-on-tone effect. The image is apparent but not overpowering.

EMBOSSING

Embossing involves raising or lowering items on your project. Most embossing uses the raised impression, but don't overlook the creative depressed side of your embossing. Embossing is typically divided into two groups: dry and heat.

Dry embossing uses a template or object, a stylus, and paper. The template or object is traced to create an impression that can be used either raised or depressed. Dry embossed items can be chalked, sanded, painted, inked, and more to accent or add depth. Templates can be purchased in a variety of designs or created from things you have around the house.

Heat embossing uses ink, powders, a heat tool, a stamp, and the project's surface. The ink should be a slow-drying ink, such as an embossing or watermark ink, so you have time to apply the powder before the ink dries. Embossing powders come in fine to ultra thick in a variety of colors. The stamped image often determines the best type of powder to use. For example, for a detailed image you should use either fine or regular embossing powders to achieve a clear result. After stamping and applying the embossing powder, apply heat to allow the powder to melt with the ink.

For extra fun, try embossing your favorite adhesive, such as glue dots or adhesive tabs. Apply your adhesive in a pattern or design, sprinkle on your embossing powder and heat set. Also, make a hit on your next card by mixing in a scent such as orange (from a sugar-free drink mix) or cinnamon.

ADDITIONAL TIPS:

- Decorate a glass votive candle holder by stamping an image, applying embossing powder, and heat setting it. Be careful not to get your heat tool too close to the glass or let the glass get too hot-it may crack.

- For a quick background, purchase pre-embossed paper and apply ink to the paper with a make-up sponge. I love doing this with leaf patterns for fall. The effect is very colorful. It reminds me of the piles of leaves we had in front of our house growing up.

- Make your own dry embossing template using your favorite punches. You can either punch out the shape to create a design, or take the punched item and adhere it to another paper to create a raised template. This technique not only saves you money but allows you to create a template to match the occasion.

CREATIVE TECHNIQUES

Stamping involves basic techniques and a lot of creativity. Whether you are creating a resist with heat embossed images or stamping on other surfaces, the results are different each time.

We've shown you some fun projects where bleach is used instead of ink. This method removes the color from the paper and produces a different result each time, based on the amount of bleach used and the dye in the paper. Ink lifting removes the ink from the project. Instead of adding ink to the stamp, you use it to remove ink from the paper. It creates a similar effect to bleach stamping.

Stamping on clay and dominoes allows you to create your own accents, jewelry, and much more. Clay creates a dimensional stamped image. Dominoes provide a smooth surface on which to stamp. Make sure to use inks that are made for this surface or the ink will not adhere.

For an extra challenge, try making your own stamps. You can use basic materials like foam or sponges or invest in rubber and other stamp products. Making your own stamps allows you to express your creativity and create the perfect image for your project.

ADDITIONAL TIPS:

● When stamping with bleach, use a piece of felt as your stamp pad. Felt provides a smooth, solid surface than paper towels, and will more evenly coat the stamp with bleach.

● Another ink lifting technique is stamp kissing. You'll need two stamps for this technique. Apply ink to one stamp and then touch an uninked stamp to the inked stamp, then stamp your image. The uninked stamp removes the ink from the inked stamp to create a unique image. You can also ink both stamps and then the second stamp's image is transferred to the first stamp when they kiss. This technique works best with solid stamps rather than line art stamps and produces a layered stamped look.

ADDING TEXTURE

Texture can be added to projects in a variety of ways, including tearing, crumpling, dimensional glaze, and glitter. Texture adds depth to your project and can make the difference between blah and wow!

Look for fun projects that showcase crumpling, tearing, dimensional glaze, liquid appliqué, glitter, layering paper, and using mesh.

ADDITIONAL TIPS:

- Try mixing multiple types of texture to create a collage-type effect.

- Use mesh to create a paper finish by painting over the mesh and then removing it. The paint creates a pattern that you can see and feel.

STITCHING

Whether you stitch by hand or with a machine, stitching adds a handmade touch to any project. You can use standard embroidery stitches or simple back-stitching to highlight a portion of a project or create a fun border.

If you are like me and sewing is the last thing you want to do, look for stickers and rub-ons that mimic stitching. It's a quick and easy way to get the hand-stitched look without the work!

ADDITIONAL TIPS:

- Stitch a shape on your paper craft using a template as your guide. For example, if you want to stitch a star, grab a template with a star and then use a paper piercer and poke holes every 1/4" along star's edge. Remove the template and use the holes to stitch a star.

- When stitching text, lightly pencil in the text on the item to stitch. When finished stitching, erase any visible writing marks.

ACCENTS

There are so many accents available to purchase or make yourself. Accents can be the focal point of your project or add the finishing touch. Some accents double as ways to adhere items to your project, such as eyelets and brads. Other accents have been around for years and are popping up in new ways, such as shrink plastic.

You'll find ideas for using ribbon, pre-made accents, eyelets, brads, tags, and more. I love the creative uses these designers have for standard things-who would have thought to create a musical note with two eyelets? Let your imagination go wild after looking at these fun ways to add accents to your creations.

ADDITIONAL TIPS:

- Use ribbon to create a background. This is a great way to use ribbon scraps. Decide on the pattern and then adhere the ribbon. Mix and match colors, patterns, and widths to add variety.

- If you don't have a brad color to match your project, use a mini-glue dot and apply embossing powder to the glue dot. Heat set and you'll have an instant brad.

PAPER FINISHES AND AGING

Earlier we looked at using stamps to create backgrounds. Here we show you how to create patterns and designs using finishes. Most of these ideas use products you have around the house as a means of applying color to your paper, like, shaving cream. The techniques are simple and the results unique each time.

Aging is another way to add patterns or designs to paper and other mediums, such as ribbon. You can age with ink, dyes, paint, sandpaper, and more. Aging can be dark or light depending on the project. You'll often hear aging referred to as distressing or sanding, but regardless of how you modify your project, it will take on new qualities.

Decoupage and collage often go hand-in-hand. Decoupage has been around for years and is often used to adhere one item to another, such as paper to metal. It can be used to create layers on a project, for collage purposes. Collage is a free-form layering of items related to each other. It allows you to create a unique background or display similar items. Both decoupage and collage remind me of vintage or heritage items, but they can be used for any era and on any project. Let your creativity loose and see what you come up with!

ADDITIONAL TIPS:

● For a softer look when aging with ink, use a make-up sponge or your fingertip to apply the ink. The sponge absorbs most of the ink and applies a lighter amount to your project.

● When working with paper finishes, to make the most of the product you are using, plan to make several sheets of paper at one time. For example, if you are doing shaving cream marbling, you can do three or four sheets from one batch.

PATTERNED AND SPECIALTY PAPERS

Paper manufacturers spend a lot of time creating papers that coordinate with each other, which can help us by taking the guesswork out of what looks good together. The right combination of patterned papers can create a fun or elegant project that requires little else in the way of embellishments.

Vellum and transparencies can be used to add softness or layering to a project. They are perfect for printing your sentiment or quote on with your printer. Vellum can be found in a variety of colors and textures.

ADDITIONAL TIPS:

- For a quick card, use double-sided paper. Make the card base from one side and accents or matting from the other side. The colors and patterns are coordinated so they'll always match perfectly.

- When printing out images or text on transparencies, make sure you have the correct transparency type for your printer (laser or inkjet). For inkjet printers, select reverse print in your software application so you can print on the rough side of the transparency where the ink will adhere better.

ALTERED PROJECTS

When I think of altered projects, I think of altered books. In reality, many projects are altered, such as composition books, coin holders, or trays. Some altered projects start as blank items, such as spiral-bound books created specifically for altering. Others served a purpose before they were altered, such as composition books. Regardless of how it started, an altered project takes on a life of it's own. It can have hidden pockets, windows, include pictures and journaling, use aging techniques or unique binding.

ADDITIONAL TIPS:

- Look for interesting packaging when you go to the grocery store. I pick up mint tins at the check-out and then cover them (when empty) with paper or metal tape to create a clever gift wrap or mini-book container.

  - Children's board books are fun to alter and provide a thick surface to work on. Also, they usually have fewer pages than a normal book so they are not as overwhelming to learn with.

DESIGN CHALLENGE

Everyone likes a challenge now and then and that's exactly what we've done here. We've asked several designers to look at things in a new way. Whether they took an existing idea and adapted it to another theme or created a cool gift wrap from an every day item, their ideas may get you thinking about how you can modify projects you love for new uses.

ADDITIONAL TIP:

- Hold your own design challenge. Pull out a favorite project and list all the ways you can modify it-color, sentiment, accents, or occasion. Save those notes for future reference or create one of the ideas while it is fresh in your mind.

Stamping Basics

Stamping involves an image, color, and surface. Whether you create your own stamp or buy them, stamping provides versatility and variety in your paper-crafting projects.

INK TYPES

TYPES OF INK

Here's a rundown of the basic types of ink pads and their uses, plus tips for selecting the perfect ink type for your needs.

DYE INK

This type of ink dries quickly on all types of paper, and most dye inks are great for children as they are non-toxic and washable. With the exception of archival dye ink pads (perfect for scrapbooking), some dye inks are not permanent and will fade over time. Use dye ink with detailed stamps or for stamping on glossy paper or vellum. Don't use dye ink for embossing, as it dries too quickly, and don't use non-permanent dye ink with markers and watercolors, as it may smear.

PIGMENT INK

Pigment ink is thicker than dye ink, and it's slow-drying (great for embossing). Pigment ink colors are vivid and fade-resistant, and many are made specially for stamping on surfaces like glass, wood, or fabric. Use pigment ink for embossing and for richer color. Most pigment inks won't dry on glossy paper or vellum unless you emboss them.

PERMANENT INK

This ink is opaque and quick-drying, and it works great on slick surfaces like plastic. It's also great for home décor stamping, including surfaces like walls, furniture, or glass. Permanent ink will stain clothing and is not available in as many colors as other inks.

EMBOSSING INK

Specifically designed for embossing, this ink is often lightly-colored and very slow drying. Embossing ink is available in ink pads and ink pens. Although not as versatile as other types of ink, this ink is the most ideal for embossing.

BRUSH MARKERS

Apply the ink of the brush marker directly on the parts of a broad surface stamp. Press the stamp to the paper as you would in the basic technique. Marker ink may dry quickly on the stamp, so remoisten the ink before you stamp by huffing (exhaling) on the stamp. If the marker ink beads up on the stamp, clean the stamp, then rub the surface with fine sandpaper to remove any residue that may have built up.

BRUSH MARKERS

BRAYERS

This technique creates rainbow, faded, or multicolored images. Apply different colors of ink to a rubber or foam roller either from ink pads or markers, and then roll the brayer onto the stamp. Apply the inked brayer directly onto paper for back-grounds.

BRAYERS

WATERCOLORS

Using watercolors adds a nice, soft touch to stamped images. Stamp your design with archival or waterproof ink, or heat emboss it to keep the ink from smearing. Color the outer edge of the stamped image with watercolor pencils, markers, or crayons, and then blend the color toward the center with a wet paintbrush or blender pen. Here's how:

WATERCOLORS

INK PADS

Stamp the image with a water-based dye ink pad, and then lightly stroke the outline with the paintbrush to add the color to the rest of the image.

MARKERS

Apply color to the surface of the stamp with the brush markers, and then stamp the image. Pull color from the outside to the center of the image with the paintbrush. Or, stamp the image and then color it with brush markers.

PENCILS AND CHALK

Color a stamped image with chalk or colored pencils, and then use the paintbrush to intensify and blend the colors. Just wipe the blender pen on scrap paper between colors.

MASKING

Create an uncluttered layered design by masking the stamped images as you layer them. Masking will create dimension by giving the illusion of stamped images appearing behind other stamped images. Here's how to create this look:

❶ Stamp the image you want to appear in the foreground. Stamp the identical image on scrap paper and cut it out with fine-tip scissors.

❷ Place the cut-out image over the original stamped image using repositionable adhesive. Stamp another design over the mask, and then remove the mask to reveal the layered images.

Color Me Beautiful

Infuse your stamped projects with a splash of color.

When I bought my first house, I painted every wall white. Not from some urban desire for minimalism, but from a complete lack of trust in my ability to use color. The powerful effects of color in our everyday lives are undeniable, and color has that same strong impact on our stamped projects. When I stamp an image, I'm reminded of that first naked house, in need of a confident and creative eye for color. So let's take the mystery out of adding color to stamped images. From vivid violets to subtle siennas, we'll look at just a few methods of using color to make simply gorgeous artwork.

WATERCOLORS

Watercolors are very easy to use—they make almost anything look good, and with watercolors, it's easy to fix any mistakes you make. To begin, color the outer edge of your stamped image with watercolors, and then blend the color toward the center with a wet paintbrush or blender pen. For a delicate effect, first paint onto a scrap of watercolor paper, then lift the color from there and use it to color your stamped image. You can easily mix the colors on the scrap paper, too.

Everyone Smiles

For a beautiful handmade background, use watercolor paper and blend two or three of your favorite colors.

Designer: Allison Strine

SUPPLIES

Sticker: Everyone Smiles, *Wordsworth*

Other: black ink (for stamp), watercolor paper, blue and purple watercolor paints, purple and white cardstock, paintbrush, water, palette, adhesive, scissors

INSTRUCTIONS

❶ Wet paintbrush and rub into light blue paint.

❷ Paint onto scrap of watercolor paper; lift color from scrap paper and color one section of background paper.

❸ Repeat with violet and color other section of background.

❹ Blend two colors together with smooth strokes and water.

❺ When dry, add sticker. Mat with purple, then white cardstock.

Travel

Look outdoors for inspiration. Natural colors—those borrowed from the earth, sea, and sky—convey a feeling of earthy simplicity and comfort.

SUPPLIES

Globe rubber stamp: *Above the Mark*

Alphabet rubber stamps: Davinci, *Hampton Art Stamps*

Ink: Ms. Green, ColorBox, *Clearsnap*

Travel collage paper: *Karen Foster Design*

Other: gold and copper pens, black ink, black embossing powder, watercolor paper, olive green and brown watercolor paints, brown cardstock, paintbrush, water, palette, postcard charm, embossing heat tool, adhesive, scissors

INSTRUCTIONS

1 Stamp globe on watercolor paper with green ink.

2 Load paintbrush with water and small amount of olive green paint; apply over entire design, mixing with brown paint where desired. Let dry.

3 Add more paint as desired.

4 Trim closely; mat with patterned paper. Mount on brown cardstock.

5 Stamp letters on watercolor paper with black ink; heat emboss.

6 Color sections of letters with pens. Trim closely; mount on globe.

7 Add charm.

Brush Markers

Color your stamped images fabulously with brush markers. Since they're water based, these brushes remain wet longer. You can color a big stamp surface and then stamp the image. When coloring an already stamped image, apply light pressure to control the amount of color flow and use a blending pen to soften and blend colors. Store flexible-tip brush markers horizontally to keep the pigments evenly distributed.

Birthday Tags

Keep your design balanced by using colors at the same intensity (the amount of pure color).

SUPPLIES

Rubber stamp: present, *Denami Design*

Ink: Coal Black, Ancient Page, *Clearsnap*

Brush markers: ZIG Color Brush Twin, *EK Success*

Assorted fibers, beads, glitter glue: *Magic Scraps*

Alphabet tiles: Primary Tiles, *Creative Imaginations*

Other: clear embossing powder, white tags, orange and green patterned paper, white cardstock, pop-up dots, embossing heat tool, adhesive, scissors

INSTRUCTIONS

1 Stamp present on white cardstock with black; heat emboss.

2 Color presents with soft-colored markers.

3 Add light coat of glitter glue; trim and let dry.

4 Color tags with markers; blend.

5 Mount presents on tags with pop-up dots.

6 Adhere letters and beads to tags.

7 Mat tags with patterned paper; add fibers.

Love Beauty

Enhance the impact of a color on a stamped image by repeating that color in a cardstock mat. Here, subtle shades of red in the leaves are complemented by the mat.

SUPPLIES

Rubber stamps: leaves, *Stampin' Up!*

Ink: Coal Black, Ancient Page, *Clearsnap*

Copper leafing pen: *Krylon*

Mini frame: *Nunn Design*

Other: black embossing powder; watercolor paper; olive green, brown, orange, and red watercolor paints; red and kraft cardstock; skeletonized leaf; word charms; paintbrush; water; palette; embossing heat tool; adhesive; scissors

INSTRUCTIONS

❶ Stamp leaves on watercolor paper with black ink; heat emboss.

❷ Apply small amount of water over each design.

❸ Load paintbrush with water and small amount of olive green paint. Apply over entire design, mixing with brown, red, and orange where desired. Let dry.

❹ Cut out leaves as desired and line edges with pen; mount on kraft cardstock. Adhere to the red cardstock.

❺ Line skeletonized leaf with pen. Adhere leaf to frame; adhere frame to kraft cardstock.

❻ Attach word charms to leaf.

Party!

Choose colors that communicate the right emotion for the accent or page. Convey excitement with a jumble of many colors that share the same lightness/darkness or value.

SUPPLIES

Rubber stamp: Time2Fly, *Uptown Design*

Ink: Coal Black, Ancient Page, *Clearsnap*

Brush markers: ZIG Color Brush Twin, *EK Success*

Party! sticker: Chalk Talk, *Creative Imaginations*

Other: clear embossing powder, white and light green cardstock, pink patterned paper, pop-up dots, embossing heat tool, adhesive, scissors

INSTRUCTIONS

❶ Stamp collage pieces on white cardstock with black; heat emboss.

❷ Color stamped squares with soft-colored markers.

❸ Adhere sticker sentiment to white cardstock; mount on stamped image with pop-up dots.

❹ Mat with light green cardstock.

❺ Mount on pink patterned paper; adhere to light green cardstock.

1 Corinthians 1:4

Designer: Linda Beeson

SUPPLIES

Rubber stamps:
(Start Stampin' Leaves set)
Hero Arts

(I Always Thank God)
PrintWorks

Pigment ink: black, ColorBox, *Clearsnap*

Dye ink: Creole Spice, Kaleidacolor, *Tsukineko*

Clear embossing powder: *Stamp La Jolla*

Cardstock: purple, *Bazzill Basics Paper*

Other: scissors, brayer, white cardstock, adhesive, embossing heat tool, foam tape

Finished size: 5" square

INSTRUCTIONS

❶ Make purple card.

❷ Ink brayer with Creole Spice and roll onto white cardstock.

❸ Cut into 3" square, then into four squares. Adhere square to card.

❹ Stamp sentiment with black on white cardstock; emboss.

❺ Tear bottom of sentiment block. Mat with scrap of brayer-colored paper; tear bottom and adhere to card with foam tape.

❻ Stamp leaf on scrap of brayer-colored paper with black; emboss.

❼ Cut out leaf; adhere to card with foam tape.

One

Designer: Nichole Heady

SUPPLIES

Rubber stamps: (Classic Alphabet set, Lovely Leaves set) *Stampin' Up!*

Dye ink: Pumpkin Patch, Spectrum Pad, *Stampin' Up!*

Cardstock: Ultrasmooth White, *Stampin' Up!*

Fonts: Corel (Schindler Small Caps, Vivaldi) *WordPerfect*

Other: computer with printer, paper trimmer, bone folder

Finished size: 4¼" x 5½"

INSTRUCTIONS

❶ Print sentiment on Ultrasmooth White cardstock. *Note: Omit second "one" in quote.*

❷ Cut to size; fold.

❸ Stamp leaf with Spectrum pad.

❹ Stamp "one" within sentiment. *Note: Use different shade for each letter.*

The Wonder of Watercolor

Adding color to your projects can be simple—and stunning!

The beauty of stamping is that in moments you can add an image to any project. Adding color to the image is quick and easy as well, whether you work with brushes or blender pens. And the choice of color scheme is completely yours!

To prepare to watercolor, stamp the image with archival or waterproof ink or heat emboss it to keep the ink from smearing. Next, color the outer edge of the stamped image with watercolor pencils, markers, chalks, or inks; then blend the color toward the center with a wet paintbrush or a blender pen. We've created some fun projects to help you learn more about these techniques. So dive in, and put some color in your life!

Flower Cube

Designer: Alice Golden

SUPPLIES

Plain white memo cube

Flower stamp: Garden Flowers sketch, *Hero Arts*

Coal ink: Ancient Page, *Clearsnap*

Watercolor pencils: *Derwent*

Blender pen: *Dove Brushes*

Purple gingham ribbon: *Impress Rubber Stamps*

Repositionable paper: Post-It Notes, *3M*

Others: black fine-tip marker, rubber bands

Finished size: 3½" cube

Coloring with Pencils or Chalk

Prepare a palette by coloring stripes of watercolor pencils or chalks on a paper plate or other surface. Dip a blender pen into the colors as you need them, using the pen to add, intensify, and blend the colors (see "Blender Pen Tips" before you begin).

STAMP MASKED IMAGE

1. Wrap rubber bands around cube to keep it in place, and stamp first image in center of one side of cube. *Note: Don't stamp images on side where adhesive holds papers together.*

2. To create mask of flowers, stamp them on repositionable paper.

3. Cut out image. This mask will be used to create a dimentional effect when stamping.

4. Position mask over flowers on memo cube. Stamp flowers on each side of masked image, overlapping slightly. Repeat this step on two other sides of cube. To fill in space along bottom, draw grass blades with a black marker.

COLOR IMAGE

5. To color image, pick up colors on a blender pen. Blend colors to create soft, realistic hues and variations.

6. Add shading with watercolor pencils. Tie finished cube with ribbon.

MATCHING GIFT CARD

This memo cube makes a great gift to set by the phone at home or office. Create a matching gift card by stamping the flower image on cardstock, watercoloring the bouquet, tying it up with a ribbon, and adhering it to a card. This ties the whole gift together beautifully!

BLENDER PEN TIPS

- Before changing colors, wipe the blender pen clean on scrap paper.
- Be careful not to pick up too much color. If you do, simply wipe the blender tip on scrap paper.
- For a realistic blended look, layer color on top of color.
- Start with lighter colors, then gradually add darker colors.
- Limit the number of colors. Generally, three basic colors differing in intensity and value will give life and interest to any stamped image.
- Blender pens do not work on glossy or clay-coated paper or cardstock.

Coloring With Ink

To color using stamping ink, put a drop or two on the lid of the inkpad and apply it with a blender pen as Emily did in this card. As an alternative, you can stamp the image with a water-based dye ink, then lightly stroke the outline with the blender pen to spread the outline color through the rest of the image.

A Line-Up of Flowers

Designer: Emily Call, courtesy of Stampin' Up!

SUPPLIES

All supplies from Stampin' Up!

Cardstock: Confetti White, Kraft, Orchid Opulence

Natural hemp

Rubber stamps: "Love" from All-Year Cheer I set; flowers in bottles from Simply Sweet set

Ink pad refill bottles: Brilliant Blue, Forest Foliage, More Mustard, Orchid Opulence, Real Red

Blender pen

Finished size: 4¼" x 5½"

INSTRUCTIONS

1 Stamp image on white cardstock.

2 To prepare a palette, place a few drops of ink on lid of inkpad or paper plate.

3 Watercolor image with blender pen (see "Blender Pen Tips: on p. 19). You can create shadows. . .

. . . or highlight details. Mat with orchid cardstock and tie hemp around ends.

4 Make card base from Kraft cardstock. Mount flower piece on cardbase. Stamp "Love" on card.

Julie Chacra says that with Stampin' Up! ink pads, all you have to do is press the top lid down firmly so it touches the raised felt pad. You'll end up with a smudge of ink on the lid. Then, just take a small damp- ened paintbrush, gather up the smudge of ink, and immediately apply the color to your stamped image. It's that simple. If you're using a regular ink pad with a hard, inflexible lid, all you have to do is smudge the ink pad lightly on a small styrofoam or plastic plate (or any old non-porous surface). Then, gather up the ink with a dampened brush to color. To help with this, she keeps a water bottle close by, and uses it to put a tiny drop of water next to the smudge of ink. She touches the brush to the water, then the ink.

Ornament Christmas Wishes

Designer: Kriss Cramer

SUPPLIES

Rubber stamps: *Hero Arts* (Merry Christmas Ornaments, Merry Christmas and Happy New Year)

Pigment ink: *Stampin' Up!* (Basic Black); Encore!, *Tsukineko* (Ultimate Metallic Silver)

Other: cardstock (plum, white, silver metallic), watercolor pencils, adhesive, blender pen, scissors, sil- ver glitter glue, stipple brush

Finished size: 5½" x 4¼"

❶ Make card from plum cardstock. Stipple with Ultimate Metallic Silver.

❷ Stamp Merry Christmas Ornaments with Basic Black on white cardstock. Color with watercolor pencils; blend. Accent stamped image with silver glitter glue.

❸ Mat stamped image with silver metallic; adhere to card front.

❹ Stamp Merry Christmas and Happy New Year with Ultimate Metallic Silver inside card.

Water Color Tips & Tricks

Learn the how-tos for painting with watercolors and get our reader's best tips for cleaning your rubber stamps.

Painting With Watercolors

Did you ever want to be an artist but couldn't make it past the paint-by-number projects? Now you can create miniature works of art with the help of your stamping supplies and a paint-brush. With these simple techniques you'll be painting in no time—and the recipients of your masterpieces will be soon raving about their friend the talented artist.

Friendship Greeting

Designer: Lori Bergmann

SUPPLIES

Rubber stamps: (Friends Block) *Stampendous!*

Specialty paper: (140 lb. watercolor) *Strathmore Artist Papers*

Patterned paper: (Spring Plaid) *Scrapbook Wizard*

Cardstock: (yellow, white)

Adhesive: (glue stick)

Color medium: (watercolor markers) ColorBrush Twin, *EK Success*

Tools: (medium-tip paintbrush) BrusH2O Watercolor, *EK Success*; scissors, fine-mist spray bottle

Finished size: 6¼" x 5"

INSTRUCTIONS

❶ Make card from white cardstock.

❷ Cut Spring Plaid paper to fit card front; adhere.

❸ Color Friends Block with watercolor markers; lightly mist and stamp on watercolor paper.

❹ Pull color to center of hearts and flowers with wet paintbrush; let dry.

❺ Mat with yellow cardstock; adhere to card front.

DESIGNER TIPS

Be sure the spray bottle is on the finest mist possible for best results.

Hold the spray bottle about two feet from the stamp to reduce excess water and prevent colors from running together.

Touch up washed-out or missing parts of the stamped image with watercolor markers after the image dries.

Bonus Idea

For a watercolor look with defined lines, stamp the image with watermark ink and emboss with black. Then color the image using a paintbrush and ink pads or try using Ranger Industries' Perfect Pearls pigment inks. Ranger Industries, 800/244-2211, *www.rangerink.com.*

Asian Landscape

Designer: Lori Bergmann

SUPPLIES

Rubber stamps: (Landscape Scroll) *Duncan*

Pigment ink: (Onyx Black) VersaFine, *Tsukineko*

Cardstock: (black)

Patterned paper: (Asian Collage) *DMD, Inc.*

Specialty paper: (140 lb. watercolor) *Strathmore Artist Papers*

Paint: (Antique Gold) Rub n' Buff, *American Art Clay Co.*

Color medium: (watercolors) Aquarelle Fine Watercolour Tubes, *Pebeo*

Accents:
  (Asian charm) *American Traditional Designs*
  (bamboo strip) *Global Solutions*
  (gold tassel) *Arnold Grummer*
  jump ring

Adhesive

Tools: (medium-tip paintbrush) BrusH2O Watercolor, *EK Success;* scissors, fine-mist spray bottle

Other: wedge sponges

Finished size: 3½" x 6"

INSTRUCTIONS

❶ Stamp Landscape Scroll on watercolor paper with Onyx Black.

❷ Mist stamped image with water; apply watercolors to image with paintbrush, let dry, and cut out.

❸ Mount stamped image on Asian Collage paper; cut out.

❹ Mat with black cardstock.

❺ Wrap Gold tassel around each end of bamboo strip; adhere strip to top of black cardstock.

❻ Apply Antique Gold to charm; attach charm to tassel with jump ring.

Happy Mother's Day

Design: Suzanne Iabelle-Tracy

SUPPLIES

Rubber stamps:
  (daisy, swirl) *Magenta Rubber Stamps*
  tulip

Watercolor crayons, *Lyra Aquacolor*

Ink pads:
  Graphite Black, Brilliance, *Tsukineko*
  Lagoon Blue, VersaColor, *Tsukineko*

Clear embossing powder

Watercolor paper

8½" x 11" cardstock:
  Pumpkin
  Rust
  Turquoise

Adhesive pop-up dots

Miscellaneous items: paintbrush, scissors, double-sided tape, ruler

INSTRUCTIONS

❶ Stamp two daisies and two tulips on the watercolor paper with Graphite Black ink. Heat emboss the flowers with clear embossing powder.

❷ Color in the flowers with the watercolor crayons and blend with a wet paintbrush.

❸ Cut out the flowers and mount them on a piece of pumpkin cardstock with adhesive pop-up dots.

❹ Trim the pumpkin cardstock to 4¾" x 1¾" and mat it with rust cardstock.

❺ Trim the turquoise cardstock to 6¼" x 3" and stamp swirls on it with Lagoon Blue ink. Mat it with pumpkin cardstock.

❻ Print "HAPPY MOTHER'S DAY" on rust cardstock using your favorite font (the designer used Bradley's Hand, Microsoft) or your own handwriting. Trim the cardstock to 7¼" x 9", and then fold it in half lengthwise so the wording is at the bottom front of the card.

❼ Adhere the matted blocks together (see photo).

Health & Peace Postcard

Designer: Susan Neal

SUPPLIES

Rubber stamps:
  (Health & Peace) *Wordsworth*
  (Daisy) *Inkadinkado*
  (Postcard) *River City Rubber Works*

Chalk ink: Ocean Blue, ColorBox, *Clearsnap*

Watercolor crayons: (blue, yellow) *Lyra*

Other: white glossy cardstock, scissors, spray bottle

Finished size: 3½" x 5"

INSTRUCTIONS

① Make white glossy postcard.

② Stamp Health & Peace with Ocean Blue on glossy side; let dry.

③ Color daisy stamp with watercolor crayons; mist with water and stamp on card. Repeat two times. *Note: Stamp partial images for unique design.*

④ Ink edges with Ocean Blue.

⑤ Stamp Postcard with Ocean Blue on back of card.

⑥ Repeat step 3, stamping flower in opposite corners; let dry.

Chalking

Chalk provides soft color when shading, aging, or tinting. A variety of applicators, such as brushes, make-up applicators, sponges, your fingertip, and swabs change the look and effect chalk has on your project.

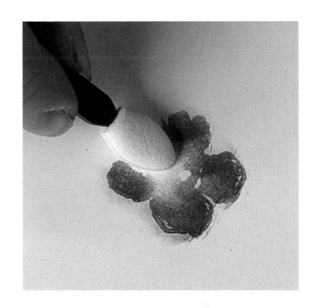

Balloons

Designer: Kathleen Paneitz

SUPPLIES

Rubber stamp: Balloon, *Hero Arts*

Pigment ink:
(red, yellow, green) VersaColor, *Tsukineko*

(orange) *Stampabilities*

Embossing powder: Holographic, *Ranger Industries*

Cardstock: 2 Tone, *Paper Adventures* (red)

Chalk: (red, orange, yellow, green) *Craft-T Products*

⅛" hole punch: *McGill*

Other: cream cardstock, ribbon, scissors, adhesive, embossing heat tool

Finished size: 4½" square

INSTRUCTIONS

1 Make red card.

2 Stamp Balloon with orange, yellow, green, and red on cream cardstock; emboss.

3 Tear edges of stamped cardstock. Chalk balloons and edges with corresponding colors; adhere to card.

4 Punch two holes on fold; thread ribbon through holes and tie bow.

Easter Blessings

Designer: Jenny Grothe

SUPPLIES

Rubber stamps: *Close To My Heart* (Little Things Matter set, Easter Blessings to You sentiment)

Watermark ink: VersaMark, *Tsukineko*

Dye ink: Clover Meadow, *Close To My Heart*

Cardstock:
(white) *Provo Craft*
(Sky Blue) Double Dipped, *Making Memories*

Patterned paper: Popsicle Stripe, *Doodlebug Design*

Chalk: *Craft-T Products* (pink, yellow, orange, blue)

Other: raffia, adhesive, adhesive dots, scissors, cotton swab or make-up applicator, hole punch

Finished size: 6" square

INSTRUCTIONS

1. Make Sky Blue card.

2. Stamp stems with Clover Meadow on white cardstock. Stamp flowers with watermark ink and apply chalk. *Note: Stamped image will appear darker.*

3. Tear top edge, mat with Popsicle Stripe strip and cut to fit front of card.

4. Tear top of Popsicle Stripe; adhere to card front.

5. Stamp sentiment with Clover Meadow; apply yellow chalk. Trim around sentiment, punch holes and string raffia.

6. Adhere sentiment to card with adhesive dots, wrap raffia around card front, and adhere ends.

Eggs

Designer: Nichol Magouirk

SUPPLIES

Rubber stamps:
(Polka Dots and Pinstripes, Tiny Blocks, Window Screen background) Textures and Patterns, *Hero Arts*
(Happy Easter sentiment) *Savvy Stamps*

Dye ink: black, Memories, *Stewart Superior Corp.*

Chalk ink: (Rouge, Lime Pastel, Wisteria, Tangerine, Turquoise) ColorBox, *Clearsnap*

Textured cardstock: (Romance, Peach, Aloe Vera, Splash, Wisteria) *Bazzill Basics Paper*

Oval punch: *Emagination Crafts*

Stick pin: *Making Memories*

Other: white cardstock, adhesive

Finished size: 7" x 3½"

INSTRUCTIONS

1. Make Romance card.

2. Punch oval from each color of cardstock.

3. Stamp ovals with corresponding ink. *Note: Place ovals on scratch paper before stamping.*

4. Adhere eggs to bottom of card; trim.

5. Stamp sentiment with black on white cardstock, mat with Peach and trim.

6. Stick pin through sentiment; adhere to card.

Good Friend

Designer: Jenny Grothe

SUPPLIES

Rubber stamps:
(flowers) *Stampin' Up!*
(sentiment from Bouquet of Smiles set) *Hero Arts*

Chalk ink: (Spring Pansy, Petunia Pink, Aspen Mist, Thatched Straw) VersaMagic, *Tsukineko*

Cardstock: (purple, ivory, white)

Textured cardstock: (Splash) *Bazzill Basics Paper*

Color medium: (colored pencils)

Fibers: (purple) Adornaments, *EK Success*

Adhesive

Tools: scissors

Finished size: 6" square

INSTRUCTIONS

① Make card from purple cardstock.

② Tear Splash cardstock; adhere to card.

③ Randomly stamp flowers on white cardstock with Spring Pansy, Petunia Pink, Aspen Mist, and Thatched Straw. Ink edges with Aspen Mist; adhere to card.

④ Stamp sentiment from Bouquet of Smiles set with Spring Pansy on ivory cardstock; color with colored pencils. Ink edges with Spring Pansy; cut out. Mat with purple cardstock. Ink edges of purple cardstock; adhere to card.

⑤ Tie fibers around card.

Friends

Designer: Jenny Grothe

SUPPLIES

Rubber stamps:
(Starry Night Swirl) *Close To My Heart*
(Conversation Dots set, Graphic Brush Strokes) *Hero Arts*

Pigment ink: (Graphite Black) Brilliance, *Tsukineko*

Chalk ink: (Tea Leaves, Pink Petunia) VersaMagic, *Tsukineko*

Cardstock: (Kraft) *Bazzill Basics Paper*

Textured cardstock: (Baby Pink) *Bazzill Basics Paper*

Patterned paper: (Green Engraving) *Anna Griffin*

Paper accent: (Tag Types) Sticko, *EK Success*

Fasteners: (silver brads) *Lasting Impressions for Paper*

Adhesive

Tools: scissors

Finished size: 5½" x 4¼"

INSTRUCTIONS

① Make card from Kraft cardstock; ink edges with Tea Leaves.

② Stamp Starry Night Swirl with Pink Petunia on Baby Pink cardstock. Ink edges with Tea Leaves; adhere to card.

③ Stamp Graphic Brush Strokes on Green Engraving with Tea Leaves and Pink Petunia; ink edges with Pink Petunia. Attach to card with brads.

④ Stamp Conversation Dot on tag with Graphite Black; adhere to card.

A Cheery Hello

Designer: Jenny Grothe

SUPPLIES

Rubber stamps:
   (Word Blocks set, Handwritten Notes set) *Hero Arts*
   (butterfly) *Magenta Rubber Stamps*

Dye ink: (Desert Sand, Sunny Yellow) *Close To My Heart*

Cardstock: (white, ivory) *Provo Craft*

Yellow glass rectangle: *Heidi Grace Designs*

Adhesive: Diamond Glaze, *JudiKins*

Chalk: (brown, orange, yellow) Stampin' Pastels, *Stampin' Up!*

Other: tan cardstock, jute, scissors, adhesive, cotton swab or make-up applicator

Finished size: 5½" x 4¼"

INSTRUCTIONS

① Make white card; trim tan cardstock and adhere to card.

② Stamp "Hello" shadow on tan cardstock with Sunny Yellow and Desert Sand.

③ Cut ivory cardstock square and tear diagonally; stamp butterfly in center with Desert Sand.

④ Chalk torn edge and butterfly; adhere to card.

⑤ Stamp "Hello" sentiment with Desert Sand; adhere glass piece over "Hello" sentiment.

⑥ Tie jute around front flap of card.

Keep The Glow

Designer: Jenny Grothe

SUPPLIES

Rubber stamps:
   (sun) *Magenta Rubber Stamps*
   (Keep the Glow) *Hero Arts*

Dye ink: Close to Cocoa, *Stampin' Up!*

Chalk: *Craf-T Products* (yellow, orange)

Cardstock:
   (orange/yellow two-tone) *Paper Adventures*
   (white) *Provo Craft*

Patterned paper: *Cross My Heart*

Other: raffia, scissors, adhesive, cotton swab or make-up applicator

Finished sizes:
   Large card: 4¼" x 5¾"
   Small card: 2½" x 3¼"

INSTRUCTIONS

① Make large white card.

② Adhere patterned paper to front of card.

③ Trim orange/yellow cardstock into small card.

④ Stamp sun on white cardstock; color with chalk. Trim sun and adhere to small card.

⑤ Stamp sentiment on white cardstock; trim and mat with orange/yellow cardstock.

⑥ Adhere small card to large card and add raffia. Adhere sentiment over raffia inside small card.

Leafy Wishes

Designer: Nichol Magouirk

SUPPLIES

Rubber stamps: (Pinstripe Background, Poetic Prints Real Leaves, With Sympathy) *Hero Arts*

Chalk ink: (Dark Moss, Yellow Ochre, Amber Clay) ColorBox, *Clearsnap*

Cardstock: (white, vintage green, olive green)

Specialty paper: (Artistic Scrapper handmade) *Creative Imaginations*

Adhesive: foam squares, glue stick

Tools: scissors

Other: sponge

Finished size: 4¼" x 5½"

PREPARE & STAMP

1 Make card from vintage green cardstock.

2 Trim handmade paper to slightly smaller than card.

3 Randomly stamp leaf design with Dark Moss on handmade paper, stamping off edges of paper.

4 Adhere handmade paper to card.

EMBELLISH

1 Ink Pinstripe Background with Yellow Ochre; ink edges with Amber Clay. Ink leaf stamp with Dark Moss; stamp leaf on surface of inked Pinstripe Background stamp. Stamp layered image on white cardstock.

2 Trim stamped image; mat with olive green cardstock.

3 Stamp sentiment with Dark Moss on white cardstock. Ink with Amber Clay.

4 Mat sentiment on olive green cardstock; adhere to card.

5 Adhere matted leaf image to card with foam squares.

Background Stamping

Create your own patterned paper by stamping a pattern or randomly stamping on paper.

Sparkle Snowflakes

Designer: Teri Anderson

SUPPLIES

Rubber stamps: (Happy Holidays, Fluttering Snowflakes Fancy Notes set) *Hero Arts*

Dye ink: (Indian Corn Blue, Gray Wool) *Close To My Heart*

Snowflake accents: silver, *Amscan*

Other: cardstock (blue, white), vellum, sewing machine, white thread, scissors, adhesive

Finished size: 5½" x 4¼"

INSTRUCTIONS

1. Make card from blue cardstock.

2. Stamp Happy Holidays with Gray Wool along top and bottom of slightly smaller rectangle of white cardstock.

3. Stamp Fluttering Snowflakes with Indian Corn Blue on white.

4. Cut vellum to fit over stamped images; stitch.

5. Adhere snowflake accents to vellum.

6. Adhere white cardstock to blue card.

Season of joy

Designer: Leslie Elvert

SUPPLIES

Rubber stamps:
  (ornament from Sparkling Season set) *Stampin' Up!*
  (Printers Type Upper and Lower Case Alphabet) *Hero Arts*
  (Buttons Alphabet) *PSX*

Dye ink:
  (Basic Black, Real Red) *Stampin' Up!*
  (Olive) Exclusive Inks, *Close To My Heart*
Cardstock:
  (Real Red) *Stampin' Up!*
  (Olive) *Bazzill Basics Paper*
Snaps: red, *Stamp Doctor*
Other: white cardstock, ribbon, eyelet-setting tools, scissors, adhesive

Finished size: 5½" x 4¼"

INSTRUCTIONS

1. Make card from white cardstock.

2. Stamp images at random with Olive and Real Red ink.

3. Adhere ribbon to strip of Olive cardstock. Attach snaps, adhere to card.

4. Stamp "Season of JOY" on card.

5. Mat card with Real Red cardstock.

Wrapped Up In Holiday Cheer

Designer: Amy Eng

SUPPLIES

Rubber stamps:
(Florentine Scroll background) *Hero Arts*
(Holiday Cheer) *Impress Rubber Stamps*
Watermark ink: VersaMark, *Tsukineko*

Other: cardstock (green, burgundy), silver embossing powder, embossing heat tool, ruler, adhesive, scissors, embossing pen

Finished size: 4" x 6½"

INSTRUCTIONS

❶ Make card from green cardstock; cut ¾" strip off right side of card front.

❷ Randomly stamp Merry Christmas on card front with watermark ink.

❸ Draw line on right edge of burgundy cardstock rectangle with embossing pen and emboss; adhere to inside of card.

❹ Cut strip of burgundy to fit around card; stamp with scroll background and emboss.

❺ Wrap strip around card, adhere ends together in back.

Merry Christmas Toile

Designer: Summer Ford

SUPPLIES

Rubber stamps:
(Toile) *Stampabilities*
(Loopy Letters alphabet) *EK Success*
Dye ink: (Baroque Burgundy, Mellow Moss) *Stampin' Up!*
Patterned paper: (floral, red) *Anna Griffin*
Fibers: *Lion Brand Yarn*

Other: ivory flecked cardstock, ribbons, sewing machine, ivory thread, green blender pen, scissors, adhesive

Finished size: 5" x 7"

INSTRUCTIONS

❶ Make card from ivory flecked cardstock.

❷ Cut red paper to fit card front.

❸ Stamp Toile on smaller rectangle of ivory cardstock with Mellow Moss; adhere to red paper.

❹ Cut rectangle from red paper and slightly smaller rectangle from floral paper. Tear window in center of each, making floral window larger.

❺ Adhere red rectangle to stamped ivory rectangle. Adhere torn floral rectangle.

❻ Stamp "Merry Christmas" in window with Baroque Burgundy.

❼ Zigzag-stitch around edges.

❽ Wrap ribbon and fibers around stamped blocks; attach charm. Adhere entire block to card front.

Victorian Holly Box

Designer: Barbara Greve

SUPPLIES

All supplies from Plaid unless otherwise noted.

Rubber stamps: Anna Griffin, All Night Media ("For" and "From" from Greetings set, Hollyberry Background)

Pigment ink: green, Anna Griffin, All Night Media

Embossing ink: clear, Emboss, *Tsukineko*

Embossing powder: gold, All Night Media

Vellum: Clouds, *The Paper Company*

Ribbon: Anna Griffin, All Night Media

Punch: Holly Corner, All Night Media

Fabric adhesive: Fabri-Tac, *Beacon Adhesives*

Jewelry adhesive: Gem-Tac, *Beacon Adhesives*

Other: metallic gold paper, gold cording, scissors, ruler, embossing heat tool, piercing tool, scoring tool, vellum adhesive, pillow box

Finished size: 7" x 4¼" x 1"

INSTRUCTIONS

❶ Stamp Hollyberry Background with green on pillow box.

❷ Cut 2½" strip of metallic gold paper; punch holly along sides. Adhere around center of box.

❸ Adhere box end, using fabric adhesive.

❹ Tie ribbon around box.

❺ Stamp For and From on vellum with clear; emboss. Cut into tag and adhere to strip with vellum adhesive.

❻ Pierce hole through each top corner of box. Thread gold cord through holes to create handle; knot ends inside box and secure with jewelry adhesive.

Stamped Flowers

Designer: Nichol Magouirk

SUPPLIES

FOR LAVENDER CARD:

Cardstock: lavender, light lavender, *Bazzill Basics Paper*

"Thank You Very Much" stamp: *Hero Arts*

Chalk inks: green, orange, yellow, *Clearsnap*

FOR GREEN CARD:

Cardstock: light green, very light green, *Bazzill Basics Paper*

"Thank You" stamp: *DeNami Design*

Chalk inks: green, dark purple, light purple, *Clearsnap*

For both:

White card: *Impress Rubber Stamps*

Wildflower stamps: *Hero Arts*

Black ink: *Clearsnap*

Watermark ink: Versamark, *Tsukineko*

Other: black brads, sponge

Finished size: 4¼" x 5½"

INSTRUCTIONS

❶ Trim cardstock to fit card. Tear bottom edge if desired.

❷ Stamp cardstock several times with wildflower stamp and watermark ink. Clean stamp.

❸ Layer different colors of chalk ink on wildflower stamp. Stamp cardstock once.

❹ Sponge edges with black ink. Adhere to card.

❺ Stamp "Thank you" on light colored cardstock; trim. *Note: Tear edges if desired.*

❻ Sponge edges with black ink. Adhere to card with brads.

May Hope Fill Your Heart

Designer: Jenny Grothe

SUPPLIES

Rubber stamps:
  (May Hope Fill Your Heart) *Stampin' Up!*

  (Hope from Express It) Magnetic Date Stamp, *Making Memories*

Pigment ink: (Sahara Sand, Hint of Pesto, Red Magic, Midnight Black) VersaMagic, *Tsukineko*

Cardstock:
  (Lava) *Bazzill Basics Paper*

  (Tan, Brown) *DMD, Inc.*

Patterned paper: (Green Plumes) *Anna Griffin*

Adhesive: glue stick

Tools: scissors, ruler

Finished size: 5½" x 4¼"

INSTRUCTIONS

1 Make card from Lava cardstock.

2 Cut Tan cardstock slightly smaller than card front; ink edges with Hint of Pesto and adhere.

3 Cut 3" square of Brown cardstock. Randomly stamp "hope" with Sahara Sand and Hint of Pesto ink; ink edges and adhere to card.

4 Make heart from patterned paper; ink edges with Red Magic and adhere to card.

5 Stamp sentiment with Midnight Black.

Falling Leaves

Designer: Shelene Lee

SUPPLIES

Rubber stamps: (leaves, leaf outline from Leaves set; botanicals script from Botanicals set) *Stampin' Up!*

Dye ink:
   (Really Rust) Classic Stampin' Pad, *Stampin' Up!*
   (Autumn Leaves) Kaleidacolor, *Tsukineko*

Watermark ink: VersaMark, *Tsukineko*

Cardstock: (Really Rust, Ultrasmooth Vanilla) *Stampin' Up!*

Adhesive: Mono, *Tombow*

Pigment powder: gold, Pearl Ex, *Jacquard Products*

Other: gold metallic cord, ribbon, paintbrush, scissors, make-up sponge, hole punch

Finished size: 5½" x 4¼"

CARD

1 Make card from Really Rust card-stock.

2 Stamp leaves with Autumn Leaves and script with Really Rust randomly on Ultrasmooth Vanilla.

3 Tear one edge; sponge with Really Rust.

TAG

1 Stamp script with Really Rust on Ultrasmooth Vanilla; cut rectangle and cut adjacent corners to make tag. Stamp leaf with Autumn Leaves on tag.

2 Stamp leaf outline with watermark ink on tag.

3 Apply pigment powder with paintbrush.

4 Tear bottom edge of stamped tag; mat with Really Rust and tear bottom edge.

5 Punch hole at top and thread on gold metallic cord; knot.

FINISH

1 Wrap gold ribbon around stamped cardstock; string tag on ribbon and tie bow.

2 Adhere stamped cardstock to card.

Erica

Designer: Christi Spadoni

SUPPLIES

All supplies from Close To My Heart unless otherwise noted.

Rubber stamp: In Friendship's Garden

Ink: (Red Velvet, Olive, Buttercup)

Cardstock: (White, Olive, Ultra White, Red Velvet)

Pink striped paper

Decorative chalk

Black pen: ZIG Millennium, *EK Success*

Waterbrush: *Yasutomo*

VIBRANT BACKGROUNDS

For vibrant stamped backgrounds like this one, stamp on a slightly padded surface like a magazine or a mouse pad. The designer used dye ink to stamp the flowers, pressing the stamp down for a few seconds allowing the ink to penetrate the paper. She also varied the direction of the images and stamped them on the edges of the paper to create her own patterned paper look.

Sunflower Portrait

Design: Karen Potts

SUPPLIES

Rubber stamps: (Sunflower) Botanicals Super Set, *Close To My Heart*

Ink pads: (Autumn Terracotta, Black, Garden Green, sunflower Yellow)

LAYERING STAMPS

These layered sunflower stamps were used to create a simple patterned paper for this layout while complementing the photograph's colors. Here's how to create this look:

❶ Stamp the spiky petals with Sunflower Yellow ink.

❷ Stamp the circle image inside the petals with Autumn Terracotta.

❸ Stamp the splatter image on top of the center circle with Black ink.

❹ Stamp the stem with Garden Green, lining it up under the flower head.

STAMPING TIP

Achieve a "randomly stamped" look by stamping the image upright, sideways and upside-down.

Family Photo

Designer: Leslie Elvert

SUPPLIES

Rubber stamps: Love and Wildflowers set, *Close To My Heart*

Dye ink: (Aspen Green, Desert Sand) Exclusive Inks, *Close To My Heart*

Watermark ink: VersaMark, *Tsukineko*

Marker: Aspen Green, *Close To My Heart*

Eyelets: brown, *Making Memories*

Fonts:
  (Beautiful) *twopeasinabucket.com*
  (Bradley Hand ITC) *Microsoft*

Other: jute, cardstock (natural, green, brown)

CREATE DEPTH WITH STAMPED IMAGES

Randomly stamp the same image without re-inking the rubber to add depth to your stamped background paper. The various ink intensities will create the illusion of dimension on your flat surface. Stamp another image in a deeper color over the previously stamped images to create even more depth. For continuity, choose inks that match the background of your photographs.

STAMPING OFF

Stamping off will produce a lighter, more subdued stamped image, ideal for backgrounds. Simply stamp once or twice on scrap paper directly after inking to reduce the ink intensity, and then stamp on the desired paper or surface.

Just the right words for creating just the right cards

You know that feeling you get when you know what you want to say but you don't know how to say it? When it comes to handmade greeting cards, I've discovered an amazing new concept for coming up with the perfect sentiment for every occasion. When you're at a loss for words, just use someone else's! Thousands of resourceful and clever people have already come up with pithy sayings, beautifully expressed, so take advantage of their way with words.

ONLINE

Naturally, the Web is a tremendous resource when searching for the perfect expression for a handmade card. For a vast archive of sayings from practical to inspirational try *www.quote-land.com* or *www.quotationreference.com*. There are even Web sites that specialize in sentiments especially for stampers, like *www.versalog.com* and *www.verseit.com*. Visit *www.followyour-dreams.com* for inspirational sayings on topics such as love and friendship. If you're a quote addict, sign up to receive an email quote a day. I like to start my day off right with a positive sentiment from *www.terimartin.com*.

BOOKS

Also available for inspiration are many profound and provocative quote books. *Reader's Digest's Quotable Quotes* offers such soothing-to-the-self-esteem witticisms as "We are all worms, but I do believe I'm a glowworm" (Winston Churchill). For words to inspire and motivate, peruse *The Change-Your-Life Quote Book* by Allen Klein. From *Phillips' Book of Great Thoughts and Funny Sayings* by Bob Phillips, we learn that "To exercise is human; not to is divine" (Robert Orben). One of my other favorites is *I Love You Verses and Sweet Sayings* by Bessie Pease Gutmann (pictured here).

ALPHABET STAMPS

Use alphabet stamp sets to recreate a favorite quote. Mix and match sizes and typefaces for a unique and personalized look. For smallish alphabets, try the versatile letter sets from Hero Arts, and the unique Pixie alphabet sets from PSX. For making a strong statement, I love using the graphic Montreal alphabet set from Green Pepper Press and any of the sets from Wordsworth Art Stamps.

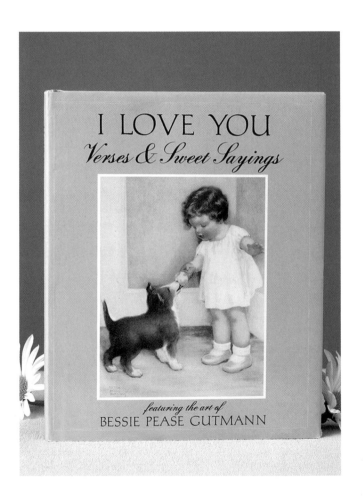

QUOTE STAMPS

If you're crazy about ready-to-stamp quotes, you're in luck. Many rubber stamp companies offer unique and inventive quotes, designed to complement the emotion evoked by the sentiment. For a classic quote, beautifully expressed in calligraphy, check out the designs of Wordsworth. River City Rubber Works is the company to buy from when you're looking for offbeat, hilarious expressions, such as the sloppily scrawled, "well... this day was a total waste of makeup." From My Sentiments Exactly!, you'll find an inspiring and eclectic mix of creatively designed sentiments, from the humorous to the heartfelt.

WEB SITES

Here's a selection of even more Web sites featuring indispensable phrases for all occasions.

www.twopeasinabucket.com
www.oneliners-and-proverbs.com
www.famous-quote-famous-quotes.com
www.quotationspage.com

Quote stamps

Cards with quote stamps

Bonus Idea

Make a matching tag using the heart stamp from the Signs of Spring set from Close To My Heart.

Mother's Day Dots

Designer: Jenny Grothe

SUPPLIES

Rubber stamps: (Circle Pop alphabet) *Hero Arts*

Pigment ink: (Pink Petunia, Magnolia Bud) VersaMagic, *Tsukineko*

Cardstock: (Sherbet) *Bazzill Basics Paper;* (white)

Patterned paper: (Baby Pink Mini Gingham) Snip Its, *Pebbles Inc.*

Fibers: (pink satin ribbon) *The Robin's Nest*

Adhesive

Tools: scissors, hole punch

Finished size: 5½" x 4¼"

INSTRUCTIONS

❶ Make card from Sherbet cardstock.

❷ Cut rectangle of patterned paper; tear top and bottom and adhere to card.

❸ Stamp "happy mothers day" on white cardstock with Circle Pop alphabet using Pink Petunia. Stamp plain circle between words using Magnolia Bud; adhere to card.

❹ Tie knots in ribbon; adhere to top and bottom edge of white cardstock.

Cock a Doodle Doo

Designer: Gretchen Schmidt

SUPPLIES

Rubber stamps:
(Fancy, Grade A) *Stampabilities*

(Antique Lowercase and Uppercase alphabets) PSX, *Duncan*

Dye ink: (Close to Cocoa) *Stampin' Up!*

Pigment ink: (Black) VersaColor, *Tsukineko*

Cardstock: (Deep Red, Tumbleweed) *Making Memories*

Patterned paper: (Brown Tattered Tweed) Sara Horton, *Tumblebeasts*

Color medium: (colored pencils) *EK Success*

Accents: (red staples) *Making Memories*

Fibers: (orange fibers, twill ribbon)

Adhesive: double-sided tape

Tools: ruler, scissors, stapler, pencil, eraser

Finished size: 4¼" x 5½"

INSTRUCTIONS

❶ Make card from Tumbleweed cardstock.

❷ Cut Deep Red cardstock to fit card front. Cut strip of patterned paper and adhere to left side. Wrap fiber around left side and staple in place.

❸ Stamp rooster on Tumbleweed with Black; color with colored pencils. Draw line along top contour of rooster with pencil. Stamp "cock a doodle doo" on line with Black; erase line. Stamp "happy" under rooster. Trim; tear top and bottom edges of piece. Ink edges with Close to Cocoa and adhere to card.

❹ Stamp "Valentine's Day" on twill ribbon with Black. Adhere to bottom of rooster piece and add staple.

❺ Stamp "to you" below twill ribbon with Black.

Take a Chance

Designer: Jenny Grothe

SUPPLIES

Rubber stamps: (large heart from Tags with Words set, small heart from Handwritten Caps set) *Hero Arts*

Chalk ink: (Sahara Sand) VersaMagic, *Tsukineko*

Pigment ink: (Cardinal) VersaColor, *Tsukineko*

Cardstock: (black, cream, oatmeal)

Fibers: (cream embroidery floss)

Dimensional glaze: Glossy Accents, *Ranger Industries*

Adhesive

Tools: ruler, scissors, hole punch

Finished size: 4" square

INSTRUCTIONS

❶ Make 3½" x 3¼" card from oatmeal cardstock; ink edges with Cardinal.

❷ Lightly stamp small hearts repeatedly with Cardinal. Stamp large hearts with Sahara Sand.

❸ Stamp large heart on cream cardstock with Cardinal. Trim, leaving ⅛" border; mat with oatmeal. Punch hole in top and add floss. Adhere floss ends behind card so tag hangs over top.

❹ Adhere card to square of black cardstock.

We've Moved

Designer: Allison Strine

SUPPLIES

Rubber stamps: Stencil alphabet, *Fusion Art Stamps*

Solvent ink: Ultramarine, StazOn, *Tsukineko*

Patterned paper: Blueprints, *Karen Foster Design*

Mosaic tile stickers: Tile's Play, *EK Success*

Eyelets: *Making Memories*

Other: cardstock (navy, blue), adhesive, eyelet-setting tools, embossing heat tool, scissors

Finished size: 6½" x 5"

INSTRUCTIONS

❶ Make blue cardstock card.

❷ Stamp "WE'VE MOVED" with Ultramarine on mosaic tile stickers; heat set.

❸ Mat rectangle of patterned paper with navy cardstock; trim to fit card front and adhere.

❹ Secure eyelets in corners of card; adhere stamped tiles.

Holiday Package

Designer: Teri Anderson

SUPPLIES

Rubber stamps:
(present) *Magenta Rubber Stamps*
(Happy Holidays, Holiday Stripes) *Hero Arts*

Dye ink: (True Black, Red Velvet) *Close To My Heart*

Chalk ink: (Charcoal, Burnt Sienna) ColorBox Fluid Chalk, *Clearsnap*

Cardstock:
(Ivy) *Bazzill Basics Paper*
(Red) *Provo Craft*

Vellum: *Provo Craft*

Adhesive: glue stick

Tools: scissors

Finished size: 4¼" x 5½"

INSTRUCTIONS

❶ Make card from Red cardstock. Stamp Holiday Stripes with Red Velvet on card front.

❷ Stamp present with True Black on Ivy cardstock; repeat on red cardstock.

❸ Cut stamped red into pieces; adhere diagonal piece over corresponding sections on stamped Ivy. Trim and ink edges with Charcoal.

❹ Adhere stamped present to vellum; cut out. Stamp Happy Holidays with True Black around edges of present; ink edges with Burnt Sienna and Charcoal. Adhere to card front.

Merry

Designer: Lisa Schmitt

SUPPLIES

Rubber stamps:
(Christmas Words) *American Art Stamp*
(Buttons Lowercase Alphabet) PSX, *Duncan*

Watermark ink: VersaMark, *Tsukineko*

Dye ink: (True Black) *Close To My Heart*

Cardstock: (Willow Green, Deep Red) Double Dipped, *Making Memories*

Patterned paper: (Christmas Stripe) *Doodlebug Design*

Fibers: (green ribbon) *May Arts*

Adhesive: (foam squares) *Making Memories*; glue stick

Tools: (square die, die-cut machine) Sizzix, *Provo Craft/Ellison*; sicssors

Finished size: 5½" x 4¼"

PREPARE

❶ Make card from Willow Green cardstock. *Note: Fold dark green to outside.*

❷ Die-cut small square from Deep Red cardstock and large square from Willow Green.

❸ Stamp Christmas Words with watermark ink on Deep Red square; over stamp "merry" with True Black. Adhere Deep Red square to light side of Willow Green square.

EMBELLISH

❶ Cut Deep Red rectangle slightly smaller than card front.

❷ Mat with light side of Willow Green.

❸ Cut rectangle of Christmas Stripe paper; adhere to top of Deep Red rectangle.

❹ Adhere ribbon at bottom of Christmas Stripe; adhere all to card front.

❺ Adhere stamped square to card front with foam squares.

Christmas Noel

Designer: Lori Fairbanks

SUPPLIES

Alphabet rubber stamps*

Watermark ink pad*

8½" x 11" red cardstock

Embossing powder*

Gold pigment powder*

Embossing heat tool

Gold cord*

Gold foil

Gold eyelets: four ⅛", sixteen 1⁄16"

Eyelet setter and hole punch

Miscellaneous items: scissors, adhesive, ruler, hammer

*Sugarloaf Products Anita's Art Stamps stamps; Tsukineko VersaMark ink pad; Stampendous! Stamp N' Bond embossing powder; Jacquard Products Pearl Ex Aztec Gold pigment powder; and Stampin' Up! cord were used in the sample project.

Finished size: 5" x 4¼"

Christmas Block Letters

Designer: Linda Beeson

SUPPLIES

Rubber stamps: alphabet*, tree bough*

Ink pads*: red, silver, white

Red fibers*

4 mini red brads*

8½" x 11" cardstock:

  Green

  Red

  Silver

  White

Foam tape*

Heart punch*

Miscellaneous items: scissors, glue stick

*Hero Arts Alphabet Blocks stamps; Delta Rubber Stampede Redwood Bough stamp; Tsukineko Brilliance Rocket Red, Platinum Planet, and Moonlight White ink pads; Lion Brand Yarn fibers; Family Treasures mini brads; 3M WorldWide Scotch foam tape; and EK Success Paper Shapers punch were used in the sample project.

Finished size: 6½" x 4¼"

Christmas Wishes

Designer: Denise Pauley

SUPPLIES

Rubber stamps: Antique Uppercase alphabet, *PSX*

Pigment ink: black, Dauber Duos, *Tsukineko*

Decorative washers: (Happiness, Imagine) Washer Words, *Making Memories*

Alphabet stickers: black sonnets, *Creative Imaginations*

Patterned paper: green/red striped, Embellishment Papers, *Making Memories*

Ribbon: red, Merry Christmas, *Making Memories*

Other: black marker, scrap paper, photo, adhesive, sandpaper, cardstock (cream, red)

STAMP YOUR JOURNALING

When journaling is minimal, try recording your memories with alphabet stamps. Save time and give the stamped images a neat, clean look by aligning the individual letters into words before impressing them on your layout.

Foam Stamps

Use foam stamps to create fun, chunky designs.

Holly & Berries

Designer: Linda Beeson

SUPPLIES

Foam stamps: (Holly Stripe set) Chunky Layers, *Duncan*

Rubber stamps:
  (leaves, berries from Christmas Poinsettia set) *Close To My Heart*

  (Noel) *Art Impressions*

  (Tiny Noel) *American Art Stamp*

Dye ink: (black, Cherry Red, Pine Tree Green, Soft Green) Memories, *Stewart Superior Corp.*

Gift box: white, Paper Basket, *PrintWorks*

Other: ribbon, cardstock (green, red), glossy white paper, adhesive, scissors, green eyelet, eyelet-setting tools, texture sponge

Finished sizes
  Box: 3⅜" x 5¾" x 1¾"
  Tag: 1⅝" x 2¼"

BOX

❶ Apply Pine Tree Green to box with texture sponge.

❷ Stamp stripes on front, back with Soft Green.

❸ Stamp Noel on sides with Pine Tree Green.

❹ Stamp holly and berries on front, back over stamped stripes with Cherry Red and Pine Tree Green.

TAG

❶ Apply Pine Tree Green to glossy white paper with texture sponge.

❷ Stamp stripes with Soft Green.

❸ Stamp leaves and berries over stamped stripes with Cherry Red and Pine Tree Green.

❹ Stamp Tiny Noel with black.

❺ Cut into tag; mat with red and green cardstock.

❻ Set eyelet; thread ribbon through eyelet, and tie bow.

ACRYLIC PAINT

ACRYLIC PAINT

Use a paintbrush or the flat side of a cosmetic wedge sponge to apply paint to the various parts of the stamp, using separate brushes or sponges for different colors. Stamp the image onto your surface firmly, and then lift the stamp off carefully. When finished, clean the stamps well with paper towels and warm water.

PAINT & FOAM STAMP HINTS

▪ Use a separate sponge to apply and blend each color to the stamp.

▪ Work quickly as acrylic paint dries very fast. Reapply paint for each impression.

▪ Fill in any incomplete areas in your stamped image with a small paintbrush.

▪ Clean the stamp well with water and a paper towel or use a baby wipe for quick paint cleanup.

Swirl Stocking Wrap

Designer: Cheryl McMurray

SUPPLIES

Foam stamp: Swirl Stocking, *Delta Rubber Stampede*

Rubber stamp: Small Spiral, All Night Media, *Plaid*

Pigment ink: Frost White, ColorBox, *Clearsnap*

Swirl sticker: Santa's Coming Borders, *Doodlebug Design*

Alphabet stickers: Mini Letters School, Sticko, *EK Success*

Hole punch: ¼", *McGill*

Acrylic paint: (Opaque Red, white) Ceramcoat, *Delta*

Other: large sheet brown paper, tan cardstock, shrinkable plastic, silver mini brad, 2 small foam paintbrushes or sponges, newspaper, ruler, baking sheet, oven, scissors, adhesive

Finished sizes
  Card: 5¾" x 4¼"
  Wrap: 30" x 20"

CARD

1. Make card from tan cardstock. Trim ¾" off bottom front of card.

2. Adhere border sticker to top of card front, and along bottom inside edge.

3. Stamp stocking on shrinkable plastic with Opaque Red and white. Let dry.

4. Punch hole through stocking loop. Cut out stocking and bake, following manufacturer's instructions.

5. Attach stocking to card with brad.

6. Adhere alphabet stickers to card to spell sentiment.

WRAP

1. Randomly stamp stocking on brown paper with Opaque Red and white.

2. Randomly stamp swirls on paper with Frost White. Let dry.

DESIGNER TIPS

- Stamp partially on and off of the outer edges of wrapping paper to achieve a continuous look. Place newspaper or scrap paper underneath the paper to catch any excess paint or ink.

- The Swirl Stocking stamp from Delta Rubber Stampede has been discontinued. If you can't find the stamp, substitute the image as follows:

  Try another stamp with a bold, simple design for best results.

  Use a different stocking stamp such as the Chunky Layers Stocking & Frame set from Duncan Enterprises or the Holiday Basics set from Stampin' Up!

Jolly Snowman
Switch Plate

Designer: Rhonda Black

SUPPLIES

Foam stamps: (Snowflake Time, Snow Angel) Chunky Layers, *Duncan*

Plastic paint: (Light Blue, Bright Blue, Pumpkin, Fudge Brown, black) Paint for Plastic, *Plaid*

Other: switch plate, paper plate, foam paintbrushes, hair dryer (optional)

Finished size: 2¾" x 4½"

INSTRUCTIONS

Let paint dry between all steps. Use hairdryer to speed drying time.

❶ Stamp square background from Snowflake Time with Light Blue, starting at top and stamping partial background as needed.

❷ Stamp snowman body from Snow Angel (omit wings) with Bright Blue.

❸ Stamp snowflakes from Snowflake Time with Bright Blue.

❹ Stamp eyes, nose, arms, and buttons from Snow Angel on snowman with desired paint colors.

Bonus Idea

Coordinate your room further by creating a matching outlet cover.

Nature's Garden Window Clings

Designer: Rhonda Black

SUPPLIES

Foam stamps: (Sun, Dragonfly) *Duncan*; (Butterfly, Inchworm, Rose) Simply Stamps, *Plaid*

Paint: (Bright Pink, Pink, Purple, Turquoise, Light Purple, Green, Bright Green, Orange, Yellow) Paint for Plastic, *Plaid*

Vinyl: (½ yd. clear)

Tools: foam paintbrush, scissors, palette, ruler

INSTRUCTIONS

Test vinyl to find side that clings best. Stamp designs on opposite side so pictures will stick to window.

❶ Stamp on vinyl and let dry.

❷ Cut out each shape leaving ¼" border around stamped design.

Bonus Ideas

■ Try using colored vinyl to add variety to your window clings.

■ Make a set of window clings for every season—flowers for Spring, a day at the beach for Summer, leaves for Fall, and snowflakes for Winter.

■ Personalize your window pictures by stamping messages with alphabet stamps or using stamps that represent sports, dance, or your favorite music.

How to stamp on fabric

Always wanted to try stamping on fabric? Not sure where to start? Learn the basics to create impressive clothing and accessories for all ages.

CHOOSE AND PREPARE FABRIC

Pay close attention to the weave and surface texture of the fabric you wish to stamp. The tighter the weave and smoother the texture, the cleaner the stamped image will be. Cotton and other natural fibers work best. Fabrics such as twill, denim, and some cotton fabrics will give cleaner images but will absorb less ink and give a more muted look. Coarse or porous fabrics absorb ink quickly and require an ample amount for a clear, defined image. Use caution, as too much ink will make the fabric stiff.

Wash and dry your fabric before you stamp to allow for shrinkage. Do not use fabric softener.

CHOOSE INK OR PAINT

Use a fabric-specific (craft) ink or acrylic paint mixed with a textile medium for the best results.

In some instances, it's a good idea to stamp on darker colored fabric with white ink or paint first, then overstamp with a second color. This allows the top layer to be less affected by the fabric color underneath.

PLACE CARDBOARD UNDER FABRIC

LOAD STAMP WITH PAINT

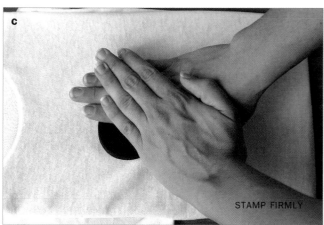

STAMP FIRMLY

FILL IN WITH BRUSH

CHOOSE STAMPS AND DESIGN

Use rubber, foam, or acrylic stamps with broad designs. Small details may get lost on fabric.

Practice stamping on a scrap of similar fabric to get a feel for the amount of ink or paint needed and how much pressure to apply. If the edges of the stamp show around the stamped image on the practice piece, trim closely around the stamp image with a craft knife.

If you're going to stamp several images on your project, it's helpful to stamp images on scrap paper or adhesive notes first, and then cut them out and arrange them on your fabric until you achieve the desired design. Once you've decided on placement, simply remove the paper and stamp in its place.

STAMP

To prevent your ink or paint from bleeding through the fabric, place a protective sheet of waxed paper-covered, smooth cardboard directly beneath the layer on which you're stamping (see Figure a).

Ink the stamp or load it with paint by dipping a wedge sponge or sponge brush lightly into the paint and tapping it onto the stamp's raised image (see Figure b). Stamp firmly (see Figure c). Reload the stamp with ink or paint as needed, generally after each application.

Use a fine paintbrush and paint, an ink pad, or matching fabric pen to fill in any holes as needed (see Figure d).

HEAT SET AND CARE

Press the back of the fabric with a warm iron (no steam) or follow the ink manufacturer's instructions to make stamped images permanent.

Launder stamped wearables according to the fabric manufacturer's instructions, turning items inside out to prevent fading or cracking.

Spring Jumper

Designer: Tresa Black

SUPPLIES

Rubber stamps: (Maggie's Daisy set) *Stampendous!*

Fabric paint: (White, Pink, Yellow, Black) *ZimPrints*

Jumper: (100% cotton blue)

Tools: stamp positioner, scissors, paintbrush

Other: pencil, white card-stock, disposable palette, waxed paper–covered card-board, wedge sponges

Finished size:
   child size 24 months

INSTRUCTIONS

Wash and dry jumper prior to stamping. Do not use fabric softener. Place cardboard under fabric while stamping.

❶ Stamp flowers along jumper bottom with White; fill in with White.

❷ Stamp butterfly with White; allow to dry and paint inside Pink.

❸ Dip pencil eraser in Yellow; stamp flower centers.

❹ Dot flower centers Black with end of paintbrush.

Hip Capri Pants

Designer: Tresa Black

SUPPLIES

Rubber stamps:
(Tendril Stencil, Stencil) *Duncan*

(decorative corner flourish)
Magenta Rubber Stamps

Fabric paint: (Brown) *ZimPrints*

Capri pants: (93% cotton, 7% spandex beige)

Other: disposable palette, waxed paper-covered cardboard, wedge sponge

Finished size: junior size 9

INSTRUCTIONS

Wash and dry pants. Do not use fabric softener. Place cardboard under fabric while stamping.

Stamp on pants pockets and leg bottoms as desired.

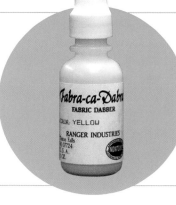

Latest & Greatest

CREATE WASHABLE FABRIC PAINT

Transform Delta's Ceramcoat acrylic paint into washable fabric paint with the help of Ceramcoat Textile Medium from Delta. This essential product allows you to stamp permanent beautiful designs on fabrics. Thanks to Ceramcoat Textile Medium, your work won't crack or bleed when washed! Simply prewash fabric, mix acrylic paint with the textile medium, apply paint, heat set with an iron for 20 seconds, and your stamped fabric is washable! Suggested retail $2.59–$6.49. 800/423-4135, *www.deltacrafts.com.*

FABRIC MAGIC

In order to stamp images on fabric with the results you've always wanted, you'll need to know the magic word: Fabra-Ca-Dabra! This fabric ink by Ranger Industries is permanent for clothes, sneakers, photo album covers, and more. Make personalized gifts that are destined to be well-loved. Available in 12 colors, you'll be able to create any design you envision with satisfying results. And this acid-free, nontoxic paint cleans up like magic—just use soap and water. Suggested retail $4. 800/244-2211, *www.rangerink.com.*

ENDLESS POSSIBILITIES

Try using VersaCraft from Tsukineko the next time you stamp on fabric, paper, wood, leather, walls—almost anything you can think of! Simply apply ink to a rubber stamp using your choice of the 32 solid pads, two 12-color pads, 32 one-inch cubes, or 31 dual-tipped markers available. Then, stamp on the porous surface of your choice and heat set using an iron or heat tool. VersaColor is water-based, nontoxic, acid-free, and archival. Suggested retail $2.60–$17.80. 425/883-7733, *www.tsukineko.com.*

Cherry Kitchen Trimmings

Designer: Vickie Clontz

SUPPLIES

Foam stamps:
    (Garden Cherries, Cherries) *Duncan*
    (Square Checkerboard) *Delta Rubber Stampede*

Acrylic paint: (Bright Red, Medium Foliage Green, black, Light Ivory) Ceramcoat, *Delta*

Textile medium: *Delta*

Cotton tablecloth: ivory, Home, *Target*

Square cotton napkins: ivory, Home, *Target*

Rickrack: Atom Red, *Coats & Clark*

Varnish: Satin Interior, Ceramcoat, *Delta*

Other: sponge brushes, paper towels, waxed paper, paintbrush, craft knife, paper plates, scissors, fabric adhesive, 4" terra cotta pot, 7" terra cotta saucer, artist gesso

Finished sizes:
    Tablecloth: size to fit table
    Centerpiece height: 5½"
    Curtain panel: 9½" square

INSTRUCTIONS

Prior to stamping, wash and dry all fabrics without fabric softener. Iron if needed. If you skip washing and drying the fabrics, paint may not adhere.

PREPARE

❶ Cut off two rows of the checkerboard stamp; trim edges to be even with checks. Repeat, cutting one row off stamp. *Note: Single row will be used on centerpiece.*

❷ Cover work surface with waxed paper.

❸ Mix each paint color with textile medium.

TABLECOTH & CURTAIN PANELS

❶ Stamp checkerboard with black along edge of tablecloth. Repeat until one side is finished. *Note: Let paint dry before moving to stamp other sides of tablecloth. Repeat until border is complete.*

❷ Stamp Garden Cherries with Medium Foliage Green and Bright Red in corner of tablecloth. Repeat for each corner.

❸ Stamp Cherries with Medium Foliage

Green and Bright Red above border along sides. *Note: Space cherries about 17" from corner image and continue along entire side.*

❹ Repeat until one side is finished. *Note: Let dry before continuing to next side. Stamp remaining sides.*

❺ To make curtain panel, repeat step 1 around entire edge of napkin, let dry.

❻ Repeat step 3, stamping Garden Cherries in one corner of napkin; let dry.

❼ Repeat steps 1–4 to create number of curtain panels needed to fit length of window.

CENTERPIECE

Let paint dry thoroughly between all coats and steps.

❶ Paint pot and saucer with gesso; let dry.

❷ Apply Light Ivory basecoat to pot and saucer; let dry. Repeat if desired.

❸ Apply black to checkerboard stamp; stamp pot rim and let dry.

❹ Stamp Cherries with Medium Foliage Green and Bright Red on side of pot; repeat on opposite side. *Note: Make sure pot is upside down before stamping cherries.*

❺ Stamp single checkerboard with black on saucer rim; let dry.

❻ Repeat step 4, stamping cherries inside saucer. Spray saucer and pot with varnish; let dry.

❼ Adhere rickrack around base of saucer.

Bonus Ideas

- Make napkins to match your cherry kitchen by tying rick-rack around folded black-and-white checked cloth napkins. Secure a button to the center of the bow with adhesive. The rickrack napkin ring easily slides on and off of the napkin!

- Serve Cherry Surprises to your guests at a special brunch or afternoon tea. Then send them home with a jar of cookie mix and the recipe so that they can create their own little piece of cherry heaven!

CHERRY SURPRISES

Makes 5 dozen 1" cookies

    ½ cup sugar
    ½ cup finely-chopped nuts
    2¼ cups sifted cake flour
    6 oz. dried cherries
    1 cup butter, softened
    1 tsp. vanilla
    Red crystal sugar

Preheat oven to 350º. Cream butter and vanilla in large bowl. Add sugar, nuts, flour; mix well. Wrap dough in waxed paper; chill. Roll to ¼" thickness on lightly floured surface and cut into pieces. Place dried cherry in center of piece and form into ball. Roll in red crystal sugar and place on ungreased cookie sheet. Chill for 15 minutes. Bake 15–20 minutes.

Note: To create a Cherry Surprise cookie mix, layer appropriate measurements of sugar, nuts, flour, and cherries in a quart jar. Cookie mixes containing nuts will stay fresh for three months.

DID YOU KNOW?

According to the Cherry Marketing Institute, Americans consume more than 260 million pounds of cherries per year! New research indicates that eating tart cherries may help reduce pain from arthritis and headaches.

The Possibilities of Heat Embossing

Add dimension, sparkle, and never-ending fun to all your paper projects.

What is Heat Embossing?

Heat embossing is the easy and versatile technique of combining inks, embossing powders, and heat to make raised designs on paper. The effect is similar to the lettering on an embossed wedding invitation. Here's how it's done:

- Apply ink to paper, using rubber stamps and an inkpad.

- Sprinkle embossing powder over the wet areas, working quickly so the powder grains will stick. Shake off the excess.

- Melt the powder using a heat embossing heat tool (a special heat gun made for this purpose). When cool, the melted powder will dry into a glossy, raised image.

The following projects will help you explore the many creative possibilities of heat embossing. Let's get started!

Happy Hello

Designer: Emily Call, courtesy of Stampin' Up!

SUPPLIES

All supplies from Stampin' Up! unless otherwise noted.

More Mustard cardstock

Stamps: sunflower, "a happy hello", Little Layers set

Dye ink: More Mustard

Watermark ink: VersaMark, *Tsukineko*

Clear detail embossing powder

Square metal-edged tag

Silver brad

Silver wire

Adhesive foam dots

Other: stipple brush, needlenose pliers, 1/16" hole punch, paper towel, heat embossing tool

Finished size: 4¼" x 5½"

INSTRUCTIONS

❶ Make More Mustard card base. Stamp flower on tag and randomly across card front using watermark ink.

❷ Sprinkle clear embossing powder over stamped areas. Shake off excess. Melt with heat embossing tool.

③ Dip stipple brush into More Mustard ink and lightly pounce embossed flowers. This will create a shadow effect. Stamp "a happy hello" with More Mustard ink, in lower corner of tag.

④ Punch holes in top corners of tag. Thread wire through holes, and curl ends with pliers.

⑤ Insert mini brad in card front. Adhere tag to card with adhesive foam dots.

Sunflower Stationery Box

Designer: Emily Call, courtesy of Stampin' Up!

SUPPLIES

All supplies from Stampin' Up! unless otherwise noted.

More Mustard cardstock

Confetti Tan stationery box

Stamps: large flower, leaf, Just My Type set

Watermark ink: VersaMark, *Tsukineko*

Embossing powder: Clear, Leaf Green, More Mustard

Round vellum metal-edged tag

Creamy Caramel eyelets

Adhesive foam dots

Other: jute, string, heat embossing tool

Finished size: 6" x 4½" x ½"

INSTRUCTIONS

① Punch out and assemble box. Randomly stamp and emboss leaves on box front, using watermark ink and clear embossing powder. Stamp large flower on cardstock and emboss with Creamy Caramel embossing powder.

② While melted powder is still wet, sprinkle more powder over flower.

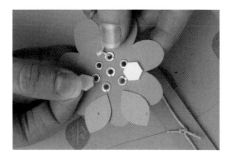

③ Melt powder again, using heat embossing tool. Cut out. Stamp and emboss two leaves with Leaf Green embossing powder. Cut out.

④ Place tag over flower center. Punch holes through both layers and set seven eyelets. Stamp "for you" on Confetti Tan cardstock scrap left over from box. Cut out and punch hole in one end. Thread string through tag and one eyelet in flower; tie.

⑤ Cut strip of More Mustard cardstock and tie around box with jute. Adhere embossed leaves behind flower. Adhere flower to box center with adhesive foam dots.

If I could, I'd comb the sky and collect the stars...

Wishing Star

Designer: Nichole Heady

SUPPLIES

All supplies from Stampin' Up! unless otherwise noted.

Ultrasmooth White cardstock

Blank paper

Stamps: star from Teeny Tinies stamp set, large ball from The Shape of Things stamp set, medium ball from Little Shapes stamp set

Dye ink: Almost Amethyst, Bliss Blue, Brocade Blue

Watermark ink: VersaMark, *Tsukineko*

Sterling Silver embossing powder

Font: Carefree, "Write Me A Memory" CD

Blue fiber

Adhesive foam dots

Other: 1/16" hole punch, new pencil with eraser, heat embossing tool

Finished size: 5½" x 4¼"

INSTRUCTIONS

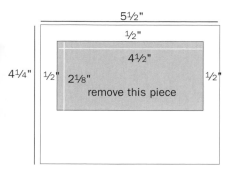

5½"

½"

4½"

4¼"   ½"   2⅛"

½"

remove this piece

TEMPLATE CUTTING DIAGRAM

1 Print "If I could, I'd comb the sky and collect the stars . . ." on Ultrasmooth White cardstock. Make card base. Cut template from paper, following diagram. Cover front of card with template.

2 Stamp large and medium-sized balls over template, using Bliss Blue and Brocade Blue ink. *Note: This technique is called masking.*

3 Stamp small balls with pencil eraser and Almost Amethyst ink. Remove template.

4 Cover small scrap of cardstock with watermark ink.

5 Sprinkle scrap with Sterling Silver embossing powder. Melt with heat embossing tool.

6 Stamp into melted powder with small star stamp.

7 Cut out star to make charm. Punch hole in one point and tie with fiber.

8 Adhere star charm to card with adhesive foam dots. Adhere end of fiber to back of card.

Shades of Autumn Stationery Set

Designer: Alice Golden

SUPPLIES

For All:

Watermark ink: VersaMark, *Tsukineko*

Copper embossing powder: *PSX*

Heat tool

For Cards:

Cream cards

Rubber stamps:
  Rectangle blocks; Block Group #3, *Stamp It!*

  (*Cairo* from Mail and Tag Art set), No. 07849, Venetia Graphic, New Zealand Immigration, *Limited Edition Rubberstamps*

  Leaf on script background (see "Stamp Sources")

Dye ink: Artprint Brown, Brown; Memories, *Stewart Superior*

Metallic pigment ink: Champagne, Honeydew, Satin Rose; Encore!, *Tsukineko*

Low-tack tape: BLOCKit!, *Stamp It!*

Copper foil tape

Deckle-edge scissors

For tin:

Sycamore Leaf rubber stamp: *A Stamp in the Hand*

Embossing powder:
  Detail Gold, *Ranger Industries*
  Metallic Bronze, *JudiKins*

Brown tin box

Copper ribbon

Other: dryer sheet, old paintbrush

Finished sizes:
  Tin box 5¾" x 6¾"
  Cards 4¼" x 5½"

CARDS

❶ Trim bottom front edge of card with deckle-edge scissors.

❷ Adhere copper foil tape to inside bottom of card.

❸ Stamp and heat-emboss rectangle blocks on card front, using watermark ink and copper embossing powder.

❹ Mask area outside embossed blocks with low-tack tape (see Figure a).

❺ Stamp a collage of images over rectangles, using assorted stamps and ink. Remove tape.

❻ Repeat steps 1–5 to make more cards, varying the stamped collage on each.

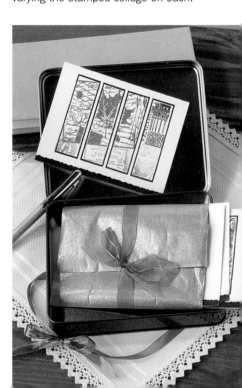

a

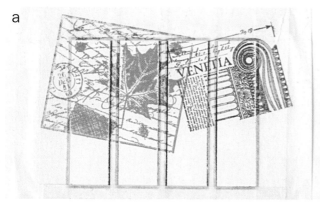

Mask rectangles and stamp.

TIN

See Figures b–d.

1. Wipe tin box with dryer sheet to prevent static.
2. Stamp lid with watermark ink.
3. Sprinkle stamped image with gold, copper, and bronze embossing powders, brushing off excess after each color with paintbrush. *Note: Be sure leaf is entirely covered with powder.*
4. Emboss with heat tool.
5. Place cards inside box and tie with ribbon.

b

Stamp lid.

c

Add embossing powder.

d

Heat emboss.

STAMP SOURCES

The leaf on script background stamp used in the project has been discontinued by Hero Arts. The good news is that we found some great leaf and script background stamps from other sources:

- Pressed Leaves Collection (Delta Rubber Stampede, 800/423-4135, www.rubberstampede.com)
- Assorted leaves (Stamp It! 757/425-0721, www.stampit.com)
- Background Script, In the Beginning, Kawani Script, The Equitable (Limited Edition Rubberstamps, 650/594-4242, www.limitededitionrs.com)

TIPS FROM ALICE

- Do not hold the tin box while heat embossing. The box may heat up and burn your hand.
- Use bold images when stamping metal. They tend to show up better than finely-detailed images.
- If you aren't satisfied with your stamped image prior to embossing, wipe the ink off the metal surface and start over.

Bonus Ideas

- Create a winter-themed tin and cards. Emboss a snowflake on a blue, silver, or white tin box, using pearlescent silver powder.
- Personalize a tin box with alphabet stamps. Keep cards or crafting supplies inside.

Gold Holly Gift Set

Designer: Kathleen Paneitz

SUPPLIES

Gold metallic paper: Canford, *Daler-Rowney*

Holly stamp: *Stampabilities*

Gold ink pad: ColorBox, *Clearsnap*

Jeweled gold embossing powder: *Mark Enterprises*

Gold cabachons: *Jones Tones*

Gold brads: *Avery*

Miniature adhesive dots: *Glue Dots International*

Other: red gift bag, gold thread, gold mesh fabric

Finished sizes:
    Bag: 5¼" x 8¼"
    Tag: 3¼" x 2⅞"

Embossed Elegance Box & Tag

Designer: Sande Krieger

SUPPLIES

White cardstock

Patterned paper:
(script) *Mille Rouge*
(Provence (striped), *7gypsies*

Vellum

Box: Ashlyn Gift Box; Jolee's By You, *EK Success*

Rubber stamps: Christmas Tree Script, Holly Sprig, *DeNami Design*

Dye ink: Vermillion Lacquer, Chartreuse Leaf; Nick Bantock, *Ranger Industries*

Embossing powder: clear fine, Rich Red, *Ranger Industries*

Accents:
Red ribbon: *May Arts*
Decorative brads: *Making Memories*
Green thread

Other: heat tool, hole punch, sewing machine, sponge, vellum adhesive

Finished sizes:
box 2¼" x 3¼" x 3¼",
tag 5" x 3"

BOX

❶ Stamp Holly Sprig twice on vellum with green ink; heat-emboss with clear powder. Trim to 1½" squares. Repeat, using red ink and red embossing powder.

❷ Cut two 1½" squares from each patterned paper and adhere to box lid. Adhere green stamped squares over striped squares and red stamped squares over script patterned squares, using vellum adhesive.

❸ Cut ¾" wide strip of striped paper long enough to wrap around box. Cut ½" wide strip of script paper and zigzag-stitch to wider strip. Adhere stitched strip around box.

❹ Tie box closed with ribbon.

TAG

❶ Cut tag from cardstock. Cut script paper to same size. Adhere striped paper vertically over half of script paper.

❷ Stamp and heat-emboss Christmas Tree Script on vellum with red. Sponge

green ink around edges and heat-emboss with clear powder. Adhere to paper piece.

❸ Add brads to bottom corners and adhere piece to tag.

❹ Punch holes through top corners and add ribbon for hanger.

With Love Valentine

Designer: Cheryl Mcmurray

SUPPLIES

Cardstock (Celery green, Pale yellow, Royal blue)

White vellum, *Paper Adventures*

2" square no-slip rug pad

2" square acrylic stamp block, *Paper Adventures*

Alphabet rubber stamps, Antique Lowercase Alphabet stamps, *PSX*

Ink pads:
   (Moss Green) *Stampin' Up!*
   (Silver) *Stampendous!*

Silver embossing powder, *Stampendous!*

Punches:
   ($^1/_{16}$" hole) *McGill*
   (heart) Folk Heart, Paper Shaper, *EK Success*

Embossing pen

Folk Heart Paper Shaper, *EK Success*

Embossing heat tool

5" length 24-gauge silver craft wire, *The Beadery*

Medium-sized heart template

Adhesive: Memory Book Glue Dots, *Glue Dots International*

Miscellaneous items: adhesive dots, scissors, double-sided tape, scrap paper, ruler

INSTRUCTIONS

1 Adhere the piece of no-slip rug pad to the acrylic stamp block with double-sided tape.

2 Stamp the rug pad stamp twice on pale yellow cardstock with Moss Green ink, leaving a small border in between.

3 Trace the heart template on scrap paper and cut it out. Place the heart on pale yellow cardstock and stamp over it with the rug pad stamp and Moss Green ink.

4 Remove the heart, and then carefully trim the three stamped images, leaving a small border around each.

5 Adhere the stamped images to celery green cardstock (see photo). Trim the green cardstock, leaving a $^1/_8$" border.

6 To make the card, cut a 6½" x 8½" piece of royal blue cardstock and fold it in half widthwise.

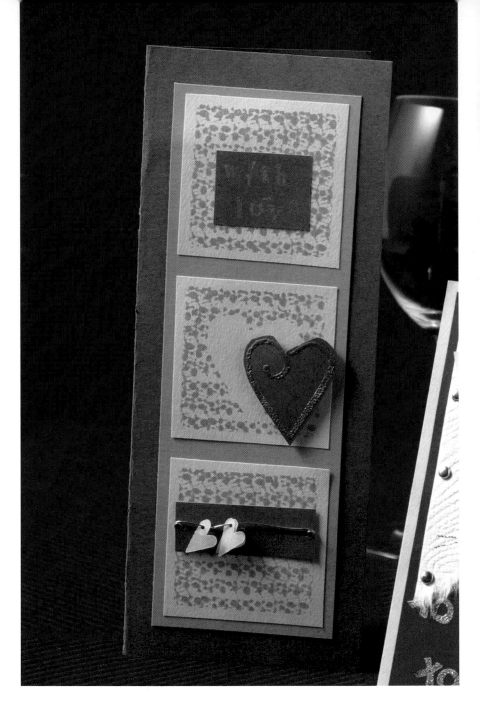

7 Adhere the celery green piece to the front of the card.

8 Stamp "with love" on a small piece of royal blue cardstock with the alphabet stamps and silver ink.

9 Trace a heart on royal blue cardstock and cut it out. Draw a curly outline of the heart with the embossing pen (see photo). Heat-emboss the design with silver.

10 Cut a ¾" x 2" piece of royal blue cardstock. Punch three hearts from vellum, then punch a hole in the top corner of each heart. Punch a hole in each side of the royal blue cardstock.

11 Thread the vellum hearts onto a 5" length of silver craft wire and insert the ends into the holes in the royal blue cardstock. Wrap the wire around the cardstock and bend the ends in back to secure (see photo).

12 Adhere the pieces to the front of the card (see photo).

RUG PAD SOURCES

No-slip rug pads are made of rubber mesh and used under rugs to keep them from sliding. You'll also find similar rubber material used for lining shelves and placemats. Look for this material at your local Home Depot or other hardware and department stores.

XO Wax Seal Valentine

Design: Kathleen Paneitz

SUPPLIES

Paper:
  (Cream handmade) *Pulsar Paper*
Cardstock:
  Red cardstock
  (Gold metallic) *Daler-Rowney*
  Tan print
  (Tan two-tone) *Daler-Rowney*
  (White vellum) *Daler-Rowney*
6 gold mini brads, *Impress Rubber Stamps*
XO rubber stamp, All Night Media, *Plaid*
Gold glitter glue, All Night Media, *Plaid*
Watermark ink pad, VersaMark, *Tsukineko*
Gold embossing powder, *Mark Enterprises*
Embossing heat tool
Burgundy wax seal, *Mark Enterprises*
Gold key charms, *PSX*
Gold thread
Miscellaneous items: bone folder or scoring blade, scissors, glue stick, white craft glue, ruler, computer with printer

MAKE THE MINI ENVELOPE

1 Transfer the envelope pattern onto the wrong side of the tan print paper. Assemble the envelope.

2 Line the exposed part of the inside of the envelope with gold metallic paper.

3 Wrap the envelope with gold thread and tie key charms onto the ends of the thread.

4 Melt the wax seal with the embossing heat tool until the top is soft. Press the XO stamp into the soft wax, and then lift it straight off.

5 To attach the wax seal, slightly melt the bottom with the embossing heat tool, and then press it onto the envelope.

6 Print your message on vellum using your favorite font (the designer used CK Script, "The Best of Creative Lettering" CD Combo, Creating Keepsakes) or your own handwriting. Trim the message and insert it into the mini envelope.

MAKE THE CARD

1 Trim the tan two-tone paper to 8½" x 6", then fold it in half widthwise.

2 Trim the red cardstock and adhere it to the front of the card.

3 Stamp the XO stamp randomly onto the red cardstock with watermark ink. Heat-emboss the designs with gold.

4 Tear the handmade paper diagonally and adhere it to the front of the card with gold mini brads (see photo).

5 Apply gold glitter to the XO's on the card and wax seal.

6 Adhere the mini envelope to the card.

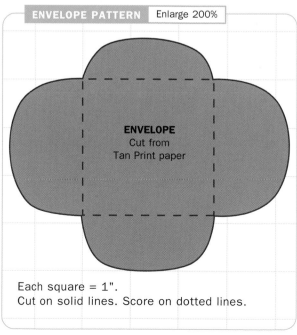

ENVELOPE PATTERN Enlarge 200%

ENVELOPE
Cut from
Tan Print paper

Each square = 1".
Cut on solid lines. Score on dotted lines.

Perhaps they are not stars in the sky

but rather openings where

our loved ones shine down

to let us know they are happy.

Celestial Sympathy

Designer: Nichole Heady

SUPPLIES

Rubber stamps: (In the Sky set, Border Builders set) *Stampin' Up!*

Dye ink: Basic Black, Classic Stampin' Pad, *Stampin' Up!*

Embossing powder: silver, *Stampin' Up!*

Cardstock: (Night of Navy, Ultrasmooth White, More Mustard) *Stampin' Up!*

Font: Fraternity, "Becky Higgins Creative Clips and Fonts" CD, *Creating Keepsakes*

Pen: silver, ZIG Painty Pen, *EK Success*

Air art tool: Inkworx, *Stampin' Up!*

Other: watermark ink, embossing heat tool, poker chip, adhesive, clothespin, scissors, small scrap matching cardstock, sponge, computer and printer

Finished size: 4¼" x 5½"

INSTRUCTIONS

❶ Make card from Night of Navy cardstock.

❷ Ink stars with silver pen; stamp on card front. Spray card with pen and air art tool.

❸ Print quote on Ultrasmooth White and More Mustard cardstock.

❹ Cut Ultrasmooth white quote into strips; adhere to card.

❺ Cut "stars," "loved," and "happy" from More Mustard cardstock.

❻ Adhere words over corresponding words on white strips.

❼ Make medallion (see "How to Make Medallion") and adhere to card.

HOW TO MAKE MEDALLION

❶ Ink cardstock scrap with watermark ink; emboss with silver. *Note: Layer 2–3 times* (see Figure a).

❷ Stamp sun into warm embossed layer; let cool and remove (see Figure b).

❸ Cut out stamped impression; sponge with black and adhere to poker chip (see Figure c).

❹ Holding poker chip with clothespin, ink edges with watermark ink and emboss with silver. Adhere to card when dry (see Figure d).

EMBOSS PAPER

IMPRINT WITH STAMP

CUT OUT IMPRINT

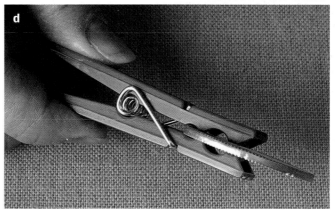

HOLD POKER CHIP WITH CLOTHESPIN TO INK EDGES

Thick Embossing Powders

a

RUB ON INK

b

SHAKE ON POWDER

c

MELT POWDER

① Coat the desired surface with embossing ink (Figure a).

② Sprinkle on thick embossing powder (Figure b).

③ Melt the powder with an embossing heat tool (Figure c).

④ While the powder is still wet, sprinkle on another coat. Re-melt with the heat tool.

⑤ Repeat this process until the desired thickness is achieved, usually about 3–5 coats, and then let the powder cool.

Tips for embossed accents

Convert ordinary scrapbook accents into artistic expressions with a few shakes of embossing powder and a little help from your heat tool.

If you love using thick embossing powder but don't have the right watermark or embossing ink on hand (or want a less messy alternative), you can get the same results by running the stamped image through a Xyron machine before sprinkling on the powder.

Colorful Embellishments

Designer: Julie Leedy

SUPPLIES

Embossing ink, punched shape or die cut, embossing powder, embossing heat tool, rubber stamps (optional)

INSTRUCTIONS

① Completely ink shape with embossing or watermark ink (or see the tip for using a Xyron machine instead of an ink pad).

② Sprinkle embossing powder over entire shape; heat with embossing heat tool.

③ Repeat at least 3–5 times.

Turn a plain-Jane punched shape, tag, or die cut into a unique embellishment with a little embossing ink and powder.

Bonus Ideas

★ Try using gold and silver embossing powders for a cool gilded finish.

★ Stamp a small image into the embossing powder while it's still warm but not liquid. Press the stamp down until the powder is almost completely cooled.

Latest & Greatest

ULTRA THICK FOR EXTRA DIMENSION

To get even more dimension out of your embossing, try Ultra Thick Embossing Enamel by Ranger Industries. Its powder grains are bigger than most other embossing powders, making thicker layers. For varied effects, apply 1–3 layers. A single layer produces a grainy appearance. Two layers give a thick, enameled look. Three layers create an almost solid effect. For an interesting reverse embossing, stamp an image into three melted layers.

Embossed Leaves

Designer: Suze Weinberg

SUPPLIES

Interference Green thick embossing enamel*

Gingko leaf rubber stamp, *Suze Weinberg's Ultra Thick*

Embossing heat tool

Ink pads: black, teal

Glitter glue

7 small jewels

8½" x 11" paper:

    Embossed background

    Purple cardstock

    Turquoise cardstock

    White cardstock

Corner punch

Miscellaneous items: plastic bowl or storage container, double-sided tape, white craft glue, tweezers, glue stick, scissors, ruler

EMBOSS THE DESIGN

❶ Pour the green embossing enamel into the plastic bowl or storage container.

❷ Ink the mat board with black until it is completely covered. Place the mat board inked side down in the embossing enamel until it is thoroughly covered. Lift it out with the tweezers.

❸ Heat with the embossing heat tool until melted and tacky. Place the mat board in the embossing enamel and coat again. Remove with the tweezers. Repeat three times.

❹ Apply teal ink to the stamp. Heat the embossing enamel on the mat board and press the Gingko leaves stamp into it (see photo).

❺ Embellish the embossed images with glitter glue and adhere the jewels.

ASSEMBLE THE CARD

❶ Mat the embossed mat board with white and then purple cardstock. Adhere the embossed mat board at an angle to the embossed paper and trim it to 4½".

❷ Adhere rhinestones to the embossed paper (see photo).

❸ Cut a 5" square of purple cardstock and a slightly smaller square of turquoise cardstock. Punch the corners of the squares with the corner punch, and then adhere them together.

❹ Adhere the embossed paper to the cardstock.

Puppy Love

Designer: Teri Anderson

SUPPLIES

Rubber stamps: (Antique Lowercase alphabet) *Duncan*

Dye ink: (Black) Exclusive Inks, *Close To My Heart*

Watermark ink: VersaMark, *Tsukineko*

Chalk ink: (Charcoal) ColorBox Fluid Chalk, *Clearsnap*

Embossing powder: (Clear) Ultra Thick Embossing Enamel, *Ranger Industries*

Color medium: (Black marker) ZIG Writer, *EK Success*

Cardstock:
  (Red) *Bazzill Basics Paper*
  (blue, yellow, black, ivory)

Accents:
  (letter tiles) Foofabets, *FoofaLa*
  (yellow, red, blue buttons) *SEI*
  (craft metal) *Making Memories*
  (clear beads) *Darice*

Stickers: (multi-colored letters) *SEI*

Fibers:
  (green ribbon) *May Arts*
  (black)

Adhesive

Tools:
  (flower punch) Whale of a Punch, *EK Success*
  (label maker) *Dymo*
  scissors, heat tool, stapler

Other: (staples) *Making Memories*; photos

ADD TEXTURE TO ACCENTS

Emboss texture right onto your layout to create a background for accents. Thick embossing on the flower petals and added marble beads create dimension and interest.

Embossed Snowflake

Designer: Lori Fairbanks

SUPPLIES

Rubber stamp: Snowflakes set, *Stampin' Up!*

Alphabet stamps: Pixie, Antique Lowercase, *PSX*

Pigment ink: gold, ColorBox, *Clearsnap*

Solvent ink: Ultramarine, StazOn, *Tsukineko*

Watermark ink: VersaMark, *Tsukineko*

Embossing powder: Ultra Thick Embossing Enamel, Suze Weinberg, *Ranger Industries* (clear, Interference Blue, white)

Other: CD tin, cardstock, scrap paper or cardboard, embossing heat tool, paintbrush

Finished size: 5½" x 4¾"

PREPARE

① Apply Ultramarine directly to tin. Let dry.

② Apply watermark ink to top lid.

③ Sprinkle clear powder over lid; heat.

④ Sprinkle Interference Blue and white powder over lid while powder is heating. *Note: Use heat tool to spread melted powder over surfaces.*

STAMP

① Stamp snowflake on melted powder with gold; let cool before removing stamp.

② Reheat stamped image to melt down powder.

③ Repeat 2–4 times to create marbled look with faint appearance of snowflakes.

④ Tear cardstock strip; apply gold to strip.

⑤ Stamp "cds" with Ultramarine, sprinkle clear powder, and heat.

⑥ Reheat powder on tin; place word strip in melted mixture.

⑦ Stamp snowflake in center of tin with gold; let cool, harden.

DESIGNER TIPS

■ Apply multiple coats of solvent ink if you're using a preprinted tin but don't worry about completely or perfectly covering any print.

■ Internet service provider tins that come in the mail work well for this project.

■ Work on a piece of cardboard bigger than the project to protect your work surface.

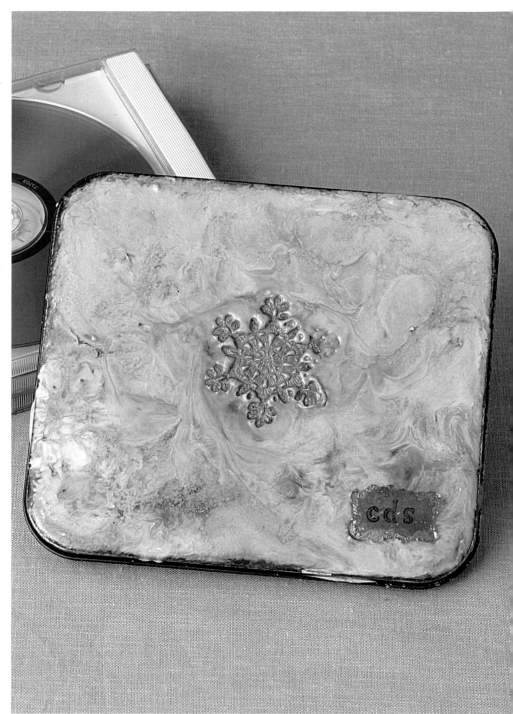

Bonus Idea

Create a CD of holiday tunes as a special gift for family or friends. Personalize the tin with the recipient's name.

Marbled Bracelet

Design: Suze Weinberg

SUPPLIES

Small cardboard squares*

Pigment ink pad in desired color(s)

Thick embossing enamel* (in any color except black)

Embossing heat tool

Watercolor crayons

Clear lacquer

Desired jewelry findings

Small rubber stamp (optional)

Miscellaneous items: plastic container, tweezers, hairpin or toothpick, paintbrush for applying lacquer, scissors, ruler

*Suze Weinberg's Stamping Craft Squares cardboard squares and Ultra Thick Embossing Enamel were used in the sample project.

INSTRUCTIONS

① Pour the embossing enamel into a plastic container.

② Pat the pigment ink pad onto one side of a cardboard square until the square is thoroughly coated.

③ Quickly immerse the cardboard square in the embossing enamel, then lift it out with tweezers.

④ Melt the enamel on the square with the embossing heat tool. While the square is still warm, immerse it in embossing enamel again. Melt the enamel. Repeat 2–3 times or until the enamel is 1–2 mm thick.

⑤ While the square is still slightly warm, draw random lines of color over the embossed area with watercolor crayons.

⑥ Place the square on the work surface. Hold a hairpin or toothpick in your dominant hand and the heat embossing tool in the other.

⑦ To marbleize the enamel on the square, warm the colored surface with the embossing heat tool while you use the toothpick to pull the colors in the opposite direction from the way they were applied.

⑧ Firmly press a stamp into the warm enamel, if desired.

⑨ Seal the color with clear lacquer, and let it dry completely.

⑩ Repeat the steps using different color combinations of embossing enamel and crayons to achieve different looks.

⑪ Cut the squares into small shapes and attach them to earrings, a necklace, or a bracelet with jewelry adhesive.

Embossed Charm Pins

Design: Lori Fairbanks

SUPPLIES

Heavy cardstock or watercolor paper

Metallic gold ink pad

Clear thick embossing powder*

Pigment powder: blue, gold

6–10 small gold charms*

2 adhesive pin backs

Embossing heat tool

Miscellaneous items: waxed paper*, small container, small paintbrush, tweezers

*Ranger Industries Suze Weinberg's Ultra Thick Embossing Enamel; Yvonne Albritton Designs Just Charming charms; and Embossing Arts Co. Release Paper were used in the sample projects.

Finished size: 1¾" x 1½"

EMBOSS THE BACKGROUND

❶ Pour the embossing powder into the container.

❷ Tear two rectangles (approx. 1¾" x 1½") of heavy cardstock or watercolor paper. Note: Tear the cardstock from the front so the textured edges will show.

❸ Pat the ink pad on one side of a rectangle until it's thoroughly coated.

❹ Quickly immerse the inked side of the rectangle in the embossing powder, and then lift it out with tweezers.

❺ Place the rectangle on waxed paper and melt the embossing powder with the heat tool. Let it cool. Note: The waxed paper will catch excess powder and allow you to peel it off the paper and re-melt it.

EMBELLISH THE PIN

❶ Rub gold pigment powder on the torn edges.

❷ Add three more layers of embossing powder. While the third layer of embossing powder is still warm, lightly tap some blue pigment powder from the paintbrush on it.

❸ Add another layer of embossing powder. While the melted powder is still warm, set a charm on the piece using tweezers. Repeat to attach the other charms.

❹ To secure the charms, sprinkle a small amount of embossing powder over them and heat the powder. Repeat to further embed the charms in the powder, if desired.

❺ Adhere the pin back to the piece.

❻ Repeat steps 3–5 of "Emboss the Background" and steps 1–5 of "Embellish the Pin" to make the other pin.

Embossing with Adhesives—
A Technique That Will Stick Around

You can create so many different looks that you'll just have to keep trying something new.

Adhesive embossing is a wonderful way to create custom metal embellishments for any paper craft project (and you can use non-metallic colors as well). It's quick, easy, and affordable. In moments, you can make your own frames, brads, rimmed tags, and charms—all with supplies that you already have on hand. This terrific technique works on anything sticky. So learn the basics here, and then set off on your own adventure of discovery.

How to Emboss with Adhesives

Apply the adhesive to the project surface.

Sprinkle with embossing powder; shake off excess.

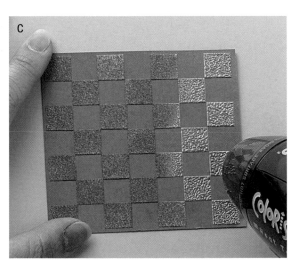

Heat set with heat tool

Soaring Spirit Card

Designer: Nichole Heady

SUPPLIES

All supplies by Stampin' Up! unless otherwise noted.

Cardstock: Barely Banana, Kraft, Old Olive

Gold brads

Dragonfly rubber stamp: Wonderful Wings stamp set

Gold Glory embossing powder

Acrylic sheet: Window sheet

Permanent black ink: StazOn, *Tsukineko*

"Grow" epoxy sticker: *Creative Imaginations*

Adhesive tabs: Vario, *EK Success*

Heating tool: Coloriser, *EK Success*

Other: 1/16" hole punch

Finished size: 4¼" square

INSTRUCTIONS

1 Make Kraft card base.

2 Cut smaller square of Old Olive cardstock. Place adhesive tabs in checkerboard pattern. Sprinkle with embossing powder and shake off excess. Heat set.

3 Mat checkerboard accent with Barely Banana cardstock.

4 Stamp dragonfly on acrylic sheet with black ink. Cut out. Adhere sticker and dragonfly to accent.

5 Punch holes and attach accent to card using brads. To conceal backs of brads, line inside of card front with Kraft cardstock if desired.

Butterfly Dreams Card

Designer: Nichole Heady

SUPPLIES

Card stock: Almost Amethyst, Bliss Blue, Gable Green, Mellow Moss, Sage Shadow, Ultrasmooth White, *Stampin' Up!*

Butterfly rubber stamp: Wonderful Wings stamp set, *Stampin' Up!*

Alphabet stickers: *Pioneer*

Sterling Silver embossing powder: *Stampin' Up!*

Black solvent ink: StazOn, *Tsukineko*

Adhesive lines: Zips, *Therm O Web*

Small square punch: *EK Success*

Ribbon: *Making Memories*

Clear shrink plastic: PolyShrink, *Lucky Squirrel*

Heat tool: Coloriser, *EK Success*

Sturdy cardboard

Finished size: 4¼" x 5½"

INSTRUCTIONS

❶ Make card base from Ultrasmooth White cardstock.

❷ Punch small squares of several shades of cardstock; adhere to cardboard in pattern shown in photo.

❸ See Figures a–c below to create faux metal-rimmed tag.

❹ Stamp butterfly on shrink plastic, cut out, and shrink in oven or with heat tool. Adhere butterfly to tag; adhere tag to card.

❺ Attach ribbon to card front. Spell "wish" with alphabet stickers.

Faux Metal-Rimmed Tag

Adhere adhesive lines to edges.

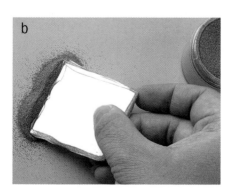

Dip in embossing powder.

Heat set with heat tool.

Bouquet of Poppies Card

Designer: Nichole Heady

SUPPLIES

Ink: Basic Black, *Stampin' Up!*

Chak: Stampin' Pastels, *Stampin' Up!*

Rubber stamps:

Flowers and stems from Spring Garden stamp set, *Stampin' Up!*

"smile" greeting from Good Times stamp set, *Stampin' Up!*

Black marker

Sterling Silver embossing powder

Gingham ribbon: *Offray*

Adhesive dots: Zots, *Therm O Web*

Watermark ink: VersaMark, *Tsukineko*

Finished size: 4¼" square

INSTRUCTIONS

❶ Make red card base.

❷ Stamp stems and flowers with watermark ink on Ultrasmooth White cardstock. Chalk stems with olive pastel and flowers with red pastel. Make small dots in center of flowers with marker. Stamp "smile" with black ink along the stems.

❸ To make faux brads, place adhesive dot in each corner, sprinkle with embossing powder, shake off excess, and heat set. Mat with Ultrasmooth White Vellum.

❹ Adhere ribbon and embossed piece to card.

Bonus Ideas

ADHESIVE OPTIONS

Discover the variety of looks you can create with these different adhesives:

■ **Adhesive dots:** Make faux mini brads without having to create holes.

■ **Foam tape:** You can imprint a stamp into this thick, pliable adhesive. Heat it to soften, stamp, then quickly add embossing powder and heat set. To highlight the image after it cools, rub on brown ink.

■ **Glue stick:** Draw patterns or rub on a background, then emboss. The thick consistency lets you create interesting textures.

■ **Hot glue:** Mix with embossing powder immediately after you've dispensed it from the glue gun, then press a stamp into it. Let the glue cool before removing the stamp.

■ **2-Way Glue:** The unique chisel tip on this adhesive works well for creating stripes and perfect borders. Sprinkle powder on quickly before the adhesive dries.

Making Scents of Embossing

Spice up your paper projects with fun textures and fragrances.

People love heat embossing because it adds eye-catching dimension to paper projects. Now, make it even more interesting by adding scents. It's easy and fun to create a variety of fragrances by mixing common kitchen ingredients such as spices, coffee, or sugar-free powdered drink mix with clear embossing powder. You can use almost any fine powder that doesn't contain sugar, which caramelizes when heated.

How to create scented embossing

Combine embossing powder and fragrance ingredient in container.

Shake container to mix.

Ink accent with embossing ink.

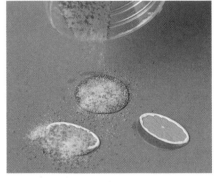

Cover accent with embossing powder mixture; shake off excess.

Heat set.

SCENTSATIONAL TIPS

- Try this technique on die cuts, accents, patterned paper, stickers, and other preprinted images. (Avoid plastic stickers because they melt when heated.)

- Use embossing pads or pens. An embossing pen, such as the VersaMarker, provides a fine point, allowing you to adhere the mixture exactly where desired.

- Store leftover mixtures in clear plastic containers. Label them so that you can identify the mixtures again. Keep your eyes open at the grocery store to see what fun new combinations you can cook up!

- Mix larger-granule ingredients such as coffee with embossing enamel or UTEE to ensure that the mixture adheres. The fine grains in regular embossing powder slide under larger particles. Embossing enamel has granules the same size as coffee.

- Try heating from underneath the object so that the granules don't blow away.

Orange You Glad Card

Designer: Nichole Heady

SUPPLIES

Cardstock: Garden Green, Ultrasmooth White, *Stampin' Up!*

Mustard patterned paper: *All My Memories*

Leaves stamp: Toille Blossoms set, *Stampin' Up!*

Embossing pen: VersaMarker, *Tsukineko*

Clear embossing powder: *Stampin' Up!*

Sugar-free orange powdered drink mix: Kool-Aid, *Kraft Foods*

Dye ink: Garden Green; *Stampin' Up!*

Accents:
  Orange stickers: Jolee's Boutique, *EK Success*
  Green mini brads: *All My Memories*

Font: Future Light, *Corel*

Heat tool

Finished size: 4¼" x 5¼"

INSTRUCTIONS

❶ Make card base from white cardstock.

❷ Stamp leaves on green cardstock with green ink. Cut rectangles of stamped green and mustard patterned paper; adhere to card.

❸ Print greeting on white cardstock and trim. Attach to card with mini brads.

❹ Emboss half-orange sticker using drink mix/embossing powder mixture; heat set. Adhere whole orange and embossed half-orange to card.

❺ To cover brads, line inside of card front with cardstock.

Simple Sentiments

Find other fruit stickers to use with these greeting ideas:

If we could choose our friends, and we searched the whole world through, we'd go bananas trying to find a better bunch than you!
      — *www.ywconnection.com*

May your new year be festive and fruitful!
      — *www.ywconnection.com*

Have a berry nice holiday season.
      — *www.ywconnection.com*

You're a grape friend!

A Cup of Cheer Card

Designer: Nichole Heady

SUPPLIES

Cardstock: Naturals Ivory, Old Olive, Ruby Red, *Stampin' Up!*

Brown velvet paper: *Stampin' Up!*

Mug stamp: Sketch an Event set, *Stampin' Up!*

Dye ink: Chocolate Chip; *Stampin' Up!*

Embossing ink: VersaMark, *Tsukineko*

Enamel embossing powder: Glassy Glaze, *Stampin' Up!*

Ground coffee

Accents:

　Tag: *Creative Imaginations*

　Square brad: *All My Memories*

　Alphabet sticker: *All My Memories*

¾" circle punch: *Marvy Uchida*

1¼" circle punch: All Night Media, *Plaid*

Adhesive: *Glue Dots International*

Other: ⅜" square punch, heating tool

Finished size: 4¼" x 5½"

INSTRUCTIONS

① Make card base from ivory cardstock.

② Punch several brown velvet paper circles and rings. Adhere randomly to card.

③ Press embossing pad on tag and sprinkle tag with coffee/embossing

enamel mixture. Shake off excess; heat set.

④ Stamp mug on olive cardstock with dye ink; trim. Adhere to tag with adhesive dots. Punch red cardstock square. Place "C" alphabet sticker on brad, and secure to square and tag. Adhere tag to card.

⑤ Print greeting on red cardstock. Trim and adhere to card.

Mix coffee and embossing enamel before embossing.

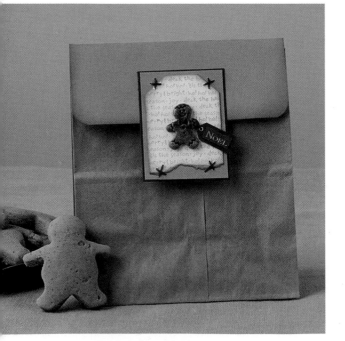

A Gingerbread Man Gift

Designer: Nichole Heady

SUPPLIES

Cardstock: Mellow Moss, Real Red, *Stampin' Up!*

Greeting stamp: Crazy for Christmas set, *Stampin' Up!*

Clear embossing powder: *Stampin' Up!*

Embossing ink: VersaMark, *Tsukineko*

Dye ink: Creamy Caramel, Mellow Moss, *Stampin' Up!*

Cinnamon

Accents:

　Tag: Naturals Ivory , Real Red, *Stampin' Up!*

　Silver mini eyelet: *Making Memories*

　Gingerbread man button: Trimming the Tree, *Jesse James & Co.*

　Noel metal charm: Christmas, *Lasting Impressions for Paper*

　Red embroidery floss: *DMC*

Adhesive: *Glue Dots International*

Other: corner rounder, heat tool, lunch bag, needle, cosmetic sponge

Finished size: 6" x 5"

Fresh as Pie Tag

Designer: Nichole Heady

SUPPLIES

Brocade Blue cardstock: *Stampin' Up!*

Rubber stamps: Checkerboard background, Classic Alphabet, "Fresh" (from Farm Fresh stamp set), *Stampin' Up!*

Embossing pen: VersaMarker, *Tsukineko*

Clear embossing powder: *Stampin' Up!*

Dye ink: Basic Black, Brocade Blue, Creamy Caramel, *Stampin' Up!*

Pumpkin pie spice

Accents:
  Pie die cut: *My Mind's Eye*
  Naturals Ivory tags: small, large, *Stampin' Up!*
  Silver eyelets: mini, regular, *Making Memories*
  Blue ribbon: grosgrain, organdy, *Making Memories*
  Green mini brads: *All My Memories*

Font: Schindler, *Corel*

Other: eyelet-setting tools, heat tool, cosmetic sponge

Finished size: 4" x 2¾"

INSTRUCTIONS

① Print greeting on small ivory tag, omitting the "M." Stamp "M" using blue ink. Sponge edges with caramel ink. Mat with blue cardstock, and sponge edges with caramel ink. Secure mini eyelet to tag.

② Stamp checkerboard image with blue ink on large ivory tag. Sponge edges with caramel ink. Mat with blue cardstock. Sponge edges with caramel ink. Stamp "Fresh" with black ink. Set eyelet in tag.

③ Color pie crust with embossing pen. Sprinkle spice/embossing powder mixture on pie, tap off excess, and heat set. Adhere to tag.

④ Thread ribbons through holes in tags and tie. Heat organdy ribbon with heat tool to shrivel. *Note: Move heat tool constantly so ribbon doesn't get too hot.*

INSTRUCTIONS

① Stamp greeting all over ivory tag with moss ink. Tear bottom of tag and sponge edges with caramel ink. Mat tag with moss and stitch X's in corners, using floss. Mat with red.

② Press gingerbread man button on embossing pad (see Figure a). Sprinkle with cinnamon/embossing powder mixture. Shake off excess and heat set. *Note: You may want to apply a second coat for added depth and texture.* Adhere to tag with adhesive dots.

③ Adhere Noel charm to red tag with adhesive dots. Attach mini eyelet to tag. Tie tag to gingerbread man with floss and adhere tag in place.

④ Trim lunch bag to 6" tall. Cut moss cardstock to 5" x 8". Adhere to back of lunch bag and fold flap over top. Punch front corners with corner rounder and sponge edges with caramel ink.

⑤ Adhere gingerbread man accent to flap.

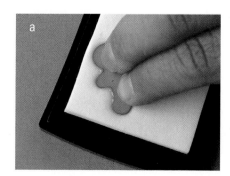

Add elegance with dry embossing

Create beautiful relief designs with this simple technique.

WHAT IS DRY EMBOSSING?

Dry embossing is a method of impressing two-dimensional designs into paper using a stencil and an embossing tool, which has a rounded tip at each end. You make depressions in the paper by pressing the tool through the cutouts in the stencil. When you turn the paper over, the depressions become raised areas, creating a relief design. The technique is called dry embossing to distinguish it from wet embossing, which uses fluids and powders to create raised effects.

SUPPLIES

Sturdy paper or cardstock

Brass stencil

Embossing tool

Other: masking or repositionable tape, light box

How to dry emboss

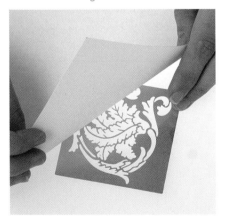

❶ Tape the stencil to the center of the light box. Lay the paper over it and tape down the edges.

❷ Hold the embossing tool like a pencil. Run the tip around the edges of the cutout areas of the stencil, applying gentle pressure. Use the size tip that best fits the areas you are working in. For crisp results, you may need to go over some areas several times.

❸ Remove the tape and turn the paper over.

EMBOSSING TIPS

- Before you begin, rub the surface of the paper with waxed paper to ease the movement of the embossing tool. Or use a rolling ball embossing tool, which moves across paper with less drag.

- If you don't have a light box, try taping the stencil and paper to a clean, bright window.

- Once you start embossing, don't move the paper or stencil until you have finished. It may be difficult to line them up again.

HOW TO ADD COLOR

Dab a cosmetic sponge on an inkpad and brush it across the highest areas of relief. Avoid getting ink in the low areas. Or, reposition the stencil over the embossing and pounce lightly with a sponge dipped in paint or ink. You can also apply chalk using an eye shadow applicator.

Bonus Ideas

- Make your stencils more versatile by using only parts of them. Emboss with a tiny section of a large stencil, or mix elements from several to create a whole new design.

- You don't need commercially made stencils to dry emboss—you can make your own with cardboard and a craft knife. Or skip the stencil altogether and make impressions using punches and a flower press! Lightly moisten a fiber-based paper like blotter or watercolor paper. Punch shapes from cardboard, arrange them on the paper, and press until dry. You can even substitute flat objects like keys and coins for the punched shapes.

Embossing with Ease

Paper Glide is a nontoxic, acid-freeproduct that conditions paper, metal, plastic, or other surfaces for embossing. This easy-to-apply mist eliminates the need for waxed paper, and lets your stylus fly over paper without breaking the cardstock fibers. Even better, there's no wax residue to interfere with adhesives and ink. Simply spray the paper or other project surface, let dry for one minute, and emboss with ease. Retail $4.95. 866/867-4064, *www.paper-glide.com*.

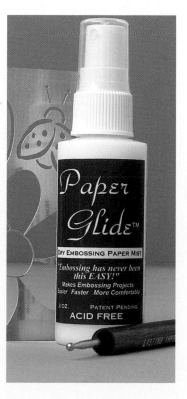

Embossing Made Easy

Embossing was never so easy or so comfortable! The new Empressor Rolling Ball Embossing Tool from EK Success has cushy soft grips and dual ballpoint tips in two sizes. The tool is designed to work equally well with most weights of paper, and sells for $9.99. 800/767-2963, *www.eksuccess.com*.

MAKE YOUR OWN LIGHT BOX

I do a lot of dry embossing, and needed an inexpensive light box. So I made one myself using materials available at home improvement stores! I found a sturdy cardboard box and cut off the lid. Then I put a battery-operated touch light in the bottom and a sheet of acrylic plastic on top. Voila! The whole thing cost less than $4.00.

—V. Penland, Clarkston, MI

Tapestry Gift Bag and Card

Designer: Jenna Beegle, courtesy of Anna Griffin

SUPPLIES

Cream cardstock

Patterned paper: Fleur Rose, Green Plumes, Pink Repousse, Anna Griffin (*Plaid*)

"A Very Happy Birthday" stamp: All Night Media, *Plaid*

Brass stencils: Medallion, Flourish Corner, Anna Griffin (*Plaid*)

Crimson ink: All Night Media, *Plaid*

Other: decorative-edge scissors, scoring tool, embossing tool, light box, sage green ribbon, ¼" hole punch

Finished sizes:
  bag 6½" x 4" x 1¾"
  card 3¾" square

CARD

Emboss four Flourish Corners on a 3⅛" cardstock square. Stamp "A Very Happy Birthday" across center. Mat with Pink Repousse paper. Make a 3¾" card base from Fleur Rose. Punch hole in corner. Adhere matted square to card.

BAG

1 Cut bag from Fleur Rose paper, following Figure a. Score, fold, and adhere.

2 Cut two 3¼" x 12" strips from Green Plumes paper using decorative-edge scissors. Adhere strips to bag where indicated.

3 Cut two 3" x 6" cardstock pieces. Emboss each with two medallions, then adhere to front and back of bag. Punch two pairs of holes in bag top (see photo). Thread ribbon through, catching in card.

a   HOW TO MAKE THE BAG

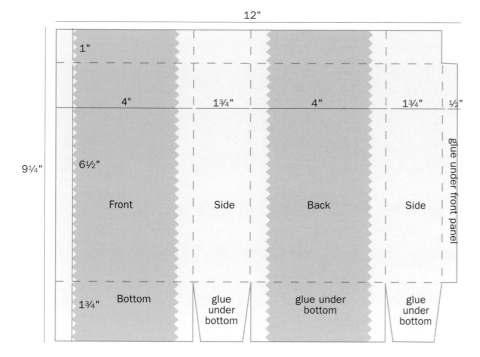

Floral Gift Box and Card

Designer: Debby Schuh, courtesy of
Anna Griffin

SUPPLIES

Cream cardstock

Patterned paper: Fleur Rouge, Striped
Fabric, Red Wreath, Green Plumes,
Persimmon Engraving, Anna Griffin
(*Plaid*)

Plume stencil: Anna Griffin (*Plaid*)

Scallop-edge scissors: *Fiskars*

Adhesive foam squares: *Therm O Web*

Other: oval paper maché box (painted),
embossing tool, light box, sage green
tulle ribbon

Finished sizes:
   box 5" x 7" x 3"
   card 3½" square

BOX

❶ Cut two 3" x 12" strips from Red
Wreath paper so that patterns align
when placed end-to-end. Adhere ends
together to make one long strip. Adhere
strip around box bottom. Overlap ends
and trim to fit (see Figure a in "How to
Cover the Box").

❷ Make one strip from two 1" x 12"
pieces of Green Plumes paper. Also join
two 12" ribbons cut from Striped Fabric
paper. Adhere Green Plumes strip to lid
rim as in Step 1. Glue ribbon strip along
the middle of rim (see photo).

❸ Make one strip from two ¾" x 12"
pieces of Red Wreath paper. Trim one
long edge with scalloped-edge scissors.
Make ¼" clips into straight edge and
adhere around lid top (see Figure b).
Fold down clipped edge.

❹ Cut cardstock oval to fit lid top.
Emboss six evenly spaced plumes on
oval; adhere to lid.

❺ Cut flowers from Red Wreath and
Fleur Rouge papers and adhere to lid
with foam squares. Tie ribbon around lid.

CARD

❶ Cut a 3¼" square from cardstock.
Emboss Plume on front. Emboss stencil
edge to make border.

❷ Mat square on Persimmon Engraving.
Cut flowers from Fleur Rouge and adhere
to front with foam squares.

HOW TO COVER THE BOX

a

b

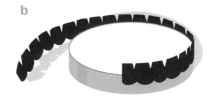

Birthday Wishes Card

Designer: Linda Beeson

SUPPLIES

Cream embossed cardstock: *K&Company*

Silver paper

"Birthdays are" stamp: *Savvy Stamps*

Black ink: *Making Memories*

Pink ink: *Stampa Rosa*

Button: Favorite Findings, *Blumenthal Lansing Co.*

Ribbon: pink/white grosgrain, pink organza, *Michaels*

Font: Scriptina, *www.scrapvillage.com*

Other: 4¼" x 5½" cream card with deckle edge, 1⁄16" and ¼" hole punches

INSTRUCTIONS

❶ Color embossed cardstock with pink ink (see "How to Add Color" on page 83).

❷ Print "Best Wishes" and cut rectangle. Tear one edge.

❸ Cut strip of silver paper; tear colored cardstock strip. Layer on rectangle.

❹ Stamp "birthdays are for wishing" on paper and trim. Punch two holes at top, thread organza ribbon through; adhere with button to rectangle.

❺ Punch two holes in rectangle. Thread grosgrain ribbon through; make bow. Adhere to card.

Embossed Baby Steps Tag Accents

Designer: Erin Tenney

SUPPLIES

Rubber stamps: (Printers Type alphabet) *Hero Arts*

Dye ink: (Brown) Distress Ink, *Ranger Industries*

Color medium: (brown chalk) *Craf-T Products*

Embossing template: (Baby feet #i155) *Lasting Impressions for Paper*

Cardstock:
  (Windy) *Bazzill Basics Paper*
  (tan)

Patterned paper: (Big Den Plaid) Den Collection, *Chatterbox*

Fibers: (assorted ribbons)

Adhesive

Tools: scissors, light box or sunny window, stylus, ⅛" hole punch, ¼" hole punch, ruler

Other: (silver staples) *Making Memories*; chalk applicator

Finished size: 3" x 9"

CREATE A FOCAL POINT

Dry embossing can make an image stand out on your accent. If you really want it to draw the eye, make sure other elements of the accent are flat or muted.

Make Your Own Envelopes

Having trouble finding an envelope or envelope template to fit that handmade card? You will always have one the right size if you make it yourself. Here's how:

❶ On cardstock, draw a rectangle that is the size of your card plus ½" to 1" in each direction.

This will be your envelope base. Follow diagram to complete the envelope.

❷ To make a liner, cut vellum or paper to the same size as the base and top flap. Trim the flap edge ½", if desired. *Note: Try using double-sided patterned paper for an instant liner.*

❸ Adhere the liner to the inside of the envelope. Score and fold down the flaps. Adhere the flaps together along the overlapping edges.

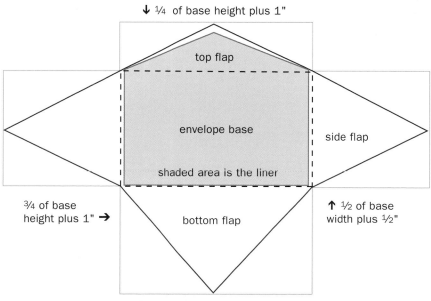

↓ ¼ of base height plus 1"

top flap

envelope base

side flap

shaded area is the liner

¾ of base height plus 1" ➡

bottom flap

↑ ½ of base width plus ½"

Cut on solid lines. Score on dotted lines.

Embossed Copper Pocket Accent

Designer: Sande Krieger

SUPPLIES

Rubber stamp: (rose) *Stampin' Up!*

Solvent ink: (Jet Black) StazOn, *Tsukineko*

Embossing template: (leaves) *Fiskars*

Cardstock: (Leapfrog) *Bazzill Basics Paper*

Patterned paper: (Peach Melba) *Scenic Route Paper Company*

Paper accents: (manila tags) *Office Max*

Accents: (scrap metal) Once Upon a Scribble; (photo turns) *7gypsies*

Fasteners: (copper brads)

Fibers: (green gingham ribbon, yellow gingham ribbon) *Offray*; (green fibers)

Adhesive

Tools: scissors, stylus, mouse pad, light box or sunny window

Other: sandpaper

Finished size: 4¾" x 3¾"

COPPER STYLE

Create striking accents with dry-embossed images on copper sheets. Emboss the image deeply for more impact, experiment with sanding to soften the look, and make it the focal point of your latest project.

Springtime Flower Tag Accent

Designer: Nichole Heady

SUPPLIES

Metal stamps: (Alphabet Stamp & Tool Kit) *FoofaLa*

Pigment ink: (Pretty in Pink, White) *Stampin' Up!*

Cardstock: (Old Olive) *Stampin' Up!*

Embossing template: (Love Without End) *Stampin' Up!*

Paper accent: ("S" sticker) *All My Memories*

Accent: (sheet metal) *American Art Clay Co.*

Fastener:
  (white eyelet) *Stampin' Up!*;
  (silver brad) *All My Memories*

Fiber: (white ribbon) *Stampin' Up!*

Adhesive

Tools: scissors, eyelet-setting tools, stylus, mouse pad, light box or sunny window, hole punch

Other: pencil, fine-grit sandpaper

Finished size: 2½" x 3¾"

MARVELOUS METAL

Dry embossing images on metal gives you a wealth of interesting looks for your layouts or cards. Use an opaque ink, like pigment ink or paint, then sand the image to create a rustic or antiqued look.

Tin Pumpkin

Designer: Janelle Clark

SUPPLIES

Rubber stamps: *Hero Arts* (Pumpkin from Autumn & Christmas Special Edition set, Thanksgiving Print)

Dye ink: Coffee Bean, Vivid!, *Clearsnap*

Craft metal sheet: copper, *American Traditional Designs*

Patterned paper: Shabby Brown, *Karen Foster Design*

Other: cardstock (brown, dark purple), scissors, stylus, antique brads, adhesive, self-healing mat

Finished size: 5½" x 4¼"

INSTRUCTIONS

❶ Make card from dark purple cardstock.

❷ Stamp Pumpkin with Coffee Bean on copper craft sheet. Place on self-healing mat and trace image with stylus. Cut out.

❸ Attach embossed pumpkin to patterned paper with antique brads.

❹ Stamp Thanksgiving Print with Coffee Bean on patterned paper; cut out.

❺ Mat with brown cardstock; adhere to card.

Embossed Velvet Wrap

Design: Susan Cottrell

SUPPLIES

44" wide fabric:

2 yd. dark green acetate-rayon velvet

2 yd. satin for backing, in desired color

Rigid foam fabric stamp*

Miscellaneous items: scissors, yard-stick, ruler, iron, sewing machine or serger, straight pins, matching thread, sewing needle, spray bottle filled with water (optional): pressing cloth, tissue paper or tear-away stabilizer

*Duncan Enterprises Cool Girl Wild Shapes fabric stamp (#12117) was used in the sample project.

CUT AND EMBOSS THE FABRIC

❶ Cut a 22" x 72" strip each of velvet and satin.

❷ From each strip, cut two 9" x 22" rectangles for the ends of the wrap, leaving one 22" x 54" rectangle for the center section.

❸ Emboss each 9" x 22" velvet rectangle with three rows of 3–4 images each (see "How to Emboss Velvet"). *Note: When planning the stamp place-ment, leave a ½" allowance along the edges for the seams.*

SEW THE WRAP

Sew the fabric pieces right sides together as instructed below. All seams are ½".

❶ Sew an embossed rectangle to each end of the 54" velvet center section, matching the 22" edges.

❷ Repeat step 1 to sew the satin pieces together.

❸ Sew the embossed velvet and satin backing together, leaving a 10" opening on one long side for turning. *Note: To help prevent the satin from shifting, place tissue paper or tear-away stabilizer between the fabric layers, carefully removing it when you turn the wrap.*

❹ For square corners, clip the corners before turning. For slightly rounded corners, do not clip them.

❺ Turn the wrap right side out. Slipstitch the opening closed.

CARE FOR YOUR WRAP

❶ Press the wrap on the satin side as needed.

❷ Dry clean only—machine or hand washing the wrap will cause the embossing to disappear.

HOW TO EMBOSS VELVET

PRECAUTIONS

■ Not all velvets are suitable for embossing. For best results use high quality acetate-rayon.

■ Practice embossing on a scrap of velvet before beginning the project.

■ Use big, bold rubber stamps, as smaller details tend to get lost in the velvet.

■ A variety of heat-resistant items other than stamps can also be used for embossing (e.g. charms, shaped wire, keys). Be sure to test them on a scrap piece of velvet first.

■ Arrange the embossed images on the fabric randomly, or position them in a uniform pattern by carefully meas-uring the placement of each image first. Random patterns may be more forgiving for beginners.

■ Leave adequate space around each image to avoid distorting it with subsequent embossing.

PROCEDURE

❶ Heat the iron to a medium-hot temperature with no steam.

❷ Place the stamp rubber side up on an ironing board. *Note: If you're using smaller images or stamps mounted on higher blocks, place a clean cutting board or piece of wood on top of the ironing board. This will give you a crisper design and keep your iron from "rocking" on the stamp.*

❸ Lightly mist the wrong side of the velvet.

❹ Press the iron firmly onto the velvet over the stamp, keeping it stationary for approx. 20 seconds. *Note: Hold the iron as steady as possible and horizontal to the ironing board.*

❺ Remove the iron by lifting it straight up, being careful not to shift the fabric. *Note: To avoid leaving steam holes on the velvet, iron it using the area of the sole plate with the fewest holes, or place a pressing cloth between the iron and the velvet.*

❻ If the velvet isn't completely dry, press it again, being careful not to shift the fabric on the stamp.

VELVET EMBOSSING MADE EASIER

The new Versa-Tool from Walnut Hollow makes velvet embossing a simple process. The tool has a disc-shaped tip that embosses permanent designs from rubber stamps. That means you can wash the velvet without erasing the embossed designs!

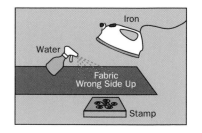

Vintage Velvet Purse

Design: Mary Lynn Maloney

SUPPLIES

Ribbon:

   1 yd. 3" pistachio rayon-acetate velvet*

   3" length decorative pink

⅓ yd. lightweight fabric for lining

Rubber stamps*: Peacock Feather, Tri-Curl

Decorative trim:

   6" length of ⅛" gold

   2 yd. tan*

1 yd. of ⅛" ivory cord*

Fabric glue or all purpose adhesive*

Spray adhesive*

½" x 1½" piece of cardboard

2 decorative beads (one with a large hole)

Miscellaneous items: tape measure, spray bottle filled with water, iron, scissors (optional): pressing cloth, tissue paper or tear-away stabilizer

*Hot Potatoes velvet ribbon and stamps; Trimtex tan rayon Snail trim; Europa Imports cord; Salis International Dr. Ph. Martin's Glue Everything all-purpose adhesive; and 3M Photo Mount spray adhesive were used in the sample project.

INSTRUCTIONS

Always let the glue dry before beginning the next step.

MAKE THE VELVET PIECE

❶ Cut the velvet ribbon in half and pull the wire edging out of both lengths.

❷ Emboss one ribbon length with Peacock Feathers.

❸ Emboss the second ribbon length with Tri-Curls.

❹ Lay the ribbon lengths side by side. Place the Tri-Curl ribbon over the Peacock Feather ribbon, so it covers about half. Adhere the Tri-Curl ribbon over the Peacock Feather ribbon with fabric glue to create one velvet piece.

❺ Trim the velvet piece to a 16" length.

ADD LINING AND TRIM

See Figure a.

❶ Cut the lining fabric to the size of the velvet piece, plus 1" on all sides. Spray the lining with a generous coat of adhesive.

❷ Adhere the lining to the wrong side of the velvet, gently pressing and smoothing it with your hands. Carefully trim the excess lining fabric. *Note: Whenever you turn the velvet piece face down, make sure the work surface is clean and free of any wet glue.*

❸ Lay the velvet piece face up with the feather side on your left. Glue the gold trim along the top raw edge of the velvet piece. Trim the excess.

❹ Cut the ivory cord to the length of the velvet piece. Glue the cord along the edge of the swirl ribbon that overlaps the feather ribbon.

MAKE THE POUCH AND HANDLE

See Figure b.

❶ Cut a 40" length of tan trim and set it aside.

❷ With the lining side up and the gold trimmed edge toward the bottom, fold the velvet piece 5" from the bottom, with the lining sides together. Glue the sides of the pouch together, stopping about ½" from the top of the pouch.

❸ To form the purse handle, insert the ends of the trim between the top corners of the pouch. Glue the trim and sides of the pouch together. Press and pinch the edges of the pouch as the glue dries.

DECORATE THE FRONT FLAP

Use the photo as a guide.

❶ Cut the flap portion of the purse into a slight curve (see photo).

❷ Cut a 6" length of tan trim and glue it along the front edge of the flap. Trim the excess. Apply a small amount of glue to the edges of the trim to prevent fraying.

❸ Wrap the piece of cardboard with leftover velvet. Wrap the pink decorative ribbon around the velvet-covered piece.

❹ Cut a 4" length of ivory cord and unravel it to make a tassel. Thread the tassel through the large-holed bead and knot it to secure. Trim excess cord from the top of the bead.

❺ Adhere the tassel to the velvet-covered piece. Glue a smaller bead next to the large bead. Adhere the embellishment to the front flap (see photo).

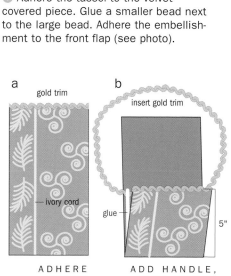

a gold trim

ivory cord

ADHERE
TRIMS

b insert gold trim

glue

5"

ADD HANDLE,
GLUE EDGES

My First Footprint Card

Designer: Valerie Pingree

SUPPLIES

Custom-made or purchased rubber stamp

Wood stamp block: *Stampin' Up!*

10–12 sheets of white facial tissue

White cardstock

Decorative-edge scissors: *Fiskars*

Pink background paper: Princess Palette, *Provo Craft*

Berry Twist Perfect Pearls: *Ranger Industries*

Adhesive: *Glue Dots International*

Black ink: *Stampin' Up!*

Other: spray bottle, cloth

Finished size: 7" x 5½"

CUSTOM-MADE RUBBER STAMP

❶ Apply black ink to baby's foot. Stamp on white cardstock.

❷ Have printing or stamp shop create rubber stamp of image.

❸ Mount stamp on stamp block.

TISSUE CASTING

❶ Saturate tissue; place over stamp.

❷ Dab with dry cloth; remove and dry for 24 hours. Color with Perfect Pearls.

CARD

❶ Make tent-fold card base using white cardstock; trim edges with decorative scissors.

❷ Adhere pink paper to card front. Adhere paper cast image.

Snowflakes

Design: Denise Pauley

SUPPLIES

Snowflake rubber stamps*
8½" x 11" paper:
   Blue cardstock
   Blue vellum*
   White cardstock
Vellum metal-rimmed tags*
Silver metallic rub-on*
Silver metallic pigment*
Silver mini brads*
Repositionable adhesive machine*
Miscellaneous items: facial tissue, adhesive dots

*Hero Arts Ornamental Snowflakes stamp set; Paper Adventures vellum; Making Memories vellum metal-rimmed tags; Craf-T Products Metallic Rub-On; Ranger Industries Perfect Pearls Silver pigment; American Pin & Fastener mini brads; and Xyron machine were used in the sample project.

Finished size: 4¹⁄₁₆" x 8⅜"

INSTRUCTIONS

❶ Stack 4 squares of tissue and sprinkle water over them until they are moist. *Note: The tissues should be saturated and moist but not soaking wet.*

❷ Press the snowflake stamps down into the stack firmly several times. *Note: Press the stamp hard enough so you can see an impression.* You may also flip the stamp over and press the tissue stack down on it. *Note: Stamping on tissue works best with stamps with bold outlines and few details.*

❸ Let the tissue stack dry, and then cut out the stamped snowflakes. *Note: The impression will become more visible and raised as the tissue dries.*

stepping & Stamping

Stamping takes on a new meaning with this fun embossing technique sent in by Kathleen Paneitz.

❶ To achieve this dimensional look, cut a piece of cardstock to fit the stamp image you want, immerse the cardstock in water, then pat with paper towel to remove excess water.

❷ Place a mousepad upside down on the floor, lay the damp cardstock on the mousepad, place the stamp on top of it, and step on the stamp. The stamp's image becomes imprinted on the cardstock, similar to dry embossing.

❸ Let the cardstock dry, then trim around the image and use it to accent cards, tags, or other paper projects.

Ink Gets a Lift

Spread on the ink and pick it back up with stamps to create intriguing reverse images.

Ink Lifting Technique

Designer: Denise Pauley

SUPPLIES

Vellum: (clear or light color)
Rubber stamp
Dye ink: (3 coordinating colors)
Tools: brayer or sponge (optional)

  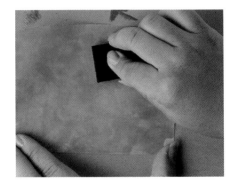

INSTRUCTIONS

❶ Apply lightest color of ink to vellum by dragging or pouncing ink pad, or applying it with brayer or sponge. Repeat with second color, allowing colors to overlap in places.

❷ Apply third color, blending with other colors to soften. *Note: Blend ink by dragging pad or smearing with brayer or sponge.*

❸ Press stamp on vellum to lift ink and leave image. Repeat as many times as desired. *Note: For crisper stamped images, clean stamp after each impression.* For more mottled, abstract images, do not clean stamp (stamp will gather ink from each impression, creating progressively darker images).

❹ Let dry.

DESIGNER TIPS

- Be sure to use pigment ink. Other ink types dry more quickly and may not work well with the ink lifting technique.

- Choose ink colors that blend well. Complementary colors such as red and green, purple and yellow, or blue and orange create muddy shades when mixed together. To make sure the ink colors blend well, test them on a scrap of vellum first.

- If you don't like the look of the stamped image, apply more ink to the vellum to erase your first attempt.

- The ink around the stamped images may bleed slightly as it dries. If the images become too distorted, try applying less ink to the vellum before stamping. Or, for heavier applications of ink, wait a few minutes before stamping to let the ink dry slightly.

- If the vellum curls when wet, flatten it under a heavy book after it is dry.

- Mat vellum with light-colored cardstock to enhance the stamped image.

Bonus Ideas

- Use only one or two colors of ink.

- Crumple the vellum after applying ink to create abstract ink patterns and texture.

- Stamp a sentiment or person's name on the vellum with alphabet stamps, then attach it to a card.

Celebrate in Style Card

SUPPLIES

Cardstock: (turquoise, white)

Textured cardstock: (yellow)

Vellum: (clear) *The Paper Company*

Foam stamps: (Dingbat set) *Making Memories*

Rubber stamp: (Celebrate) *Delta Rubber Stampede*

Dye ink: (Caribbean Blue, Salvia Blue, Yellow) Marvy Matchables, *Marvy Uchida*

Fasteners: (white brads)

Adhesive: (double-sided tape)

Tools: ruler, scissors, brayer or sponge (optional)

Finished size: 5" x 4¼"

INSTRUCTIONS

① Apply blue ink colors to vellum and stamp repeatedly with foam stamps, cleaning stamps between impressions (see "Ink Lifting Technique").

② Repeat technique on second sheet of vellum, using all ink colors. *Note: Do not clean stamp between impressions.*

③ Trim vellum into desired size strips and attach to 4½" x 3¾" piece of white cardstock, using brads and/or double-sided tape (see photo).

④ Stamp Celebrate! and ink edges of piece with Salvia Blue. Mat with yellow cardstock.

⑤ Make card from turquoise cardstock and adhere matted piece.

Bleach Stamping

Create a unique look by removing color with bleach.

Bleached Flowers

Design: Linda Beeson

SUPPLIES

Rubber stamps: flower*, miniature alphabet

Black ink pad

16 white eyelets

Eyelet setter

⅛" hole punch

8½" x 11" paper:

   Lime green cardstock

   Purple cardstock

   Red cardstock

   Turquoise cardstock

   White cardstock

   Lime green print

   Purple print

   Red print

   Turquoise print

Small white tag

Purple embroidery floss

Foam tape

Miscellaneous items: bleach, paper towels, paper plate, glue stick, scissors, ruler, hammer

*Stamps by Judith flower stamp was used in the sample project.

INSTRUCTIONS

Prepare the bleach ink pad and stamps as directed in "Bleach Stamping Basics."

❶ Stamp the flower on the four different colors of cardstock and trim each one to a 2" square. Set an eyelet in each corner of each square.

❷ Mat the flowers with white cardstock and then with the coordinating color of print paper.

❸ Stamp "TO: MOM" on the white tag with black ink and attach it through one of the eyelets with purple embroidery floss.

❹ Cut a 5½" x 11" piece of white cardstock and fold it in half lengthwise. Adhere the flowers to the card with foam tape.

BLEACH STAMPING BASICS

Create a "stamp pad" for the bleach by folding a paper towel into fourths and placing it on a paper plate. Then, slowly pour a small amount of bleach on the paper towel and let it soak in. Press the stamp into the paper towel as you would an ink pad.

Experiment with the paper color you're using to see how it reacts to the bleach. Be sure to wait a few minutes for the image to completely appear on the paper.

Vases of Flowers

Designer: Stacey Stamitoles

SUPPLIES

Rubber stamp: (Glass Vases) *Hero Arts*

Dye ink: (Black) All Night Media, *Plaid*

Cardstock: (bright blue, lime green)

Textured cardstock: (Baby Blue) *Bazzill Basics Paper*

Color medium: (watercolor pencils) *Staedtler*

Sticker: (Thanks) Phrase Café, *EK Success*

Fibers: (blue/green stripe ribbon) *Offray*

Adhesive: (foam tape) Memory Tape Runner, *Therm O Web*; double-sided tape

Tools: (bleach pen) *Clorox Company*; (blender pen) *Dove Brushes*; scissors, fine-tip paintbrush

Finished size: 4¼" x 5½"

INSTRUCTIONS

1 Make card from Baby Blue cardstock.

2 Stamp Glass Vases on lime green cardstock.

3 Color flowers using watercolor pencils. Use blender pen to blend away watercolor marks.

4 Using fine-tip paintbrush and bleach pen, color water portion of image.

5 Mat image with bright blue cardstock; adhere to card.

6 Adhere Thanks sticker to lime green; trim and adhere to card.

7 Cut two small notches in fold of card. Thread ribbon and tie bow.

Live, Discover, Enjoy

Desinger: Stacy Croninger

SUPPLIES

Foam stamp: (Paisley) *Making Memories*

Cardstock: (purple, dark blue)

Paper accent: (paint chip)

Accents: (live, discover, enjoy from Journey) Petite Signage, *Making Memories*

Adhesive

Tools: scissors

Other: bleach, paper towels, coated paper plate

Finished size: 5½" x 4¼"

INSTRUCTIONS

1 Make card from purple cardstock.

2 Stamp with bleach on dark blue cardstock. Trim to 1¼" x 1¾".

3 Trim paint chip to 5¼" long.

4 Adhere dark blue rectangles to paint chip. Adhere paint chip to card.

5 Adhere live, discover, enjoy to card.

Bonus Idea

Try using the same stamp on a different card, and use paints and a rub-on.

Bleached Dragonfly

Design: Linda Beeson

SUPPLIES

Rubber stamps: bamboo*, dragonfly*

4 gold photo corners

8½" x 11" cardstock:

   2 sheets burgundy

   Tan

   Foam tape

Miscellaneous items: bleach, paper towels, paper plate, glue stick, scissors, ruler

PSX Designs Tapestry Bamboo stamp; and *Stephanie Olin* dragonfly stamp were used in the sample project.

INSTRUCTIONS

Prepare the bleach ink pad and stamps as directed in "Bleach Stamping Basics" on page 96.

❶ Stamp the dragonfly stamp on burgundy cardstock, and then cut it into a 2½" square.

❷ Adhere the photo corners on the dragonfly square, and then mat it with tan cardstock.

❸ Cut a 4½" square of burgundy cardstock. Stamp the bamboo background randomly on the burgundy cardstock, and then mat it with tan cardstock.

❹ Adhere the dragonfly square to the bamboo background square with foam tape.

❺ Cut a 5½" x 11" rectangle of burgundy cardstock and fold it in half lengthwise. Adhere the finished square to the card.

Dreams of Freedom Postcard

Designer: Susan Neal

SUPPLIES

Rubber stamps:
   (Statue of Liberty, Dream with Faith sentiment) *Inkadinkado*

   Stars) *PSX*

   (Postcard) *River City Rubber Works*

Dye ink: Coal Black, Ancient Page, *Clearsnap*

Cardstock: *Bazzill Basics Paper* (Chili, white)

Other: adhesive, bleach, flat paintbrush, toothbrush, scissors

Finished size: 3½" x 5"

INSTRUCTIONS

❶ Cut Chili and white postcards; adhere back-to-back.

❷ Stamp Statue of Liberty and sentiment with Coal Black on Chili.

❸ Paint bleach over stamped image and sentiment with flat brush. Apply bleach to stars with brush and stamp randomly; dip toothbrush in bleach and spatter over card.

❹ Stamp Postcard and part of Statue of Liberty and stars with Coal Black on back.

Beautiful Bleached Daisy

Designer: Linda Beeson

SUPPLIES

Rubber stamps: *The Rubbernecker Stamp Co.* (chicken wire background); *Stampin' Up!* (flower); *Catslife Press* (thinking of you)

Other: bleach, paper towels, plastic plate, scissors, adhesive, cardstock (yellow gold, brown, terra cotta, red), mini copper brads, circle template

Finished size: 5½" x 4¼"

INSTRUCTIONS

❶ Make yellow gold card.

❷ Stamp chicken wire background on brown cardstock with bleach; trim and mat with terra cotta. Adhere to card.

❸ Stamp flower on terra cotta with bleach; cut out with circle template. Mat with red, then yellow gold and tear edges. Adhere to card.

❹ Stamp sentiment on red with bleach and cut into strip. Adhere to card with brads.

Forget Me Not

Designer: Linda Beeson

SUPPLIES

Rubber stamps: *Hero Arts* (Delicate Vine Background); *Rubber Moon* (Forget Me Not)

Leaf punch: *The Punch Bunch*

Other: black ink, bleach, paper towels, plastic plate, cardstock (dark purple, cream), scissors, adhesive, pop-up dots

Finished size: 5½" x 4¼"

INSTRUCTIONS

❶ Make dark purple card.

❷ Stamp leaf background on dark purple cardstock with bleach; trim and mat with cream. Adhere to card.

❸ Stamp part of leaf background on small rectangle of dark purple with bleach.

❹ Punch leaf from center of stamped piece. Mat with cream; adhere to card with pop-up dots.

❺ Stamp sentiment on cream with black and trim; adhere to card.

Creating Resists

You won't be able to resist creating resist projects!

Sunflower Dream

Designer: Tresa Black

SUPPLIES

All supplies from Close To My Heart unless otherwise noted.

Rubber stamps: (Stoneware Texture, Sunflower Garden set, dream from The Simple Things set)

Dye ink: (Indian Corn Blue, Outdoor Denim)

Embossing ink: (Tinted)

Embossing powder: (Silver)

Cardstock: (Indian Corn Blue, Outdoor Denim, Ultra White)

Fasteners: (silver eyelets)

Adhesive: no source

Tools: (round sponge, ruler, scissors, heat tool, eyelet-setting tools) no source

Other: (bleach, paper towel, sandpaper, plastic container or plate) no source

Finished size: 4¼" x 5½"

MAKE SUNFLOWER PIECE

❶ Sponge Indian Corn Blue and Outdoor Denim ink on Ultra White cardstock to create mottled background. Stamp Stoneware Texture with both colors to create speckles.

❷ To make bleach stamp pad, fold paper towel in fourths and place in plastic container; pour on bleach.

❸ Stamp sunflowers repeatedly with bleach; dry with heat tool.

❹ Stamp center on sunflowers with Indian Corn Blue.

❺ Trim to finished size of card and tear sides.

ASSEMBLE CARD

❶ Make card from Indian Corn Blue cardstock. Sand horizontally and vertically to create look of denim. Sand edges and adhere sunflower piece.

❷ Stamp dream on Ultra White with embossing ink; emboss. Trim and sponge image with Indian Corn Blue. Adhere to 2" x 1½" piece of Outdoor Denim cardstock. Set eyelets along bottom and double-mat with white and Indian Corn Blue.

❸ Adhere to card.

Rainbow Faces

Designer: Chris Herrmann

SUPPLIES

Rubber stamps: (Sisters) *Another Stamp Company*; (Grid) *Alias Smith & Rowe*

Dye ink: (Bikini Pink, Sailboat Blue, Sunshine) Rainbow Ink, *Posh Impressions*

Embossing ink: (Clear) Big & Bossy, *Ranger Industries*

Embossing powder: (Clear) *Ranger Industries*

Cardstock: (black, white, white glossy)

Color medium: (Pitch Black pigment pen) Adirondack, *Ranger Industries*

Paper accent: (gold photo corners)

Adhesive: (double-sided tape) Wonder Tape, Suze Weinberg, *Ranger Industries*

Tools: (sponge) Rainbow Sponge, *Posh Impressions*; (heat tool) *Ranger Industries*; ruler, scissors, water in spray bottle

Finished size: 5½" x 4¼"

INSTRUCTIONS

❶ Make card from white glossy cardstock.

❷ Stamp Sisters on white cardstock with embossing ink; emboss.

❸ Beginning with lightest color first, randomly apply ink to sponge. Continue adding colors until sponge is covered. *Note: For best results, place colors that blend well next to one another.* Spray sponge with water and apply ink to Grid stamp. Stamp Grid over embossed image. *Note: For added definition, wipe ink off embossed details.*

❹ Trim; outline edges with pen.

❺ Mat stamped piece with black cardstock. Add photo corners and adhere to card.

Resist Flower Tag Accents

Designer: Janelle Clark

SUPPLIES

Rubber stamp: (Real Star Flower) *Hero Arts*

Watermark ink: VersaMark, *Tsukineko*

Embossing powder: (clear) *JudiKins*

Color medium: (green marker) Marvy Brush Marker, *Marvy Uchida*

Watercolor paper: (White) *Strathmore*

Accent: (round metal-edge sticker tag) Metallic Accents, *DieCuts With a View*

Fibers: (yellow gingham ribbon)

Tools: (circle punch) *Family Treasures*; scissors, heat tool, paintbrush

Other: plastic plate

Finished size: 2" diameter

"RESIST"-ANCE IS BEAUTIFUL

Try the resist method to enliven all your accents. Applying ink or watercolors around a colorless embossed image creates a reverse effect that draws the eye and adds interest. Stamp images with bleach on dark cardstock, re-stamp with watermark ink, and emboss with clear for an even more dramatic resist look.

Golden Leaves

Designer: Nichole Heady

SUPPLIES

Rubber stamps: (Botanical Garden set, French Script, father from Flexible Phrases set) *Stampin' Up!*

Dye ink: (Chocolate Chip) *Stampin' Up!*

Cardstock: (Chocolate Chip, Naturals Ivory) *Stampin' Up!*

Watermark ink: VersaMark, *Tsukineko*

Pigment powder: (Gold Micro Pearl) Pearl Ex, *Jacquard Products*

Finish: (Triple Thick Gloss Glaze) *DecoArt*

Paper accent: (mini tag)

Accent: (gold jump ring)

Fibers: (green ribbon) *Making Memories*

Adhesive

Tools: scissors, paintbrush

Finished size: 4¼" x 5½"

INSTRUCTIONS

❶ Make card from Chocolate Chip cardstock.

❷ Tie ribbon around card.

❸ Stamp father on mini tag with Chocolate Chip. Attach to ribbon with jump ring.

❹ Stamp leaves from Botanical Garden set; brush on pigment powder with paintbrush; apply finish.

❺ Stamp French Script on stamped leaves. *Note: The ink will resist the pigment powder and the stamped image will appear.*

❻ Cut out and mat with Chocolate Chip and Naturals Ivory cardstock.

❼ Ink rectangle of Naturals Ivory. Brush on powder; apply finish. Mount matted stamped image; adhere to card.

Stamping on Clay & Dominoes

Create your own accents using clay or dominoes and your favorite stamps!

Metallic-Finish Clay Necklaces

Designer: Laurie D'Ambrosio

SUPPLIES

Black or white polymer clay, *American Art Clay Co.*

Clay-dedicated pasta machine or roller

1–2" decorative rubber stamp (#E2102)

Square Flower Etching stamp, *Hero Arts*

Slicing blade

4" glazed ceramic tile

Sunset Gold pigment powder, *Jacquard Products*

Gloss interior varnish, Ceramcoat, *Delta*

Small stud, *Prym-Dritz* rhinestone, or other heat-resistant accent

Tiny screw eye

Permanent adhesive

Satin cording, enough to fit around your head, plus 3–4"

Matching large-holed beads

Miscellaneous items: soft paintbrush, baking sheet (optional)

PREPARE THE CLAY

1 Condition ½ of the package of polymer clay until it is warm and pliable (see "How to Condition Clay").

2 Roll the clay into a ¼" thick sheet using a pasta machine or roller. Lay the clay sheet on the ceramic tile.

3 Press the stamp into the clay, gently rolling it to get a clear image. Carefully lift the stamp straight up from the clay. Remove the excess clay from around the stamped image with the slicing blade.

4 Lightly spread pigment powder over the stamped image with your finger.

5 Twist the screw eye into the top center of the clay piece.

6 To add a stud to the image, push it into the clay and leave it in place. To add a rhinestone or other accent, push it into the clay to make an impression, then take it out for baking.

7 Place the tile on a baking sheet, if desired. Bake the clay for 30 minutes at 265º. Let it cool.

FINISH THE NECKLACE

1 Unscrew the eye from the clay pendant. Apply permanent adhesive to the eye, then screw it back into the pendant.

2 Cover the pendant with a coat of varnish, removing any bubbles before the varnish dries. *Note: If you skip this step, the pigment powder will rub off the pendant.*

3 Adhere the rhinestone or other accent with permanent adhesive.

4 Thread the pendant and beads onto the cording. Tie together the ends of the cording into a slipknot, securing it with a small amount of glue.

COMBINING COLORS

The combinations of stamps, polymer clay colors, and pigment powders are endless. Pearlescent pigment powders look pastel when applied to light-colored objects and vivid on dark objects. The white pendant in the photo is coated with Pearl-Ex Duo Green-Yellow pigment powder.

HOW TO CONDITION CLAY

If you are working with hard polymer clay, such as FIMO, you'll need to condition the clay before sculpting it. Here's how:

BY PASTA MACHINE

- Flatten the clay into a pancake shape and, beginning with the #1 setting (the thickest), run the clay through a pasta machine. Fold the sheet of clay in half and run it through again, fold first. Repeat three or four times. Increase the setting to the next level. Continue feeding the clay through the machine three to four times at increasingly higher settings until the clay is soft.

BY HAND

- Knead the clay in any way that you find comfortable. You can create snakes, twist it, and form it into a pancake or ball. I have found that the clay will condition faster if I alternate between making pancakes and forming other shapes. The thinner the clay is, the easier it is to condition.

- Before you begin crafting, put the unconditioned clay into a plastic bag, then tuck it into the pocket of your pants. The heat from your body will start the conditioning process, cutting down on kneading time.

POLYMER CLAY PRECAUTIONS

- Never work on a wood surface. Polymer clay will damage a wood table.

- Because polymer clay easily collects dirt, keep your hands, tools, and work surface clean.

- If you use a type of glue or varnish other than the types listed, test it by applying some onto a piece of baked polymer clay and allowing it to sit for several days or more. Some types of glue and varnish have adverse reactions to polymer clay. They can become sticky or erode the clay, causing any adhered pieces to come off.

Faux Stone Frame

Design: Mary Ayres

SSUPPLIES

Wood frame with 4" x 6" opening, *PGM Products*

Stone border rubber stamp, *Hero Arts*

8 oz. white polymer clay, *Polyform Products*

Acrylic paint: (Jade Green, Slate Grey, Warm White) *DecoArt*

Texturizing medium, *DecoArt*

Deckle edge scissors, *Fiskars*

#8 paintbrush, *Royal & Langnickel*

Miscellaneous items: adhesive, Gem-Tac, *Beacon Adhesives*, palette, rolling pin, waxed paper, cookie sheet, paper towels

Finished size: 5" x 7"

PAINT THE FRAME

Allow the paint to dry between steps.

❶ Basecoat the frame with 2–3 coats of Slate Grey.

❷ Mix the texturizing medium with Warm White (1:1) and dab 2–3 coats on the outside of the frame.

❸ Dilute Slate Grey with water (1:2) and paint the frame. Quickly wipe or blot the paint with a damp paper towel until the desired color is achieved.

❹ Paint random areas with Jade Green and quickly wipe or blot it with a damp paper towel until the desired color is achieved.

MAKE THE CLAY ACCENTS

❶ Knead a ball of clay and roll it out on waxed paper to a sheet approx. ¼" thick.

❷ Press the border stamp into the clay and then pull straight up, keeping the impressed design in tact. Peel the clay from the waxed paper and cut around the edge of each border with deckle-edge scissors. *Note: Repeat as needed for each border section.* Trim the pieces as needed to fit the sides of the frame.

❸ Place the clay border sections on a cookie sheet and bake at 275° for 15 minutes. Let cool.

❹ Dilute Slate Grey with water (1:1). Brush the mixture on each border section, and quickly wipe off any excess

paint with a slightly damp paper towel, leaving paint in the crevices.

❺ Brush Jade Green on the border sections in small areas and quickly wipe excess paint with a slightly damp paper towel.

❻ Glue each border section around the top of each side of the frame (see photo).

Gold Sprig Candle Wrap

Design: Trice Boerens

SUPPLIES

4" x 6" cream-colored candle

4 oz. translucent polymer clay*

Sprig rubber stamp*

Gold ink pad*

Four glass head straight pins

Miscellaneous items: acrylic brayer or rolling pin, baking sheet, oven, soft cloth, craft knife

Polyform Products Sculpey polymer clay (#010); *Delta Rubber Stampede* Engraved Collection sprig stamp; and *Clearsnap* ColorBox ink pad were used in the sample project.

INSTRUCTIONS

❶ Knead the clay with your hands to soften it.

❷ Roll the clay to a 2¼" x 13½" x ³⁄₁₆" rectangle with the rolling pin.

❸ Press the un-inked stamp into the clay in a random pattern (Figure a), then trim the clay back to a 2¼" x 13½" rectangle.

❹ Stand the clay on edge, bend it into a cylinder, and place it on a baking sheet (Figure b). Bake it in an oven following the manufacturer's instructions and let it cool.

❺ Slide the clay around the bottom of the candle. Secure the ends to the back of the candle with pins.

❻ Daub the ink pad into the stamped impressions left in the baked clay. Rub off any excess ink with the soft cloth (Figure c).

❼ Round the top edge of the clay collar with a craft knife.

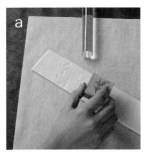

STAMP THE CLAY

FORM A COLLAR

RUB WITH INK

Inspiration Stones

Design: Susan Neal

SUPPLIES

Rubber stamps: Dream*, love script*, butterfly*, dragonfly*

Black ink pad*

Granite-colored polymer clay*

Metallic rub-ons*

Lavender and pink decorative chalk*

Craft wire: bronze, purple

Small beads or charms

Miscellaneous items: glass baking dish, oven, baking rack

*PSX Designs Dream and Affirmation Script stamps; Stampin' Up! butterfly and dragonfly stamps from the Bugs & Slugs stamp set; Stewart Superior Corporation Memories ink pad; Polyform Products Granitex clay; and Craf-T Products metallic rub-ons and chalk were used in the sample projects.

INSTRUCTIONS

❶ Knead the clay in your hands until it is pliable. Form the clay into stone shapes to fit your stamp of choice.

❷ Gently stamp one image or word(s) into each clay stone with black ink. *Note: If your first try isn't successful, simply re-knead the clay, hiding the black ink. You can only do this a couple of times before the ink will begin to recolor the clay.*

❸ Carefully move the stones onto a glass baking dish. Bake at 275° for 15 minutes for every ¼" of thickness. *Note: Do not overbake. Cool on a baking rack.*

❹ Embellish the stones by applying the following with your finger:

Love and dream stones: metallic rub-ons

Dragonfly and butterfly stones: decorative chalk

Note: Apply these liberally to the clay surrounding, but not within, the stamped words or image.

❺ Wrap bronze wire and some beads or charms around the Dream stone. Wrap purple wire around the butterfly and dragonfly stones.

DISPLAY IDEAS

Inspiration stones can be placed anywhere for a whimsical thought. Add them to a rock garden, or a dish with decorative rocks and dried flowers, lavender petals, or potpourri.

Fall Impression Magnets

Designer: Stephanie Baker

SUPPLIES

Rubber stamps: maple and oak leaves from Four Leaves set, *Close To My Heart*

Acrylic paint: Ceramcoat, *Delta* (assorted fall colors)

Polymer clay: Tan/Sand, *Polyform Products*

Antiquing medium: FolkArt, *Plaid*

All-purpose sealer: clear, Ceramcoat, *Delta*

Other: soft cloth, adhesive-backed magnet, fine-grit sandpaper, smooth glass

jar or acrylic roller, paintbrushes, ruler, baking sheet, index card, oven

Finished size: 2¼" square

PREPARE & STAMP

❶ Work clay in hands until warm and pliable.

❷ Roll flat to ¼" thickness using glass jar or roller.

❸ Shape clay into square.

❹ Stamp leaf image on clay.

FINISH

❶ Place clay on index card on baking sheet. Bake according to manufacturer's instructions; let cool.

❷ Apply coat of sealer; let dry.

❸ Paint stamped image; let dry.

❹ Sand lightly over stamped image.

❺ Apply antiquing medium with soft cloth; wipe off excess and let dry.

❻ Apply coat of sealer; let dry.

❼ Secure magnet to back.

DESIGNER TIP

Cover color discolorations in baked polymer clay by applying a neutral color of acrylic paint to the entire piece.

Domino Wisdom Necklace

Designer: Barbara Matthiessen

SUPPLIES

Secrets and Devotion rubber stamp sets: *Postmodern Design*

Little children rubber stamp: *Uptown Rubber Stamps*

Clock face with wings rubber stamp: *A Stamp in the Hand Co.*

Solvent ink: Jet Black, StāzOn, *Tsukineko*

Ink refills: StāzOn, *Tsukineko* (Olive Green, Royal Purple, Mustard)

Pigment ink: Brilliance, *Tsukineko* (Pearlescent Lavender, Sky Blue)

Adhesive: Glass, Metal & More, *Beacon Adhesives*

Gold leafing pen: 18K, *Krylon*

1½" square plastic material: Tyvek, *DuPont*

Other: two faux ivory dominoes; 1½" x 8½" strip white vellum; metal triangle picture hanger; 4½" length 18-gauge silver wire; 24" length black waxed linen beading cord; green, gold, and lavender beads; 3" square felt; rubbing alcohol; wire cutters; round nose pliers; scissors

Finished size: 1" x 2" x ¾"

COLOR

❶ Dampen felt square with rubbing alcohol. Randomly drip 2–3 dots of each ink refill color onto felt.

❷ Dab gold pen onto undotted sides of dominoes, making puddles.

❸ Dab dominoes onto inked felt, turning for random coloring. Let dry, then reapply inks as needed. *Note: Rubbing alcohol will remove ink from skin.*

❹ Color both sides of plastic square and edges of vellum with gold pen.

STAMP

❶ Stamp words on undotted sides of dominoes with Jet Black ink.

❷ Stamp clock and hand on vellum with Lavender and Sky Blue.

❸ Stamp words and saying on vellum with Jet Black. Let dry.

ASSEMBLE

❶ Beginning at right end, fan-fold vellum in ⅝" folds. At left end, fold under excess ⅜" to make a tab.

Inside

❷ Place dominoes dotted sides down, with one long side touching.

❸ Glue picture hanger tab to top of right domino.

❹ Glue vellum tab to left side of other domino.

❺ Glue plastic across dominoes, covering tabs and forming hinge. Let glue set.

❻ Fold dominoes together, making crease in plastic and forming book.

FINISH

❶ Twist ends of wire into flat spirals.

❷ Wrap wire around dominoes with spirals in front. Interlock spirals to hold book closed.

❸ Knot beading cord through picture hanger.

❹ Thread beads onto both sides of cord. Knot ends close to last bead on each side. Tie ends of cord together.

WHAT IS TYVEK?

Tyvek is the strong, flexible, plastic-like material used to make overnight delivery envelopes. Use a portion of a Tyvek envelope purchased at an office supply store, or purchase it by the yard at art supply stores like Dick Blick.

Live Brilliantly

Designer: Christi Spadoni

SUPPLIES

Rubber stamp: figure, *Dream Impressions*

Pigment ink: Crafter's, *Clearsnap* (black); *Yasutomo* (Copper Brilliance)

Acrylic sealer: *Krylon*

Waterbrush: *Yasutomo*

Adhesive: *Glue Dots International*

Adhesive: E6000, *Eclectic Products*

Acrylic paint: Kiwi, Perfect Pearls, *Ranger Industries*

Other: domino, beads, magnetic poetry, wire, embossing heat tool, cardstock (burgundy, yellow)

Finished size: 4½" x 5½"

STAMP DOMINO

❶ Lightly press smooth side of domino in Copper ink; heat set with embossing heat tool for one minute.

❷ Stamp figure onto domino with black; heat set.

❸ Press edges of domino in Copper; heat set.

❹ Paint Kiwi pigment powder on domino edges with waterbrush.

❺ Apply several layers of acrylic sealer to domino in well-ventilated area.

MAKE CARD

❶ Make burgundy card.

❷ Thread wire through beads and wrap around yellow cardstock; adhere to card.

❸ Adhere magnetic poetry.

❹ Adhere domino to card.

DOMINOES STAMPING TIPS

■ Let the domino cool for at least five minutes before handling after heat setting.

■ Press the stamp firmly on the domino and lift straight off.

■ Wipe off stamped image with a damp

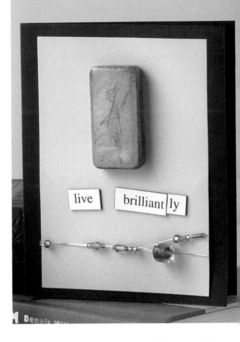

paper towel if you are unhappy with the result.

■ Use a padded envelope and request hand stamping from the post office when mailing a card embellished with a domino.

Different Hats

Designer: Janelle Clark

SUPPLIES

Rubber stamps: (Hat) Dawn Hauser, *Inkadinkado*; (Printer's Type Alphabet) *Hero Arts*

Dye ink: (Bordeaux) Ancient Page, *Clearsnap*

Cardstock: (Gold Leaf) *Bazzill Basics Paper*

Textured cardstock: (Cream, Maroon) *The Paper Company*

Patterned paper: (Romanza Gingham) *Brenda Walton, K&Company*

Accent: (ceramic tag) Collage Keepsakes, Card Connection, *Hirschberg Schutz & Co.*

Fibers: (gold ribbon)

Font: (2Peas High Tide) *www.twopeasinabucket.com*

Adhesive

Tools: scissors

Finished size: 4¼" x 5½"

INSTRUCTIONS

❶ Make card from Maroon cardstock.

❷ Cut Romanza Gingham patterned paper slightly smaller than card front; mat with Cream cardstock. Adhere to card.

❸ Stamp words on card front as desired.

❹ Print "Sis, you wear so many different hats…" and "…and you wear them all beautifully! Happy Mother's Day" on Cream cardstock. Trim into two blocks and mat each with Gold Leaf.

❺ Stamp Hat on ceramic tag; ink edges of tag.

❻ Tie ribbon on tag; adhere tag and sentiment block to card front.

❼ Stamp hat on remaining sentiment block; adhere inside card.

Inside

Domino Collage Tray

Design: Barbara Matthiessen

SUPPLIES

Rubber stamps*: background text, butterfly, clocks, dragonfly, feather, background floral, floral, tassel

Cobalt Blue acrylic paint*

Ink pads*: Moonlight White pigment, Ultramarine solvent

Stamp cleaner*

64 faux ivory dominoes

13½" x 10½" unfinished wood tray

Satin or gloss acrylic coating*

Non-water based adhesive*

Sponge paintbrush

Miscellaneous items: double-sided tape, embossing heat tool, needlenose pliers, paper towels

*Plaid Enterprises All Night Media Browning Poem (485K01), Butterfly Time Collage (601J), Dragonfly (131J), Feathers (171G), Floral Background (508F), Hydrangeas (550 H 14), and Tassel (485K05) stamps and FolkArt Artists' Pigment acrylic paint; Tsukineko Brilliance pigment ink pad, StazOn solvent ink pad, and stamp cleaner; Krylon Crystal Clear acrylic coating; and Beacon Adhesives Plexi-Bond adhesive were used in the sample project.

PREPARE THE TRAY

❶ Paint the tray Cobalt Blue with the sponge brush and let it dry.

❷ Stamp the sides of the tray with the floral background stamp using White ink. Let the ink dry overnight or set and dry it with an embossing heat tool.

❸ Apply two coats of acrylic coating following the manufacturer's instructions.

STAMP THE DOMINOES

❶ To stamp the dominoes, dab Ultramarine ink on a stamp, then lay the stamp on your work surface facing up. Press the domino, flat side down, onto

the stamp, making sure to press down firmly. Stamp the dominoes as follows:

8 each background text, feathers

4 flowers

5 each butterflies, clocks, background stems/stems with flowers

13 background flowers

7 tassels

❷ To stamp the dragonflies, place a 3" length of double-sided tape on your work surface, and lay two dominoes side by side on the tape. Stamp dragonflies across the two dominoes. Make five pairs of dragonfly dominoes.

FINISH THE TRAY

❶ Arrange the dominoes on the tray (see photo). *Note: Scatter strong design elements such as tassels, feathers, and butterflies first, and then fit in the other designs.*

❷ Apply a thin, even coat of adhesive to the back of each domino, one at a time, and adhere them to the tray.

❸ Let the glue dry completely before you use the tray.

Bonus Idea

Use ivory dominoes to create a frame. Antique the sides of the dominoes with ink, and stamp the images on them. Heat-emboss the images with clear embossing powder, and assemble them onto the frame with industrial-strength adhesive.

Make Your Own Stamps

Transform erasers, foam, or even wood into creative personal designs.

Creating your own stamps is simple and fun. Use these ideas to create some patterns and stamps of your own!

Foam Shapes

Craft foam, a thick reusable material that you find in the kids' section of local craft stores, is a great option for making simple chunky stamps. It comes in precut shapes and easy-to-cut sheets. Try these tips and techniques to create distinctive cards, background paper, or even stamped clothing:

- Use punches from your collection to make foam stamps in many shapes.

- Make bold shapes such as hearts and stars by cutting out a design penciled on the foam.

- Mount the shapes on sturdy items like empty film canisters, acrylic mounts, or wood blocks.

Clearsnap's ColorBox Stylus is a reusable foam stamp system that will mold when heated and pressed on a texture of your choice. It comes with tips in different shapes, and you can purchase moldable mats with several different patterns for creative backgrounds and designs.

COLORBOX STYLUS & MOLDING MATS

Floral Greetings Stationery

Designer: Jaime Murff

SUPPLIES

Chalk ink: Pink Pastel, ColorBox, *Clearsnap*

White craft foam: *Fibre Craft*

Flower punch and rubber-tipped hammer: Paddle Punch, Sizzix, *Provo Craft/Ellison*

Purple snaps: Forget-Me-Not dot-lets, *Doodlebug Design*

Font: 2Peas Think Small, *Two Peas in a Bucket*

Other: chopping board, 1¾" square wood block, adhesive, hole punch, eyelet-setting tools, cream paper, computer and printer

❶ Punch flower from craft foam with hammer (see Figure a). Adhere to wood block (see Figure b).

❷ Print "greetings" in top center of paper.

❸ Stamp Pink Pastel flower in each corner (see Figure c).

❹ Set snap in each flower center.

a

PUNCH FOAM SHAPES FOR STAMP

b

ADHERE PUNCHED IMAGE TO WOOD BLOCK

c

APPLY INK & STAMP

Block Carving

CHOOSE YOUR SURFACE

The most involved method of stamp making is carving stamps with images of your own design. Start by finding a medium that is suitable for your carving needs:

- Erasers have a soft surface that is easy to carve. Try art gum or pencil erasers. You can even use the eraser on the end of a pencil.

- Purchase ready to carve rubber blocks, which come in a variety of thicknesses and colors, and are available at art supply stores.

- Linoleum blocks have a hard, non-porous surface and are commonly used in printmaking. These are also available at art supply and some home improvement stores.

- Wood is a suitable hard medium, but is porous, absorbs more ink, and is more difficult to clean.

- Rubber plumber's gasket, available at home improvement and automotive stores, makes a stamp as durable as traditional rubber stamps.

TRANSFER YOUR DESIGN

Once you have chosen a medium, find an image to carve into it. Create designs that will coordinate with pre-made patterned papers or fabrics for matching cards. Recreate a child's art-work or handwriting. Or check out books or Web sites that offer free clip art. Then, use one of the following methods to transfer the image to your block:

1 Draw or trace over the image using a pencil. Turn the paper face down on the block and rub the back of the paper to transfer the graphite to the block.

2 Place the image over transfer paper on the block. Use a pen or stylus and trace the image to transfer the graphite or wax from the transfer paper to the block. *Note: Your image must be reversed to transfer properly.*

3 Wet-transfer an image to a block by saturating a cotton ball with acetone nail polish remover and patting the back of the image.

4 Heat transfer toner to the block, applying a warm, dry iron to the back of the image.

CARVE YOUR DESIGN

Now, carve out a negative of your design. Carving tools are small U or V shaped tools. You can buy them as a unit, or purchase the handle separately from the tips. Try Speedball Speedy Cut and Staedtler MasterCarve tools. Other useful cutting items are needle tools, a craft knife, or a utility blade for outlining delicate designs. For an inexpensive alternative, take the eraser out of a regular wooden pencil. Use pliers to shape the metal edges, and use this as you would any other carving tool.

Pinwheel Tessellation Card

Designer: Tracy Parlett

SUPPLIES

Carving block and block cutters: Speedy-Cut, Speedball; MasterCarve, *Staedtler* (#1, #2, #3, #5 tips)

Watermark ink: VersaMark, *Tsukineko*

Cardstock: *Stampin' Up!* (Really Rust, Old Olive, More Mustard, Eggplant Envy)

Other: clear embossing powder, embossing heat tool, craft knife, pencil, pen, tracing paper, black cardstock, paper trimmer, adhesive

TRACE & CARVE

1 Transfer pattern to carving block with transfer paper and pencil (see Figure a).

2 Begin at bottom edge of design and cut away material with block cutters and craft knife (see Figure b).

3 Carve away remaining colored designs from block (see Figure c).

STAMP

1 Stamp image on Really Rust, More Mustard, Old Olive, and Eggplant Envy cardstock with watermark ink.

2 Heat emboss.

ASSEMBLE

1 Trim Old Olive cardstock to 4¾" square, making sure stamped image is in upper right corner.

2 Trim remaining images into 2¼" squares.

3 Adhere images to Old Olive cardstock.

4 Make black card.

5 Adhere assembled color block to card.

PINWHEEL PATTERN

COLOR PATTERN

CARVE EDGE

CARVE COLORED PORTION

Snowmen Sweatshirt

Design: Barbara Greve

SUPPLIES

6 mm white or light-colored craft foam

Scroll Saw/Craft Knife Method:
 Craft knife or scroll saw with blade for close-radius cutting

 ¼" foam core board

Scissors Method:
 Scissors

 2 mm white or light-colored craft foam

Blue sweatshirt*

¾" snowflake stamp*

Six ¼" charcoal buttons

Thread:
 Charcoal

 Navy

Fabric paint*: Baby Blue Deep, Bright Blue metallic, Lamp Black, Silver Platinum, White, White metallic

Dimensional fabric paint*: Glimmer, Quick Silver

Four 1" sponge brushes

24" square thick cardboard

Stamp positioner (optional)

Miscellaneous items: ruler, lead pencil, tracing paper, craft or fabric glue*, straight pins or masking tape, needle, graphite paper, paper towels, palette, white fabric pencil or chalk, black fabric marker, flat toothpicks, hair dryer or embossing heat tool (optional)

*JustSweatshirts.com Dark Navy Sand sweatshirt; 1StopSquare.com snowflake stamp; DecoArt SoSoft Fabric and Dimensional paints; and Beacon Adhesives Fabri-Tac adhesive were used in the sample project.

MAKE THE STAMPS

See Figures a–c.

SCROLL SAW/CRAFT KNIFE METHOD

❶ Measure and cut six 1¾" x 3" rectangles each from the 6 mm craft foam and the foam core board, using the scroll saw or craft knife.

❷ Adhere each craft foam rectangle over a foam core board rectangle. Let the glue dry.

❸ Transfer the snowman pattern from p. 115 onto three foam rectangles.

❹ Cut out the shapes through both foam layers using the scroll saw or craft knife.

SCISSORS METHOD

❶ Measure and cut six 1¾" x 3" rectangles from the 6 mm craft foam, using the scissors.

❷ Transfer the snowman pattern from p. 115 onto the 2 mm craft foam three times. Cut out the snowmen with the scissors.

❸ Adhere each snowman shape over a foam rectangle. Let the glue dry.

PREPARE THE SWEATSHIRT

Prior to stamping, wash and dry the sweatshirt. Do not use fabric softener.

❶ Lay the shirt face up on a flat surface. Insert the cardboard square inside the sweatshirt, behind the design area. Smooth the sweatshirt tightly over the cardboard and secure it with straight pins or masking tape.

❷ Center and mark a 6½" horizontal line approx. ⅝" below the neck seam, using a ruler and white fabric pencil or chalk.

❸ Place three dry rectangle stamps in a row, ⅝" apart, below the horizontal line. Mark the placement of the stamps.

❹ Mark the placement for the second row of stamps ½" below the first row.

STAMP THE IMAGES

Read through all the steps before you begin stamping.

PRECAUTIONS

❶ Before you begin stamping, mark an arrow on each rectangular stamp with the black fabric marker to indicate which end is on top. When you apply a second layer to a rectangular stamped image, it's important to use the same stamp with the same end of the rectangle on top because the stamps vary slightly in shape. Also, paint residue may remain on the stamp after washing and can discolor a differently-colored image.

❷ If a stamped image is too light, stamp a second layer of paint over it.

❸ Wait until the stamped image is completely dry before applying the dimensional paint.

APPLY THE PAINT AND STAMP

❶ Squeeze the paint onto the palette, and then use the sponge brush to apply the paint to the stamp.

❷ Stamp the rectangles onto the marked areas of the sweatshirt from left to right, using different color combinations for the images (see "Paint Color Combinations" for ideas). *Note: Use the stamp positioner to help you align the stamps, if desired.*

❸ After stamping each image, wash the stamp and sponge brush and let the paint dry thoroughly before proceeding to the next step. *Note: Use a hair dryer or embossing heat tool to speed up the drying process, if desired.*

❹ Stamp the dimensional paint over some of the rectangles.

❺ Apply paint to the body area of each snowman stamp. Apply Lamp Black to the hat. Stamp a snowman onto each rectangle, aligning the bottom of the snowman with the bottom of the rectangle.

❻ Stamp the dimensional paint over some of the snowmen. Note: Do not stamp over the snowman's hat with dimensional paint.

PAINT COLOR COMBINATIONS

The sweatshirt design in the sample project was stamped with the following combinations of paint colors. Stamp your sweatshirt in the same manner, or use different paint combinations as desired.

TOP LEFT AND BOTTOM RIGHT IMAGES

Rectangle: Baby Blue Deep

Snowman: White, layered with Quick Silver dimensional paint

TOP CENTER IMAGE

Rectangle: Silver Platinum, layered with Quick Silver dimensional paint

Snowman: Baby Blue Deep

TOP RIGHT AND BOTTOM LEFT IMAGES

Rectangle: 1:1 mixture of Bright Blue metallic and White metallic, layered with Glimmer dimensional paint

Snowman: White

BOTTOM CENTER IMAGE

Rectangle: White

Snowman: 1:1 mixture of Bright Blue metallic and White metallic

---

SNOWMAN PATTERN

SNOWMAN
cut 3 from
2 mm craft foam

Each square = 1".
Cut on solid lines.

How to Make the Stamps

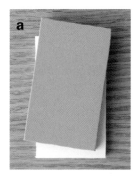

CUT RECTANGLES

TRANSFER PATTERN

CUT OUT SHAPES

Shine, Stick, and Structure

Dimensional glaze can do it all, whether you need a finish, an adhesive, or a texture.

Designer: Nichole Heady

TECHNIQUES TO TRY WITH DIMENSIONAL GLAZE

ADHESIVE: Use this super strong glue to secure fabrics, beads, glitter, and bulkier items such as dominoes to paper crafts.

DECOUPAGE: To adhere paper cutouts to surfaces and protect them as well, brush the glaze on the surface. Press the paper into the glaze and add another layer for the topcoat.

DIMENSION: Apply thickly over an entire area or in patterns to achieve a lightweight, three-dimensional appearance on the project surface. Use it to fill mini-frames or make your own faux resin words and monograms.

GLOSS: When dry, dimensional glaze is very shiny. Use it to create the illusion of glass or water elements such as puddles, raindrops, and bubbles.

INCLUSION: Achieve interesting finishes by mixing items such as glitter, tiny glass marbles, and sand into the glaze. Change the color without losing the glossiness by adding inks, dyes, watercolors, and dye powders.

Note: Although it has many uses, you'll find dimensional glaze listed under Adhesives in the Paper Crafts supplies lists.

Sweet Pear Tag

SUPPLIES

Cardstock: (Chocolate Chip) *Stampin' Up!*

Textured cardstock: (Sour Apple Watercolor Ribbed) *The Robin's Nest*

Rubber stamps: (Script from Ageless Adornments set, Sweet from Everyday Flexible Phrases set) *Stampin' Up!*

Dye ink: (Chocolate Chip) Classic Stampin' Pad, *Stampin' Up!*

Solvent ink: (Jet Black) StazOn, *Tsukineko*

Paper accent: (pear from Jolee's by You Series 1A) *EK Success*

Accent: (mini domino) Travel Games to Go, *Pressman Toy Corp.*

Sheer bag: (Organza Elements) Sonnets, *Creative Imaginations*

Adhesive:
    (dimensional glaze) Crystal Effects, *Stampin' Up!*

    Double-sided tape

Tools:
    (⅛" hole punch) Fiskars

    ruler, scissors, heat tool

Finished size: 1¼" x 2¼"

INSTRUCTIONS

❶ Make tag from Chocolate Chip cardstock.

❷ Cut Sour Apple cardstock into rectangle smaller than tag and tear bottom; adhere to tag.

❸ Stamp script on domino with Jet Black ink and heat set with heat tool. Adhere domino to tag, using dimensional glaze.

❹ Adhere pear to domino and cover pear with thick layer of dimensional glaze; let dry.

❺ Stamp Sweet with Chocolate Chip ink on tag.

❻ Place gift in bag and tie tag to bag.

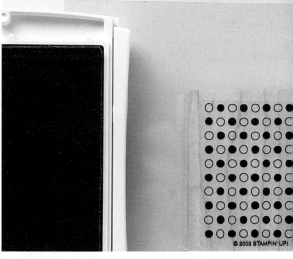

a Stamp on card

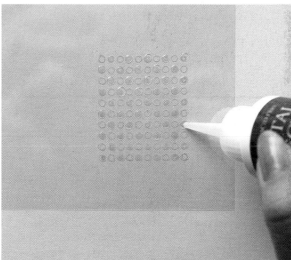

b Apply dimensional glaze to colored dots

Raindrops
Friendship Card

SUPPLIES

All supplies from Stampin' Up! unless otherwise noted.

Cardstock: (Bordering Blue, Ultrasmooth White)

Textured cardstock: (Cloud Blue Watercolor Ribbed) *The Robin's Nest*

Transparency sheet: (clear Window Sheet)

Pigment ink: (Bordering Blue) Craft Stampin' Pad

Rubber stamps: (umbrella from Fine Print set, dots from By Design set)

Adhesive:
   (dimensional glaze) Crystal Effects
   (Clear Mounting Squares) *3L*
Tools:
   (Bone folder)
   (ruler, scissors) no source

Finished size: 4¼" x 5½"

INSTRUCTIONS

❶ Make card from transparency sheet. Score and fold with heavy pressure, using bone folder.

❷ Stamp dot pattern on opposing corners of card front; let dry. To make raindrops, apply droplets of dimensional glaze to all solid dots (see Figures a–b). Let dry.

❸ Stamp umbrella on Ultrasmooth White and Cloud Blue cardstock. Cut dome from Cloud Blue umbrella and adhere to umbrella stamped on white. Trim and mat with Bordering Blue cardstock.

❹ Cut two random rectangles from Cloud Blue and adhere with mounting squares to card. Adhere umbrella piece to card center (see photo).

❺ For sentiment inside card, make matted piece same size as umbrella piece. Adhere directly behind umbrella piece to conceal text when card is closed.

A Flower for Mother's Day Card

Designer: Nichole Heady

SUPPLIES

Cardstock: (white)

Textured cardstock: (Cloud Blue, Peach, Sour Apple Watercolor Hammered) *The Robin's Nest*

Transparency sheet: (Window Sheet) *Stampin' Up!*

Shrink plastic: (white) *Lucky Squirrel*

Dye ink: (Blue Bliss Refill) *Stampin' Up!*

Accent: (large paper clip)

Fasteners:
(White Small Flowers eyelets) *Stampin' Up!*

(small clear rubber band) *Goody*

Fibers: (Celery, Sky Blue ribbon) *Making Memories*

Fonts:
(Book Antiqua) Word, *Microsoft*

(Wendy Medium) *www.fonts.com*

Adhesive:
(dimensional glaze) Crystal Effects, *Stampin' Up!*

glue stick

Tools:
(¼" hole punch) *Fiskars*

computer and printer, eyelet-setting tools, needlenose pliers, ruler, scissors, stylus, wire cutters

Finished size: 4¼" diameter

CARD

❶ To make card, cut two white cardstock circles to finished size. Set eyelets at left to join. Trim card bottom.

❷ Print sentiment, including spaces for omitted words, on Cloud Blue, Peach, and Sour Apple cardstock (see photo). Trim and adhere to card.

a Print and trim words

b Apply dimensional glaze

c Spread to edges

③ Print script words on transparency sheet and trim (see Figure a). Adhere to sentiment strips. Apply mound of dimensional glaze in center of each word (see Figure b). Spread to edges with stylus (see Figure c). Let dry.

FLOWER

① Cut flower, using pattern. Punch holes, shrink, and mold petals while warm (see Figure d).

② Mix small drop Bordering Blue ink with 1 tbsp. of dimensional glaze. Apply liberally to flower with stylus (see Figures e–g). Let dry.

③ Cut and bend paper clip to form stem with loop at one end (see Figure h).

④ To tie flower to stem, thread Sky Blue ribbon through stem loop and flower holes.

⑤ Attach flower to card using rubber band (see diagram).

⑥ Tie Celery ribbon around stem for leaves.

DESIGNER TIP

To stay in boundaries when you apply thick dimensional glaze, drop a large dab in the center and then use a stylus to pull the glaze to the edges.

d Shrink flower

e Add ink to glaze

f Mix with stylus

g Apply

h Make stem from paper clip

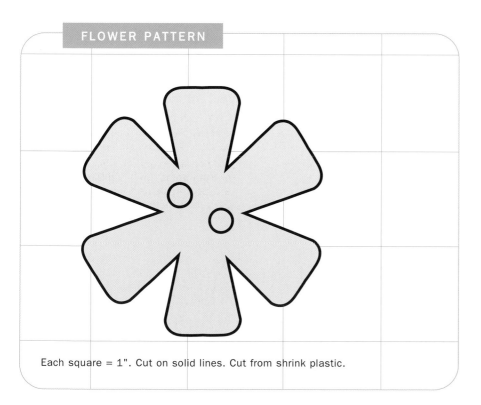

FLOWER PATTERN

Each square = 1". Cut on solid lines. Cut from shrink plastic.

ATTACH FLOWER TO CARD

① Push rubber band through top eyelet from back to front.

② Slide stem through elastic loop.

③ Push other end of rubber band through bottom eyelet from back to front.

④ Slide stem through elastic loop.

SWAK

Designer: Summer Ford

SUPPLIES

Rubber stamps: (French Writing) *Inkadinkado*; (Classic Alphabet) *Stampin' Up!*

Dye ink: (Basic Black) *Stampin' Up!*

Cardstock: (White, Red) *The Paper Company*

Paper accent: (white tag)

Fibers: (black gingham ribbon) *Offray*

Dimensional glaze: Crystal Lacquer, *Sakura of America*

Adhesive

Tools: sewing machine, scissors

Other: lipstick, white thread, paintbrush

Finished size: 6½" x 5"

DIMENSIONAL GLAZE TECHNIQUE

1 Cut rectangle of White cardstock; mat with Red cardstock.

2 Apply lipstick and kiss center of White rectangle.

3 Apply dimensional glaze to lip print.

CARD

1 Make card from White cardstock; stamp French Writing on card with Basic Black.

2 Adhere lip print rectangle to card; zigzag-stitch around edges.

3 Stamp "SWAK" on tag and ink edges with Basic Black; stitch Red cardstock border on bottom of tag.

4 Tie ribbon around bottom of card and attach tag.

Love You Always

Designer: Linda Beeson

SUPPLIES

Rubber stamps: (Letter Background, I will...) *Penny Black*; (postage cancellation) *Stampington & Co.*; (Postmark) *Just for Fun Rubber Stamps*

Dye ink: (Chestnut Brown) Memories, *Stewart Superior Corp.*; (green)

Solvent ink: (Jet Black) StazOn, *Tsukineko*

Cardstock: (Nutmeg) *Bazzill Basics Paper*

Patterned paper: (Green swirl) Heritage, *Making Memories*

Acrylic paint: (Avocado) Ceramcoat, *Delta*

Paper accents: (mini folder) Paper Reflections, *DMD, Inc.*; (paint chip)

Accents: (black swirl paper clip) *Creative Impressions*; (white shrink plastic tag) *Stampendous!*; (orange glitter, micro beads) *Art Accentz*

Fibers: (brown ribbon)

Color medium: (brown chalk)

Dimensional glaze

Adhesive

Tools: paintbrush, scissors, heat tool, large heart punch

Other: chalk applicator, paper plate, sandpaper

Finished size: 5½" x 4¼"

CARD

1 Paint folder; let dry. Stamp I will... on folder with Jet Black.

2 Stamp Letter Background on paint chip with Chestnut Brown.

3 Make card from Nutmeg cardstock.

4 Tear Green swirl paper slightly smaller than card front; ink edges with Chestnut Brown and adhere to card.

DIMENSIONAL GLAZE TECHNIQUE

1 Sand tag; chalk. Stamp Postmark on tag with Chestnut Brown.

2 Shrink tag with heat tool.

3 Coat tag with dimensional glaze; sprinkle on glitter and beads. Let dry.

4 Tie ribbon through tag.

FINISH

1 Punch heart from Nutmeg cardstock; stamp Letter Background on heart with Chestnut Brown. Adhere to folder.

2 Adhere paint chip to card. Attach paperclip to folder; adhere to card.

3 Stamp postage cancellation on card with green.

4 Adhere tag to card.

Fluffy Flowers

Designer: Nichole Heady

SUPPLIES

Rubber stamps: (Spring Flowers set) *Stampin' Up!*

Dye ink: (Old Olive) *Stampin' Up!*

Liquid applique: (White) *Marvy Uchida*

Cardstock: (Cream Confetti, Old Olive) *Stampin' Up!*

Patterned paper: (Baby Script Powder) *Daisy D's*

Color medium: (chalk) Stampin' Pastels, *Stampin' Up!*

Accent: (Best Friends charm) *Lasting Impressions for Paper*

Fibers: (blue gingham ribbon, blue satin ribbon, blue cord ribbon) *Making Memories*

Adhesive: (dots) Zots, *Therm O Web*; (glue stick)

Tools: (hole punch) *Stampin' Up!*; scissors, heat tool

Other: chalk applicator

Finished size: 5½" x 4½"

SUPER EMBOSS WITH LIQUID APPLIQUE

Use liquid applique to make images appear realistic. Try using it on stamps that include fluffy clouds, teddy bear fur, hair, tree branches, or cakes. Shade appliqued images with chalks or markers for extra zing.

LIQUID APPLIQUE TIPS

▪ Apply liquid applique sparingly, and be sure to let it dry thoroughly before heating.

▪ If you overheat applique, it will scorch or lift away from the paper. Try a few practice runs on scrap paper to get it right.

LIQUID APPLIQUÉ

LIQUID APPLIQUÉ

Stamp your image and squeeze the liquid appliqué directly on the parts you want to have a 3-D effect. For best results, wait at least three hours for the liquid to dry and use an embossing heat tool to make it puff up.

All That Glitters

Dust paper with a sparkling finish to dazzle the eye.

Designer: Denise Pauley

Glitter Finish Technique

SUPPLIES

Cardstock
Scrap paper
Adhesive machine: 510, *Xyron*
Stencil
Fine glitter in 2 colors
Repositionable tape (optional)
Brayer (optional)

INSTRUCTIONS

❶ Trim cardstock to desired size and run through adhesive machine.

❷ Remove backing to expose adhesive. Place cardstock, adhesive side up, on scrap paper.

❸ Place stencil over cardstock. Mask off area outside stencil with adhesive backing or repositionable tape.

❹ Sprinkle glitter over stencil image to cover. Press into adhesive with fingers, especially around edges. Tap excess glitter onto scrap paper. Remove masking and stencil.

❺ Sprinkle second color of glitter over background and press.

❻ Tap off excess glitter. Turn piece face down on clean sheet of scrap paper. Press with fingers or brayer to set glitter.

TIPS FROM DENISE

- To prevent the cardstock from showing through the glitter, use cardstock the same color as, or darker than, the background glitter.

- Use fine glitter to create detailed images. For a textured look, use larger-grained glitter.

Bonus Ideas

- Make your own stencils—punch or cut the images from heavy cardstock or sturdy plastic.

- To create an abstract design, cover part of the adhesive-covered cardstock with smaller pieces of cardstock, add glitter to the exposed areas, then remove the pieces. Repeat, using another color of glitter.

- Lay a piece of lace or mesh over the cardstock and shake glitter into the openings. Tap off excess, remove lace, and apply a second color of glitter.

Sparkling Snowflake Tag

SUPPLIES

Dark blue cardstock

Fine glitter: Navy, Sea Shell; UltraFine, *Art Institute Glitter*

Snowflake stencil: Events Scrapbook Templates, *Staedtler*

Magnetic word stamps: "Celebrate," "Cherish," "Holidays"; Express It, *Making Memories*

Magnetic stamp handle: *Making Memories*

Chalk ink: Indigo Velvet; Fresco, *Gary M. Burlin*

Solvent ink: Black; StazOn, *Tsukineko*

Adhesive machine: 510, *Xyron*

Accents:
   String: Bright White; Waxy Flax, *Scrapworks*

   Silver jump ring: *Gone Scrappin'*

   Small shipping tags: *Avery Dennison*

   Silver eyelet: *Creative Imaginations*

   White cotton fabric

Other: eyelet-setting tools, scrap paper, brayer (optional)

Finished size: 5" x 3"

INSTRUCTIONS

❶ Cut 5" x 3" piece of cardstock for tag.

❷ Cut 2½" x 2¾" piece of cardstock and cover with glitter finish, using snowflake stencil (see "Glitter Finish Technique"). Mat with white fabric, pulling threads to fray edges. Adhere to tag.

❸ Cut small strip of cardstock and fold over top of tag; set eyelet through center. Tie with fabric strip.

❹ Stamp shipping tags, using black ink; trim sides and rub with Indigo Velvet ink.

❺ Wrap string around large tag and knot in front. Attach jump ring and tie small tags to it.

❻ Attach tag to gift bag or box.

Winter Flurries Candle Wrap

Designer: Lucy Marino

SUPPLIES

All supplies from Close To My Heart.

Rubber stamps: A Winter Wonderland set

Dye ink: Indian Corn Blue, Pansy Purple

Cardstock: White Daisy, Indian Corn Blue

Patterned paper: Indian Corn Blue, Background & Texture Papers

Cord: Pansy Purple, Four Seasons Waxy Flax B

Adhesive: Liquid Glue

Glitter: iridescent, Prisma Glitter

Other: scissors, adhesive, clear gem, pillar candle, 1/16" hole punch, sponge

Finished size: 3" diameter
          5½" tall

❶ Measure and cut wide patterned paper strip to fit around candle with ½" overlap.

❷ Cut slightly thinner piece of White Daisy, tear long edges, and adhere to patterned paper.

❸ Stamp snowflakes on White Daisy strip with Indian Corn Blue and Pansy Purple; adhere wrap around candle.

❹ Stamp larger snowflake on White Daisy, tear edges, and sponge edges with Pansy Purple. Mat with Indian Corn Blue cardstock.

❺ Adhere glitter to snowflake; adhere gem to center.

❻ Punch holes in corners of snowflake square; tie onto candle with cord.

Happy Snowmen

Designer: Linda Brown

SUPPLIES

Rubber stamps*: Happy Winter, snowflakes, snowmen, trees, Wishing You sentiment

Ink pads*: black, blue, green

8½" x 11" cardstock:
    Blue
    White

White decorative chalk

Ultra fine silver glitter

Miscellaneous items: paper crimper, permanent/repositionable adhesive, scissors, adhesive pop-up dots

Stampin' Up! stamps from the Happy Winter set, and Basic Black, Bliss Blue, and Forest Foliage ink pads were used in the sample project.

Finished size: 4¼" x 5⅜"

Country Nativity

Designer: Debra Hull

SUPPLIES

Country nativity rubber stamp*

Black dye ink pad*

8½" x 11" cardstock:
    Light tan
    Tan

Adhesive pop-up dots

Straw pieces*

Iridescent glitter glue*

Raffia

Miscellaneous items: black pen*, colored pencils, scissors, craft knife, cutting mat, ruler, clear drying adhesive, double-sided tape

Uptown Design stamp; *Stewart Superior Corp.* Memories ink pad; *JudiKins* Straw Speckles; *PSX* Diamond Sparkles glitter glue; and *Sakura* Pigma pen were used in the sample project.

Finished size: 4¾" x 4⅛"

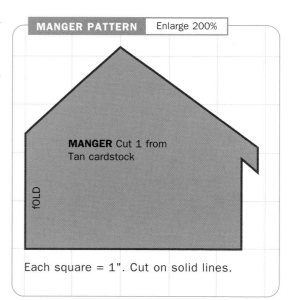

MANGER PATTERN   Enlarge 200%

MANGER Cut 1 from Tan cardstock

FOLD

Each square = 1". Cut on solid lines.

Bonus Idea

Add white dimensional paint or liquid appliqué to the lamb for texture.

Crumpling & Tearing Paper

Add texture and dimension to your paper–crumple and tear!

Great Things

Designer: Susan Neal

SUPPLIES

Rubber stamp: (To Accomplish) *Wordsworth*

Pigment ink: (Hint of Pesto) VersaMagic, (Galaxy Gold) Brilliance, *Tsukineko*

Textured cardstock: (Dark Fawn, Lemonade) *Bazzill Basics Paper*

Patterned paper: (Butterbloom) *Chatterbox*

Vellum: (Plain) *Bazzill Basics Paper*

Fasteners: (gold brads) *Making Memories*

Finish: (Sheer Gold Glaze) Paper Plus, *Delta*

Adhesive: (tabs) Herma Vario, *EK Success*; (double-sided tape)

Tools: (paper trimmer) *Fiskars*; scissors, 1⁄16" hole punch, sandpaper, paintbrush, iron and ironing board

Finished size: 5" square

INSTRUCTIONS

1. Make card from Fawn cardstock.

2. Cut Butterbloom patterned paper slightly smaller than card front; crumple, flatten, and iron on low heat.

3. Apply glaze to crumpled paper; let dry and adhere to card.

4. Stamp sentiment on vellum with Hint of Pesto; trim and mat with Lemonade cardstock.

5. Fold two corners over and attach brads. Mat with Fawn; ink edges with Galaxy Gold.

6. Adhere matted sentiment to card.

DESIGNER TIP

Be careful not to tear paper when crumpling, flattening, and ironing. For best results, test the iron heat setting on a piece of scrap paper first.

How to Make Paper Leather

Lightly spray one side of cardstock with water

Crunch moist cardstock into ball. Unfold and repeat several times. *Note: Be careful not to tear the cardstock as you work.*

Unfold; let dry flat.

Vintage Valentine

Designer: Dee Gallimore-Perry

SUPPLIES

Rubber stamps: *PSX* (Antique Alphabet); Susan Branch, All Night Media, *Plaid* (heart)

Dye ink: Basic Black, Classic, *Stampin' Up!*

Walnut ink: *FoofaLa*

Cardstock: Cinnamon, *Bazzill Basics Paper*

Patterned paper: *Rusty Pickle* (Vintage Collage, Grandpa's Letter)

Tags: *Avery Dennison*

Chalk: red, *Craf-T Products*

Other: white jute, beige thread, adhesive, hole punch, scissors, cotton swab or make-up applicator, sewing machine

Finished size: 6" x 4½"

INSTRUCTIONS

1 Make Cinnamon card.

2 Cut Vintage Collage paper to fit card front; adhere. Cut square of Grandpa's Letter paper and strip of Vintage Collage; adhere.

3 Zigzag stitch edge of square and center of strip.

4 Crumple and apply walnut ink to tags; let dry. Stamp Heart with Basic Black on each; apply red chalk.

5 Cut out heart and attach to card with white jute. Stamp sentiment with Basic Black on remaining tag; adhere.

Come Away With Me

Designer: Amber Crosby

SUPPLIES

Rubber stamp: Eiffel Tower, *Stampabilities*

Dye ink: black, *Impress Rubber Stamps*

Textured cardstock: Flamingo, *Bazzill Basics Paper*

Cardstock: *Bazzill Basics Paper* (Quartz, Blossom)

Patterned paper: Script Small, *7gypsies*

Pink twisted raffia: Twistel, *Making Memories*

Eyelets: silver, *Stamp Doctor*

Font: P22 Garamouche, *Impress Rubber Stamps*

Other: adhesive, scissors, eyelet-setting tools

Finished size: 4¾" x 6½"

INSTRUCTIONS

1 Make Flamingo card.

2 Stamp Eiffel Tower with black on Blossom; tear edges. Mat with Script Small; tear edges and adhere to card.

3 Print sentiment on Quartz; tear edges.

4 Set eyelets on each side of sentiment. Thread twisted raffia through eyelets. Adhere sentiment and twisted raffia to card; trim excess.

It's a Girl Thing

Designer: Julie Hillier

SUPPLIES

Rubber stamp: (It's a Girl Thing set) *Stampin' Up!*

Dye ink: (Black) *Stampin' Up!*; (pink)

Cardstock (pink, white)

Patterned paper: (green stripes from Apple Harvest collection) *Provo Craft*; (mosaic) *Colors By Design*

Fastener: (silver jump ring) *Making Memories*

Fibers: (green ribbon) *Offray*

Adhesive

Tools: scissors

Finished size: 4⅛" x 5½"

INSTRUCTIONS

1 Make card from white cardstock.

2 Stamp It's a Girl Thing on pink section of mosaic patterned paper with Black ink; cut out.

3 Mat with white; tear edges and ink with pink.

4 Layer patterned paper strip on green cardstock. Adhere stamped image to layered cardstock. Mat with pink cardstock.

5 Tie ribbon around cardstock; fasten with jump ring. Adhere to card.

Hello

Designer: Jenny Grothe

SUPPLIES

Rubber stamp: (Hello from Word Patterns set) *Hero Arts*

Pigment ink: (Tea Leaves) VersaMagic, *Tsukineko*

Dye ink: (brown)

Cardstock: (light green)

Textured cardstock: (Powder Blue) *Bazzill Basics Paper*

Patterned paper: (Fleur Rose) *Anna Griffin*

Accents: (staples)

Adhesive

Tools: (sandpaper) *PM Designs*; stapler, rulers, scissors

Finished size: 5½" x 4¼"

INSTRUCTIONS

1 Make card from Powder Blue cardstock.

2 Cut Fleur Rose paper slightly smaller than card. Crumple and sand creases; flatten. Ink edges with brown and adhere to card.

3 Cut Powder Blue to fit right side of card; tear left edge and adhere.

4 Stamp Hello on light green cardstock and ink edges with Tea Leaves. Staple to card.

Tricks for Tearing Paper

Most designers will tell you that an easy way to add interest to paper projects is to tear the paper instead of cutting it. But did you know there are several ways to do this? Here are some ideas:

For cardstock that is white on the back, place colored side up and tear the paper toward you to make a white edge. Tear the paper away from you to make a colored edge. Be sure to tear in a continuous motion.

For vellum, tear against the grain to make a ragged edge. Tear with the grain to make a smooth edge.

For a slightly fuzzy tear, fold the cardstock, use a cotton swab or paintbrush to apply a line of water to the fold, then pull the two sides apart.

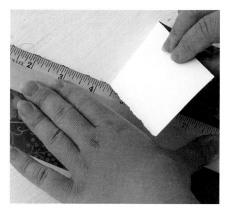

For a quick, straight tear, score the cardstock and hold a ruler securely over the crease. Pull the other side toward you, against the ruler.

For mulberry paper, make a firm crease; apply water to the crease with a paintbrush.

Tear slowly along the wet area. Let dry before applying adhesive.

For help tearing papers easily, try The Tearing Edge Tool from Stampin' Up! Simply tear the paper against the serrated edge to get an attractive torn edge. The tool retails for $19.95, and is available from a Stampin' Up! demonstrator. Call 800/STAMP UP or go to *www.stampinup.com*.

Paper Rose Birthday Bag

Design: Kathleen Paneitz

SUPPLIES

Happy Birthday rubber stamp*

Watermark ink pad*

Silver embossing powder*

Embossing heat tool

Small white gift bag

Pink tissue paper

8½" x 11" paper:

Floral print vellum

Pink cardstock

White cardstock

3 white eyelets*

Eyelet setter and hole punch

Decorative chalk*: pink, white

8 mm pearl*

Two 6" lengths sheer pink ribbon: ⅜" wide, ¼" wide

Miscellaneous items: scissors, hammer, self-healing mat, cotton swab or make-up applicator, adhesive, ruler

*PSX happy birthday stamp; Tsukineko VersaMark watermark ink pad; Ranger Industries embossing powder; Impress Rubber Stamps eyelets; Craf-T Products decorative chalk; and Westrim Crafts pearl were used in the sample project.

STAMP THE BAG

1 Trim the white cardstock to fit the front of the bag, and then trim the pink cardstock slightly smaller. Tear the right edges of both pieces.

2 Apply pink chalk to the white torn edge and white chalk to the pink torn edge, and then adhere the white cardstock to the bag (see photo).

3 Set two eyelets in the upper left corner of the torn pink cardstock, and then thread the ⅜" wide ribbon through the eyelets. Adhere it to the bag.

4 Trim the floral vellum and tear across it diagonally. Adhere it to the bag.

5 Stamp "Happy Birthday" on the pink cardstock with watermark ink and heat emboss it with silver.

6 Tear five white cardstock circles in graduated sizes. Roll each circle's edges toward the center and apply pink chalk to the edges.

7 Stack the circles from largest to smallest and adhere them together. Adhere the pearl in the center of the rose and adhere the rose to the bag.

8 Fill the bag with pink tissue paper.

MAKE THE TAG

1 Cut a 2" x 3½" rectangle of white cardstock and tear one short edge. Apply pink chalk to the torn edge.

2 Cut a slightly smaller pink rectangle. Tear one short edge and apply white chalk to it.

3 Stamp "Happy Birthday" with watermark ink and heat emboss it with silver.

4 Adhere the embossed cardstock to the tag, set an eyelet in the top, and tie it to the bag with the ¼" ribbon.

Vintage Hats

Designer: Alisa Wolcott

SUPPLIES

Rubber stamps: Three Hats, *Delta Rubber Stampede*

Ink: black, ColorBox, *Clearsnap*

Colored pencils: *Crayola*

Embossing powder: Clear Super Fine, *Ranger Industries*

Adhesive mounting squares: *3L*

Other: celery green, pale yellow, and peachy pink cardstock; scissors; adhesive

Finished size: 4½" x 5½"

Shoe Shopping

Designer: Alisa Wolcott

SUPPLIES

Rubber stamps: Four Shoes, *Delta Rubber Stampede*

Ink: black, ColorBox, *Clearsnap*

Colored pencils: *Crayola*

Embossing powder: Clear Super Fine, *Ranger Industries*

Adhesive mounting squares: *3L*

Other: blue, green, pale yellow, purple, red, and white cardstock; scissors; adhesive

Finished size: 4½" x 5½"

Layering Paper

Add depth and variety to your paper crafts by layering paper.

ABC Thank You

Designer: Linda Beeson

SUPPLIES

Rubber stamp: (Conversation Dots set) *Hero Arts*

Acrylic stamp: (Alphabet Vintage Large) *River City Rubber Works*

Dye ink: (Black) *Making Memories*

Chalk ink: (Brown) Fresco, *Gary M. Burlin*; (various colors) ColorBox Petal Point Chalk, *Clearsnap*

Cardstock: (red)

Patterned paper: (Blackboard) *Rusty Pickle*

Paper accent: (Manila folder)

Accents: (red staples) *Swingline*; (apple charm)

Fibers: (red/white striped ribbon) *Impress Rubber Stamps*; (September ribbon)

Adhesive: double-sided tape

Tools: (label maker) *Dymo*; ruler, scissors, paper sander,

Other: black label tape

Finished size: 5½" x 4¼"

INSTRUCTIONS

1 Make card from red cardstock.

2 Cut manila folder to 5" x 2¼" and round corners. Stamp Alphabet Vintage with Brown on folded paper.

3 Stamp Conversations Dots with black. Ink edges and top of paper.

4 Cut Blackboard paper to 3¾" x 4" and round corners; sand edges. Staple date ribbon to patterned paper; attach to card.

5 Tie ribbon with charm onto stamped paper; adhere to card and staple.

6 Make "Thank You" label; trim and adhere to card.

Thanks

Designer: Linda Beeson

SUPPLIES

Rubber stamps: (Harlequin Background) *Penny Black*; (Fine Line Letters Alphabet) *Hero Arts*

Dye ink: (Hot Chocolate) Oh Domino, A Country Welcome

Cardstock: (ivory)

Textured cardstock: (Nutmeg) *Bazzill Basics Paper*

Patterned paper: (Big Gallery Stripe) *Chatterbox*

Acrylic paint: (Black) Ceramcoat, *Delta*

Fasteners: (black nail heads) *Scrapworks*

Fibers: (brown/beige ribbon) *Impress Rubber Stamps*

Adhesive: double-sided tape

Tools: scissors, foam paintbrush

Finished size: 5½" x 4¼"

INSTRUCTIONS

1 Make card from Nutmeg cardstock.

2 Stamp Harlequin background on card with black paint; let dry.

3 Stamp Thanks on ivory cardstock. Tie ribbon around cardstock and attach nail heads.

4 Adhere strip of Big Gallery Stripe patterned paper and cardstock to card.

Just Moved

Designer: Nichol Magouirk

SUPPLIES

Rubber stamps: *Making Memories* (Magnetic Alphabet Set, Stenography font); *Magenta Rubber Stamps* (Key, Antique Key); *Inkadinkado* (Dawn Hauser Daydreams Key)

Chalk ink: brown, ColorBox, *Clearsnap*

Key charm: *Magic Scraps*

Jewelry tags: *American Tag*

Other: cardstock (yellow, brown), scissors, make-up sponge, adhesive, string

Finished size: 4¼" x 5½"

INSTRUCTIONS

❶ Make yellow card.

❷ Randomly stamp key stamps with brown over front of card.

❸ Ink edges of card with brown.

❹ Trim yellow cardstock; ink surface. Mat with brown cardstock.

❺ Stamp "just moved" on two jewelry tags. Tie to key charm.

❻ Attach tags and charm to inked cardstock. Adhere to card.

Family Tiles

Designer: Stacy Yoder

SUPPLIES

Rubber stamps: *Stampin' Up!* (script); *PSX* (letter stamps)

Dye ink: Classic Stampin' Pad, *Stampin' Up!* (Basic Black, Summer Sun)

Cardstock: *Bazzill Basics Paper* (Navy, Ocean, Sunflower)

Stickers: Scrabble tiles, *Limited Edition Rubberstamps*

Flower punch: *Emagination Crafts*

Eyelets: *Making Memories* (five medium blue, one large silver)

Raffia: Yellow Twistel, *Making Memories*

Spiral clip: Clipola, *Cavallini Papers*

Mesh: white, *Magic Mesh*

Other: scissors, white rick rack, fibers, square mini-brads, clear embossing powder, embossing heat tool, eyelet-setting tools, adhesive

Finished size: 5" x 6½"

PREPARE

❶ Make Navy card.

❷ Cut Sunflower cardstock to fit card front. Ink edges with Basic Black; attach to card with blue eyelets.

❸ Stamp "we've moved" on top right corner of card with Basic Black.

EMBELLISH

❶ Cut tag from Ocean cardstock. Stamp script in Sunflower on tag; emboss with clear.

❷ Cut Navy cardstock piece same width as tag; tear one edge and adhere to tag.

❸ Cut square of Ocean cardstock and triangle of Sunflower cardstock and adhere to tag. Cut small mesh rectangle and adhere to house shape. Place brads on house shape as windows.

❹ Adhere stickers spelling FAMILY to bottom of tag.

❺ Punch out flower from Sunflower card-stock; crumple then attach to tag using blue eyelet. Add spiral clip on side of tag.

❻ Cut small square of Sunflower cardstock; place near top center of tag and set silver eyelet through both layers.

❼ Thread fibers through eyelet. Adhere tag to card.

Autumn Splendor

Designer: Leslie Elvert

SUPPLIES

Rubber stamps: *Stampin' Up!* (Fall Fun set); *Hero Arts* (Printer's Lower Case); *Stamps by Judith* (small circle)

Dye ink: Classic Stampin' Pad, *Stampin' Up!* (Basic Black); Exclusive Inks, *Close To My Heart* (Desert Sand, Oak Brown)

Watermark ink: VersaMark, *Tsukineko*

Embossing powder: clear, *Stampendous!*

Cardstock: *Stampin' Up!* (More Mustard, Night of Navy, Really Rust); *Close To My Heart* (Natural)

Alphabet stickers: Nostalgiques, Jolee's Boutique, *EK Success*

Pen: black, Micron Pigma, *Sakura of America*

Fibers: *Rubba Dub Dub*

Eyelets: brown, *Making Memories*

Other: mesh

SUBTLE BACKGROUND

Stamp a monochromatic background to keep photos the focus of your layout. Choose a watermark ink and emboss a simple border with clear embossing powder. The clear powder will give the stamped design a slightly deeper hue than the background paper, creating a subtle and sophisticated look.

The World Can Wait

Designer: Michelle Tardie

SUPPLIES

Pigment ink: ColorBox, *Clearsnap* (black, silver)

Walnut ink: *7gypsies*

Embossing powder: silver, *PSX*

Cardstock: Watermelon, *Bazzill Basics Paper*

Patterned paper: Pamela Woods, *Creative Imaginations* (Gold Foundation, Burgundy Foundation)

Mesh: silver, *Magic Mesh*

Punch: Primitive heart, *Emagination Crafts*

Font: Fat Finger, downloaded from the Web

Poem: Unknown, *www.scrapangels.com/inspiration/index .php*

Foam tape: Scotch, *3M*

Other: white cardstock, scissors, embossing heat tool, computer and printer, adhesive foam squares

Finished size: 6½" x 4"

INSTRUCTIONS

❶ Make card from Watermelon cardstock.

❷ Cut rectangle of Gold Foundation and strip of silver mesh; adhere both to card.

❸ Print poem on Burgundy Foundation; tear and ink edges with black.

❹ Punch two hearts from white cardstock; ink and emboss with silver.

❺ Apply walnut ink to hearts; heat set.

❻ Adhere hearts to printed verse and printed verse to card with foam squares.

Three Flowers

Designer: Michelle Tardie

SUPPLIES

Rubber stamps: *Hero Arts* (flower); *PSX* (Antique Alphabet)

Pigment ink: Dauber Duos, *Tsukineko* (Petal Pink, Orchid, Marigold, Cool Mint)

Cardstock: Beach, *Bazzill Basics Paper*

Paper: *Sweetwater*, Farmyard Creations (cream, pink, Yellow Antique, Pink Flower Antique patterned)

Mesh: Rose, *Magic Mesh*

Square punch: *Emagination Crafts*

Adhesive: *Glue Dots International*

Other: swirl paperclip, staples, stapler, scissors

Finished size: 6" x 4"

INSTRUCTIONS

❶ Make card from Beach cardstock.

❷ Cut Pink Flower Antique to fit card front; adhere.

❸ Adhere mesh strip to card.

❹ Stamp flower with Petal Pink on Yellow Antique, Cool Mint on pink, and Marigold on cream.

❺ Punch out flowers and adhere to mesh strip.

❻ Stamp "GET WELL SOON" with Orchid at bottom of card.

❼ Staple on each side of flowers and attach swirl paper clip.

Sensational Stitches

Add a unique touch to your paper projects—sewing on paper is fun, easy, and hot!

Dust off your sewing machine and try to remember everything you learned in home economics, because stitching (both by machine and hand) is a hot trend in the world of paper crafting. Try these four, fun stitches, and start sewing up a creative storm.

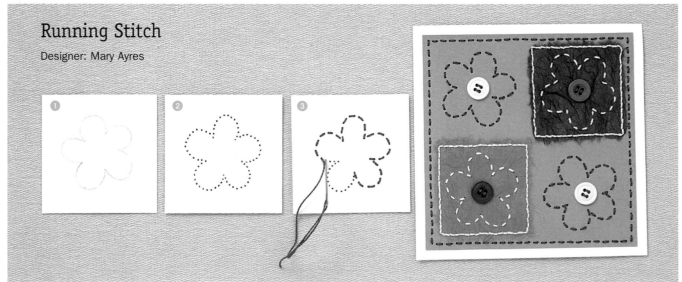

Running Stitch

Designer: Mary Ayres

❶ Lightly draw or trace a flower on cardstock.

❷ Punch holes about ⅛" apart with a needle, outlining the image. Erase the pencil lines.

❸ Thread the needle with craft thread, embroidery floss, or pearle cotton. Starting from the back, bring the threaded needle up through a hole in the image, down through the next hole, up through the next hole, and so on until you have stitched the outline of the flower. Finish with both ends of the thread in the back. Knot ends or adhere them to the back of the cardstock.

RUNNING STITCH SAMPLER

You can create running stitch accents for cards, favor boxes, or other projects. This sampler combines four blocks with buttons and a border for a fun quilted look. You can add a layer of mulberry paper for dimension and variety.

Machine Stitch

Designer: Mary Ayres

❶ Cut out the desired image or shape from cardstock. Adhere the image to the background and machine stitch around it, close to the edge. Be sure to begin and end in the same hole.

❷ You can machine stitch all sorts of images, even those with square corners. When you turn corners, make sure the machine needle is down through the cardstock so that you can make clean, sharp right angles.

MACHINE STITCH SAMPLER

If your project requires several shapes or layers, as does this layered heart sampler, stitch the shapes in order from top to bottom to avoid having to stitch through too many layers at a time. Try a variety of machine stitches like blanket stitch and zigzag. If the stitches tear the paper, increase the size of the stitches.

Hand-Stitched Edges

Designer: Mary Ayres

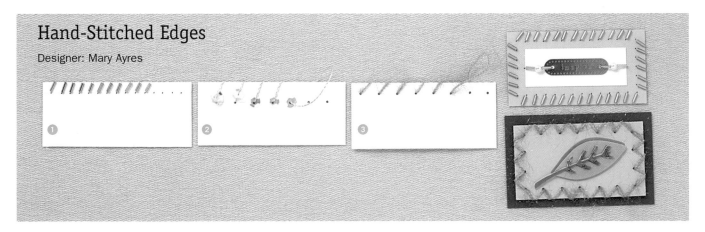

❶ Lightly draw a pencil line about ½" from the edge of the paper. Mark evenly spaced dots along the line about ½" apart. Punch holes in the marked dots, then erase the pencil line. Insert the threaded needle through first hole from back to front, leaving a short tail in back. Knot the thread or adhere it to the back of the paper. Wrap the thread around the edge of the paper, and insert the needle through the second hole.

Repeat, always stitching from the back. When finished, adhere the tail of the thread to the back of the paper.

❷ Use fun fibers or sparkly thread to make your hand-stitched edges stand out. Or try adding beads or sequins for a different look.

HAND-STITCHED EDGING SAMPLER

These fun samplers show how you can use this technique to create a natural border for greetings, images, or any other element that you want to frame.

Silk Ribbon Rosebuds

Designer: Mary Ayres

① Lightly draw a 1" vertical pencil line on paper. Beginning at the top of the line, draw five dots spaced ¼" apart. Mark a dot ¼" from the center dot on each side of the line. Punch holes through the dots, then erase the pencil line.

② Thread the needle with dark pink silk ribbon. Bring it up through A and down through B. Trim the ribbon on the back side of the paper, leaving a short tail. Repeat this step with light pink ribbon. Separate the ribbons so they lie side by side.

③ Bring the needle, threaded with three strands of green floss, up through C and down through D, passing between the two strands of pink ribbon.

④ Bring the needle, threaded with green silk ribbon, up through E and down through F. Then insert the same needle up through E again and down through G. Adhere all ends securely in back.

SILK RIBBON SAMPLER

This elegant stitch adds a gentle sophistication to any project. The careful selection of a soft pink patterned paper with this silk ribbon stitching reinforces the look and feel of the project. To vary the project, find a silk ribbon embroidery book at your local craft store and try some daisies or other flowers. Or stitch a bunch of multi-colored flowers for a refreshing summertime bouquet.

Fabulous Fabric Cards

Make a whole set of cards from one panel of distinctly designed fabric. Patricia Anderson picked Botanical Bugs from South Sea Imports to use as pockets on her thank you card set. She stitched the frayed motifs to coordinating cardstock, inked the edges, and adhered them to cards. Then she stamped "Thank You" on small aged tags tied with ribbon and tucked them in the pockets.

Doves and Heart Wedding Card

Designer: Eileen Edgar

SUPPLIES

White textured cardstock

Pink paper: *SEI*

Metallic thread: pink, white, *DMC*

Font: CK Cursive, "The Best of Creative Lettering Combo" CD, *Creating Keepsakes*

Needle

Finished size: 4" x 5½"

INSTRUCTIONS

❶ Print greeting on white textured cardstock. Make card base.

❷ Place doves and heart pattern on piece of white cardstock. Carefully outline pattern by punching holes an even distance apart. *Note: Be sure to work on an appropriate surface, such as craft foam or cork board.*

❸ Hand-stitch pattern, using pink metallic thread for heart and white metallic thread for doves. Insert needle from back at A and take a long stitch to B, then insert needle from back into C and take a long stitch to D; repeat

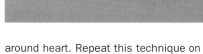
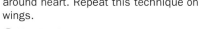

around heart. Repeat this technique on wings.

❹ Use backstitch to outline dove images.

❺ Mat with pink paper.

❻ Adhere to card.

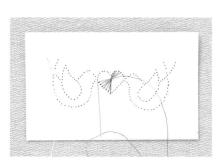

BACKSTITCH

Up at 1, down at 2, up at 3, down at 1, stitching back to meet previous stitch.

DOVES AND HEART PATTERN

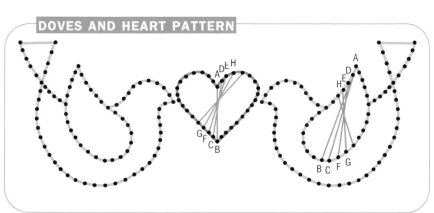

Stitch a Daisy

Designer: Maria Larson

SUPPLIES

Cardstock: cream, honeydew, lavender, light gold

White vellum

Honeydew eyelets: *Doodlebug Design*

Embroidery floss: green, purple, *DMC*

Font: CK Daydream, "Creative Clips and Fonts" CD, *Creating Keepsakes*

Other: spray adhesive, purple button, paper piercing tool, embroidery needle

Finished size: 6" square

INSTRUCTIONS

❶ Make honeydew card base.

❷ Print "Happy Mother's Day" on vellum. Cut into 5½" square and adhere to card with spray adhesive. Add eyelets.

❸ Cut flower from light gold cardstock, using pattern. Also cut 3½" x 2⅞" piece of lavender cardstock. Transfer stitching lines from pattern to both pieces. Punch holes along lines as shown.

❹ Backstitch flower, leaves and stem. Adhere flower above stem on lavender piece. Adhere button to center.

❺ Mat stitched piece with torn cream cardstock. Adhere to card.

STITCHED FLOWER PATTERN

Seed Packet Mother

Designer: Marah Johnson

SUPPLIES

Foam stamps: (Floral) *Making Memories*

Paint: (Parchment) *Liquitex*

Cardstock: (sage)

Patterned paper: (Sage Diamond) *K&Company*

Specialty paper: (Green canvas, Almond weave printable fabric) *FiberMark*

Accents: (antique mini brads) *American Label & Tag Co.*; (Seeds to Sew clipart) Click-n-Craft, *The Vintage Workshop*; (muslin strip)

Rub-ons: (Evolution Black) Simply Stated Alphabets, *Making Memories*

Sticker: (Love paper charm) Real Life, *Pebbles Inc.*

Adhesive

Tools: scissors, sewing machine, stapler, sponge paintbrush, ruler

Other: tan thread

Finished size: 3¾" x 5½"

CREATE BACKGROUND

❶ Cut 3½" x 6" rectangle of Green canvas.

❷ Cut 3½" x 3" rectangle of Sage Diamond and tear diagonally. Adhere torn paper to top of canvas.

❸ Fold down top of canvas ½" and attach ends with brads.

❹ Stamp Floral image on canvas; let dry.

❺ Print clipart on almond weave fabric, following manufacturer's instructions.

FINISH

❶ Make card from sage cardstock.

❷ Machine-stitch tag to canvas.

❸ Spell "mother" on scrap of Almond weave "fabric with rub-ons. Adhere to canvas.

❹ Attach sticker and brad to canvas.

❺ Tie knot in muslin strip and staple to top of canvas.

❻ Adhere canvas to card.

Precious Little One

Designer: Nichol Magouirk

SUPPLIES

Light blue textured cardstock

Black ink: Memories, *Stewart Superior*

Alphabet stamps: *Hero Arts*

Snap tape: *Prym-Dritz*

Buttons: *SEI*

Light blue embroidery floss: *DMC*

White thread: *Coats & Clark*

Other: white woven fabric, pencil, sewing machine

Finished size: 4¼" x 5½"

FABRIC

1 Cut 2½" x 4½" piece of woven fabric.

2 Write "Precious" on fabric with pencil. Backstitch with embroidery floss. Fray edges.

3 Stamp "Little one".

4 Stitch on buttons.

SNAP TAPE

1 Cut two snap segments from snap tape.

2 Slide top frayed edge of stitched piece between top and bottom layers of snap tape. Machine stitch in place.

3 Stitch piece to card base.

4 Stitch top edge of snap segments to top of card.

Bonus Idea

Attach the stitched cloth piece to a scrapbook page, gift bag, tag, or baby onesie.

Sweet Baby Girl

Designer: Summer Ford

SUPPLIES

Rubber stamps: (Holiday Stripes) *Hero Arts*; (Mini Solid Tag) Brenda Walton, All Night Media, *Plaid*; (Classic Alphabet) *Stampin' Up!*

Foam stamps: (Jersey Uppercase) *Making Memories*

Dye ink: (Mellow Moss, Pretty In Pink) *Stampin' Up!*

Textured cardstock: (Pear) *Bazzill Basics Paper*

Cardstock: (Solar White) *The Paper Company*

Acrylic paint: (Leaf Green, Rose Pink) FolkArt, *Plaid*

Fibers: (green, pink gingham ribbon) I; (white thread)

Adhesive

Tools: foam paintbrush, sewing machine, ⅛" hole punch, scissors

Finished size: 7" x 5⅛"

INSTRUCTIONS

① Make card from Solar White card-stock; trim Pear cardstock to fit front of card.

② Trim Solar White slightly smaller than card front. Stamp stripes on Solar White with Mellow Moss and Pretty In Pink.

③ Stamp "Girl" with foam stamps and Rose Pink paint. Lightly apply Leaf Green paint to stamps and re-stamp over word. Let dry.

④ Zigzag-stitch stamped cardstock to Pear.

⑤ Wrap green ribbon around stamped cardstock; adhere to card.

⑥ Stamp tag on Solar White with Mellow Moss; stamp "baby" on tag with Pretty In Pink; trim.

⑦ Punch hole; tie tag to card with pink ribbon.

DESIGNER TIP

Add texture to the stamped white cardstock to make it look more like fabric. Make small creases in the card-stock, hold the cardstock between your fingers, and run the Mellow Moss inkpad along the creases.

Bonus Ideas

■ Create a card to welcome a new little boy using blue ink, paint, and ribbon.

■ Stamp and embellish a photo frame to create a precious keepsake for the new parents.

The Eyelets Have It!

Choose eyelets for quick, easy, and fun accents on any project.

Designer: Nichole Heady

A few years ago, eyelets took the paper crafting world by storm. Quick and easy to use, these tiny accents became a favorite way to add dimension or capture attention. Eyelets have grown in popularity as more colors, shapes, sizes, and designs have become available—some don't even have the familiar center holes! Our tag sampler features lots of ideas to get you started. Then, say "Aye!" to your own creativity.

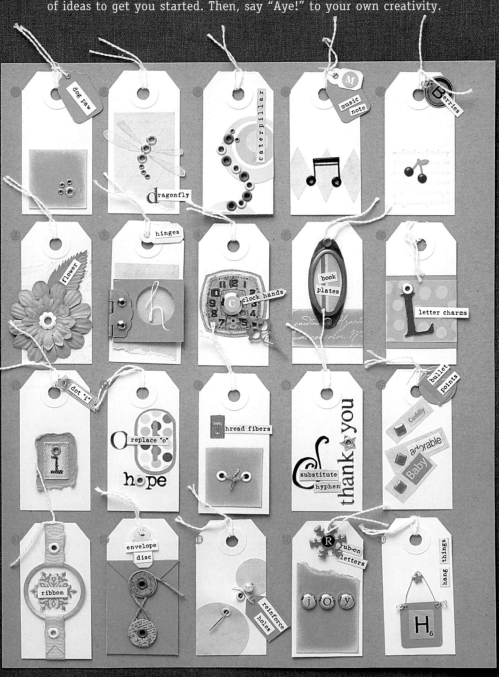

How to Set an Eyelet

① Place anywhere hole punch on spot where you want eyelet. Hit 2–3 times firmly with hammer to create hole.

② Lay eyelet upside down; place hole over eyelet.

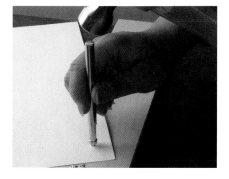

③ Place setter into eyelet, and hammer twice firmly to set eyelet in place. Remove setter, and hammer eyelet once or twice to flatten completely. Turn over.

20 FUN THINGS TO DO WITH EYELETS AND BRADS

We've set these examples on tags, but you can use them on cards, scrapbook pages, mini books, gift bags, or any project that needs a creative finishing touch.

① PAW PRINTS

Silver eyelets: ⅛" & 1⁄16", *Making Memories*

② DRAGONFLY

Silver eyelets: ⅛" & 1⁄16", *Making Memories*

③ CATERPILLAR

Eyelets: ⅛", 1⁄16", *Making Memories*

④ MUSICAL NOTES

Black eyelets: ⅛", *Making Memories*

⑤ BERRY BRADS

Wine brads: *All My Memories*

⑥ FLOWER CENTER

White flower eyelet: *Making Memories*

⑦ HINGE ATTACHMENT

Silver brads: *Stampin' Up!*

⑧ CLOCK HANDS ATTACHMENT

Silver brad: *All My Memories*

⑨ BOOKPLATE NAILS

Antique brads: *Making Memories*

⑩ CHARM ATTACHMENT

White eyelet: *Making Memories*

⑪ DOT OVER "I"

Blue eyelet: *All My Memories*

⑫ LETTER "O"

Yellow eyelet: *Making Memories*

⑬ HOLE FOR ATTACHING FIBERS

White eyelets: *Making Memories*

⑭ WORD SEPARATION

Silver star eyelet: *Stampin' Up!*

⑮ BULLET POINTS

Silver square brads: *All My Memories*

⑯ RIBBON FASTENERS

White eyelets: *Making Memories*

⑰ ENVELOPE DISC FASTENERS

Brown eyelets: *Making Memories*

⑱ HOLE REINFORCERS

Yellow eyelets: *Making Memories*

⑲ RUB-ON LETTER FRAMES

Silver brads: Creative Imaginations
Silver snowflake brad: *Boxer*

⑳ ACCENT HANGERS

Silver star brad: Tack, *Chatterbox*
Green eyelets: *Making Memories*

BRADS: EYELETS' POPULAR COUSIN

Brads are similar to eyelets in size, style, variety, and effect. The main difference is the way they're attached. Here are a few tips for using brads:

- To attach a brad, pierce a hole in the paper with a push pin or 1/16" hole punch, or make a slit with a craft knife. Press the point of the prongs through, and spread the prongs to keep the brad in place.

- Hammer a brad after it is in place for an antique look.

- Color brads with watermark ink and embossing powder. Hold with tweezers while heating.

- Color brads with permanent pens or acrylic paint.

- Dab brads with liquid glue, such as ZIG 2-Way Glue from EK Success or Crystal Effects from Stampin' Up!, then sprinkle with glitter or attach a sequin or bead.

- Sand brads and daub with brown ink for an antique look.

A Shiny Snowflake Card

Designer: Nichole Heady

SUPPLIES

Cardstock: Bordering Blue, Ultrasmooth White, *Stampin' Up!*

Patterned paper: Script, *Daisy D's*

Accents:
  Metal snowflake: *Making Memories*
  Blue eyelet: *All My Memories*

"Merry Christmas" stamp: All-Year Cheer III, *Stampin' Up!*

White pigment ink: *Stampin' Up!*

Glitter: Dazzling Diamonds, *Stampin' Up!*

Other: heat tool, sponge

Finished size: 5¼" x 4¼"

INSTRUCTIONS

❶ Create card base from white cardstock.

❷ Cut blue cardstock to fit card front. Hold eyelet upside down with tweezers, dip in ink, then stamp cardstock to create polka dot pattern. Stamp greeting; sponge edges with ink. Adhere to card.

❸ Mat script paper square with white cardstock. Ink snowflake, shake on glitter, and heat set. Adhere snowflake to paper square with eyelet. Adhere accent to card.

Painless BRAD Placement

Add brads to your projects without bending or tearing the paper. Just place the paper over a piece of corkboard or the reverse side of a mouse pad. Then make a hole with a pushpin where you want the brad to go. The brad slips right in! For more tips on using brads, see p.144.

Thinking of You Card

Designer: Nichole Heady

SUPPLIES

Ultrasmooth White cardstock: *Stampin' Up!*

Patterned paper: polka dot, *SEI*

Vellum: pink floral, *Chatterbox*

Eyelets: ⅛" white, ⅟₁₆" silver, silver pansy, *Making Memories*

"Thinking of you" sticker: Wonderful Words; Deja Views, *C-Thru Ruler*

Eyelet-setting tools

Finished size: 4¼" square

INSTRUCTIONS

① Create card base from cardstock.

② Adhere 1¾" square of polka dot paper to card.

③ Lay 2¼" square of vellum over polka dot paper. Set ⅛" eyelets in corners; set ⅟₁₆" eyelets inside ⅛" eyelets. Set pansy in center of square.

④ Adhere word sticker to card.

Bonus Idea

STICKING WITH EYELETS

Use eyelets instead of adhesive, especially on vellum or materials where the adhesive readily shows through.

Radiant Bride

Designer: Susan Stringfellow

SUPPLIES

Rubber stamp: Love Swirls, *Stampin' Up!*

Gold pearl paper, clear vellum, and cardstock: *Making Memories*

Watermark ink:
VersaMark, *Tsukineko*

Gold embossing powder: *Uptown Design*

Fibers: *Fibers by the Yard*

Gold thread: *Coats & Clark*

Punches: *EK Success*

Heart brad: *Magic Scraps*

Gold leaf: *Mona Lisa Products*

Glue pen: ZIG 2Way
Glue, *EK Success*

Bouquet sticker: *me &
my BIG ideas*

Cherish Time

Designer: Alannah Jurgensmeyer

SUPPLIES

Metal frames: *Limited Edition Rubberstamps*

Brown cardstock: *DMD Industries*

Brown patterned paper: *Karen Foster Design*

Eyelets: Stamp Doctor, *Making Memories*

Flat-top letter eyelets: Bradwear, *Creative Imaginations*

Metal accent: *Anima Designs*

Watch parts: *7gypsies*

Brown ink pad: Van Dyke Brown, Nick Bantock, *Ranger Industries*

"TIME" letter tiles: *Creative Imaginations*

Paper letters: *FoofaLa*

Diamond glaze adhesive: *JudiKins*

Gingham ribbon: *Offray*

INKED EDGES

Wipe the edge of your paper along the edge of an ink pad for a cool worn, antique look. Use brighter colors for a warm springtime, glowing look. Or, use your favorite holiday colors to add a touch of cheer.

Mommy's Girl

Designer: Katrina Lawrence

SUPPLIES

Alphabet rubber stamps: *Plaid*

Ribbon: *Offray*

Blue cardstock: *Bazzill Basics Paper*

Frame, flowers, and vellum paper: *Forget Me Not Designs*

Square nails and ID tag: *Chatterbox*

Ribbon: *Memory Lane*

Title and sentiment block: *Leaving Prints*

MAKE YOUR OWN ACCENTS

If you're looking to add a soft, handmade accent to a baby or wedding layout, stamp on ribbon, tags, acrylic figures, metal, shrink plastic, polymer clay, microscope slides, ophthalmologist lenses, or wood.

You Make My Heart Sing

Designer: Kathleen Paneitz

SUPPLIES

Rubber stamps: (Sketchbox LC alphabet) Pixie, *Duncan*; (Mini Heart) *PrintWorks*

Dye ink: (Ginger) Adirondack, *Ranger Industries*

Cardstock: (Java, Natural, Bronze, Maraschino) *Bazzill Basics Paper*

Accents: (white mesh) *Magic Mesh*; (gold music note charms)

Fasteners: (heart clip) *Making Memories*; (silver eyelets)

Fibers: (black gingham ribbon) *Offray*; (red embroidery floss) *DMC*

Fonts: (CK Stenography) "CK Fresh Fonts" CD, *Creating Keepsakes*

Adhesive: (red glitter hot glue stick) *FPC Corporation*; (foam squares) *EK Success*; (dots) *Glue Dots International*

Tools: (heart pattern paper embosser) Lil' Boss, *Paper Adventures*; (heart punch) *Emagination Crafts*; computer and printer, hot glue gun, scissors, stapler, eyelet-setting tools

Other: (red staples) *Making Memories*

Finished size: 2¾" x 5½"

MAKE TAG

❶ Make tag from Java cardstock.

❷ Adhere white mesh to tag.

❸ Emboss Bronze cardstock with heart pattern. Cut rectangle of embossed cardstock; tear top and bottom edges, adhere to tag. Adhere scrap to top of tag; trim corners to match tag.

STAMP & EMBELLISH

❶ Punch hearts from Maraschino cardstock.

❷ Set eyelet in center of each heart; thread on black gingham ribbon and knot on each side of hearts. Adhere to tag.

❸ Stamp "sing" on Natural cardstock; cut out letters and ink edges.

❹ Adhere "sing" and music note charms to tag with foam squares.

❺ Print "you make my" on Natural cardstock; cut out, ink edges, and staple to tag.

❻ Apply red glitter hot glue to tag. Stamp Mini Heart in glue; let cool and then remove stamp.

❼ Attach heart clip to top of tag with red embroidery floss.

Looking for a music note or another perfect charm? Try A Charming Place for pewter, gold, and brass charms.
A Charming *Place*,
www.acharmingplace.com.

KATHLEEN'S TIP

Apply watermark ink to your stamp before stamping in glue to make removing the stamp easier after the glue cools.

Baby Doll

Designer: Karen Burniston

SUPPLIES

Rubber stamps: artist face*, stripes*, swirl*, banana, boots*, scissors*, clock*, dancing figures*, Einstein*, flashlight*, heart*, queen*, elegant faces*, fish, sun*, wings*, script*, chopsticks*, pencil*

Eyelets*

12" x 12" paper:
  Black crackle*
  Tan patterned*

Brown pen*

Colored pencils*

Decorative chalk*

Craft wire*

Computer font*

*Twenty Two artist face, stripes, and swirl stamps; Creative Mode boots and scissors stamps; Inkadinkado clock stamp; A Stamp in the Hand dancing figures; 100 Proof Press Einstein, flashlight, heart, and queen stamps; Magdalaina elegant face stamps; Above the Mark sun stamp; Stampendous! wings stamp; Hero Arts script stamp; Rubber Baby Buggy Bumpers script, chopsticks, and pencil stamps and eyelets; Stamping Station dark crackle paper; ScrapHappy tan diamond paper; Faber-Castell pen; Sanford Prismacolor colored pencils; Stampin' Up! Stampin' Pastels decorative chalk; Artistic Wire craft wire; and CK Journaling, "The Best of Creative Lettering" CD, Creating Keepsakes, were used in the sample project.

STAMPED ACCENTS

Use combinations of your favorite stamps to create one-of-a-kind accents that reflect the personality of a featured family member or loved one. The designer made unique doll accents to celebrate her young daughter's individuality.

I'd Be Lost...

Designer: Stacy Mcfadden

SUPPLIES

Rubber stamps: *JudiKins* (Large Compass); *Stamp It! Australia* (Small Compass)

Dye ink: dark blue, Suedes Collections set, *Creative Beginnings*

Patterned paper: Harlequin Blue, Sonnets, *Creative Imaginations*

Anchor charm: *Westrim Crafts*

Square page pebble: *Making Memories*

Dimensional adhesive: *Glue Dots International*

Other: transparency sheet, textured cardstock (light blue, red), glass pebble, metal coin holder, glue stick, double-sided tape, computer with printer

Finished size: 5" x 7"

INSTRUCTIONS

1 Make light blue cardstock card. Cut Harlequin Blue paper to fit card front; adhere.

2 Stamp Small Compass with dark blue on light blue scrap square; ink edges.

3 Stamp Large Compass on red cardstock and on corner of card. Tear heart from stamped red cardstock.

4 Adhere heart, stamped square, and anchor charm to card.

5 Print sentiment and border on transparency; trim and adhere to card with double-sided tape.

6 Adhere page pebble, coin holder, and square page pebble to transparency with dimensional adhesive.

Velvet Hearts

Designer: Susan Neal

SUPPLIES

Rubber stamps: *DeNami Design* (Love Script); *PSX* (Curly-Q Heart)

Dye ink: Cardinal, Ancient Page, *Clearsnap*

Cardstock: *Bazzill Basics Paper* (Brick, white)

Patterned vellum: Through The Years, *Deja Views*

Velvet paper: Tomato, *SEI*

Other: silver metallic paper, 2 red brads, square punch, iron, adhesive, scissors, iron

Finished size: 5½" x 4¼"

INSTRUCTIONS

1 Make Brick cardstock card.

2 Place stamp rubber side up; lay velvet paper face down on stamp. Apply heat with iron to back of paper for 30 seconds. *Note: Use steam setting on iron.*

3 Repeat step 2, two times; use square punch to cut out hearts.

4 Adhere hearts to metallic paper strip. Mat with white cardstock and patterned vellum.

5 Stamp Love Script with Cardinal Red on white cardstock. Adhere hearts and stamped script to card.

6 Tear piece of patterned vellum. Secure vellum with red brads over Love Script.

Little Chicks

Designer: Janelle Clark

SUPPLIES

Rubber stamp: (Chick) *Delta Rubber Stampede*

Dye ink: (Coal Black) *Ancient Page, Clearsnap*

Textured cardstock: (Chiffon, Aloe Vera) *Bazzill Basics Paper*

Cardstock: (White) *Fiskars*

Color media: (Spanish Orange, Yellowed Orange colored pencils) Prismacolor, *Sanford*

Fasteners: (yellow brads) *Lasting Impressions for Paper*

Fibers: (yellow gingham ribbon)

Font: (2Ps Spacey Jane) *www.twopeasinabucket.com*

Adhesive

Tools: scissors, computer and printer

Finished size: 5½" x 4½"

INSTRUCTIONS

❶ Make card from Aloe Vera cardstock.

❷ Print "happy easter" on Chiffon; cut out.

❸ Stamp printed Chiffon with Chick six times with Coal Black; color with colored pencils.

❹ Adhere ribbon around Chiffon. Mat with white cardstock; adhere to card.

❺ Attach three brads to card.

Smell the Flowers

Designer: Gretchen Schmidt

SUPPLIES

Rubber stamps: (Antique Lowercase alphabet) *PSX, Duncan;* (flower and flower shadow from Little Layers set) *Stampin' Up!*

Dye ink: (Orange) *Stampabilities*

Cardstock: (White) *Making Memories*

Textured cardstock: (Limeade, Festive) *Bazzill Basics Paper*

Patterned paper: (Go-Go Boots) Together, Collection III, *KI Memories*

Color medium: (black marker)

Acrylic paint: (Titanium White) VanGogh, *Royal Talens*

Accents: (orange, purple, green buttons) *Hillcreek Designs*

Fibers: (white ribbon) *Offray*

Font: (Evergreen) *www.twopeasinabucket.com*

Adhesive: double-sided tape, dots

Tools: scissors, wedge sponge, computer and printer

Finished size: 4¼" x 5½"

INSTRUCTIONS

❶ Make card from White cardstock.

❷ Cut Go-Go Boots paper to fit card; adhere.

❸ Stamp "fun sing" on patterned paper with Titanium White.

❹ Print "Take Time to Smell the Flowers this Spring" on white cardstock. Trim and stamp flower and flower shadow with Orange. Mat with Festive and Limeade; attach to card.

❺ Stamp "joy smile" on Limeade; stamp "happy" on Festive.

❻ Apply Titanium White to patterned card with sponge.

❼ Draw border on stamped white cardstock with black marker.

Accordion Card

Designer: Patty Jahromi

SUPPLIES

All supplies from Close To My Heart unless otherwise noted.

Rubber stamps: (In Friendship's Garden, Oriental Foliage)

Dye ink: (Desert Sand, Red Velvet) Exclusive Inks

Cardstock: (Colonial White, Bark)

Patterned paper: (Asian Background, Red
Velvet B&T)

Accents: (butterfly)

Fibers: (hemp)

Adhesive

Tools: (sponge dauber, paper scorer, hole punch, scissors) no source

Finished size: 3¾" square

INSTRUCTIONS

❶ Score 12" x 3" strip of Bark card-stock every 3". Fold to make accordion.

❷ Stamp In Friendship's Garden with Desert Sand on three pieces of Colonial White cardstock; tear edges. Apply Desert Sand ink to cardstock with sponge dauber.

❸ Stamp Oriental Foliage on Colonial White cardstock with Red Velvet; sponge with Desert Sand.

❹ Adhere five alternating squares of patterned paper to accordion. Adhere alternating poem and foliage images to squares.

❺ Stamp 3¾" square of Colonial White cardstock with Oriental Foliage; mat with Bark cardstock.

❻ Adhere butterfly accent to accordion; mount accordion on Bark square.

❼ Punch holes through sides of Bark square; thread hemp through holes and tie bow.

Inside

French Script Heart

Designer: Nichole Heady

SUPPLIES

Rubber stamps: *Stampin' Up!* (Bold Shapes set, Memory of the Heart set, French Script background)

Dye ink: Classic Stampin' Pads, *Stampin' Up!* (Real Red, Basic Black)

Cardstock: *Stampin' Up!* (Real Red, Ultrasmooth White, Basic Black)

Other: adhesive, scissors

Finished size: 4½" x 4¼"

INSTRUCTIONS

① Make white cardstock card.

② Stamp heart with Real Red on scrap of Ultrasmooth White cardstock. Stamp filigree with Real Red over heart. Tear edges.

③ Adhere stamped image to Real Red cardstock; trim. Mat with Basic Black cardstock.

④ Cut two thin strips Ultrasmooth White cardstock; tie in knots around opposite corners. Mat with Real Red cardstock.

⑤ Stamp French Script with Basic Black on card front. Adhere stamped image to card front; tear bottom edge.

All You Need is Love

Designer: Denise Pauley

SUPPLIES

Rubber stamps: *Delta Rubber Stampede* (Swirl Heart); *Impress Rubber Stamps* (Small Hearts); *Posh Impressions* (flower); *Ma Vinci's Reliquary* (It's My Type Large lowercase alphabet); *Making Memories* (date)

Solvent ink: Jet Black, StazOn, *Tsukineko*

Chalk ink: Vatican Wine, Fresco, *Gary M. Burlin*

Patterned paper: Sonnets, *Creative Imaginations*

Handmade paper: white, *Black Ink*

Pewter heart sticker: *Magenta Rubber Stamps*

Metal flowers: *Carolee's Creations*

3 large tags: *Impress Rubber Stamps*

Small tag: *DMD Industries*

5 metal brads: *Making Memories*

Twill tape: *7gypsies*

Other: pink cardstock, adhesive, scissors

Finished size: 3¾" x 5¼"

INSTRUCTIONS

① Make pink cardstock card.

② Tear bottom of large tags.

③ Cut rectangle of patterned paper to fit tags. Tear long edges and crumple; adhere to tags.

④ Stamp Swirl Heart and Small Hearts with Vatican Wine on patterned paper; cut out.

⑤ Cut out two squares handmade paper; tear and ink bottom edge. Adhere stamped and handmade paper squares to tags.

⑥ Stamp date with Jet Black on patterned paper. Adhere metal heart sticker to tag; attach date strip with brads. Stamp sentiment with Jet Black.

⑦ Secure stamped small tag and metal flowers with brads. Knot twill tape through front tag. Adhere tags to patterned paper, tear edges; adhere to card.

Traveler's Trunk

Designer: Jenny Grothe

SUPPLIES

Rubber stamps: *Hero Arts* (Letters); *Stampin' Up!* (By Definition)

Craft ink: brown, *Tsukineko*

Walnut ink: *Pebbles in my Pocket*

Eyelets: pewter, *Making Memories* (round, 2 square)

Cardstock: *Provo Craft* (Tan, White)

Stickers: travel, *Sandylion*

Mesh: brown, *Magic Mesh*

Other: spiral paper clip, library card pocket, hemp, raffia, adhesive, eyelet-setting tools, small paintbrush

Finished size: 4¼" x 5½"

INSTRUCTIONS

❶ Make Tan card.

❷ Place library card pocket in walnut ink; remove and let dry. *Note: Mix walnut ink according to instructions.*

❸ Stamp definition with brown on pocket; adhere to card. Set square eyelets on each side of pocket; string raffia and hemp and knot ends.

❹ Adhere mesh to corner; apply stickers. *Note: Set stickers so only part is on page; trim excess.*

❺ Cut white cardstock square to fit pocket. Secure eyelet; thread hemp and attach paper clip.

❻ Apply walnut ink to edges of card and tag with paintbrush.

Bonus Idea

Create a tag or matching gift wrap using the extra stickers and a few findings.

Think Pink

Designer: Darcy Christensen

SUPPLIES

Pink block patterned paper: *American Crafts*

Lime green paper

Pink vellum

Patterned slide mounts: lime green, pink script, pink striped, *K&Company*

Daisy punch: *Emagination Crafts*

White eyelets: *Making Memories*

Silver flower eyelets: *Coffee Break Design*

Pink fibers: Adornaments, *EK Success*

Adhesive foam dots: *Glue Dots International*

White crochet thread: *Coats & Clark*

Font: Courier New, *Microsoft*

Finished size: 8¼" x 4¼"

INSTRUCTIONS

1 Make card base from patterned paper.

2 Punch out centers from slide mounts. Make tag from each center piece by trimming two corners and setting white eyelet.

3 Punch daisies from lime green paper and patterned paper scrap. Adhere to tags with flower eyelets (see photo).

4 Print "mom" on vellum, spacing letters about 4"apart. Cut each letter into 1¼" x 1¾" rectangle; adhere behind a slide mount window.

5 Wrap each slide mount with pink fibers. Adhere ends to back. Tie tags to fibers with crochet thread.

6 Adhere slide mounts and tags to card with adhesive foam dots.

Flower Gift Box

Designer: Lori Bergmann

SUPPLIES

Cardstock: cream, green, pink

Floral patterned wrapping paper

Paper maché heart box

Acrylic paint: Fuchsia Pearl, White Pearl, *Delta*

Circle punches: large, medium, *Marvy Uchida*

Green pastel pencil: *Faber-Castell*

Chalk: green, pink, *EK Success*

Blender pen: *EK Success*

Foam paintbrush: *Plaid*

Decoupage adhesive: *Duncan*

Other: adhesive foam dots, craft adhesive, paintbrush, pencil, cotton swab

Finished size: 3" x 3" x 1½"

BOX

❶ Paint inside of box with two coats of Fuchsia pearl. Pounce with White Pearl, using foam paintbrush.

❷ Decoupage outside of box with torn pieces of wrapping paper, following adhesive manufacturer's instructions.

FLOWER

❶ Transfer flower base pattern to cream cardstock. Shade center with pink chalk (see Figure a).

❷ Cut out. Gently curl petal edges down around pencil (see Figure b).

❸ To make petals, punch five large circles from cream, and five medium circles from pink cardstock. Chalk center of petals with pink. Curl up sides of petals with cotton swab (see Figure c).

❹ Adhere cream petals to flower base (see Figure d). Adhere four pink petals over cream ones.

❺ Completely curl last petal and adhere to flower center (see Figure e).

❻ Transfer leaf pattern to green cardstock. Cut out; chalk edges with green. Write "to" and "mom" with pastel pencil; set with blender pen. Adhere leaves to box with craft adhesive.

❼ Place adhesive foam dots under curled edges of flower base. Adhere flower to box.

a

Shade flower base center

b

Curl down base edges

c

Curl petals up

d

Adhere petals to base

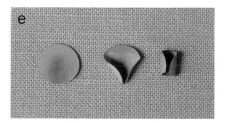

e

Curl last petals

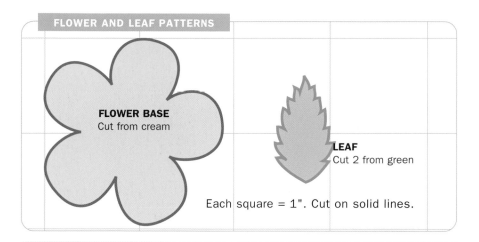

FLOWER AND LEAF PATTERNS

FLOWER BASE
Cut from cream

LEAF
Cut 2 from green

Each square = 1". Cut on solid lines.

Designer Thumbtacks

Now, your message board can sport the sharpest thumbtacks on the block—made by you! **Wendy Thomas** shares her fun decorator idea for creating these classy tacks that can be matched to any décor.

Gather up flat-head thumbtacks and ¾" metal washers. Stamp an image on cardstock, punch it out with a circle punch, and adhere it to the washer. Cover the entire top with dimensional adhesive and let it dry. Flip the washer, image side down, and adhere the thumbtack head inside the washer hole.

To display your nifty new thumbtacks, cut a square piece of cork sheet, mat it with a rectangle of red cardstock, and fold the excess over the cork front. Stamp a sentiment on white cardstock and adhere it to the folded-over red cardstock. Layer a length of sheer ribbon across the sentiment and embellish it with red heart brads.

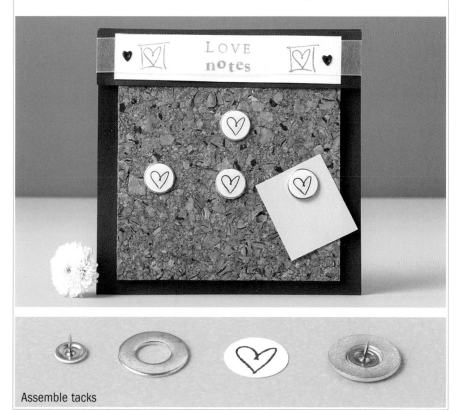

Assemble tacks

Unlimited Custom Embellishments—Just Cut, Color, and Shrink.

Design your own dimensional accents with shrink plastic.

It's easy and fun to make jazzy shrink plastic adornments from shapes cut from inexpensive plastic sheets. You can customize them to match your project perfectly by detailing them with the same rubber stamps, punches, inks, chalks, or colored pencils. If your creation needs holes, just use a paper punch. Follow the manufacturer's instructions to shrink your piece in the oven or with a heat tool until it lies flat. Shrink plastic will shrink to 45% of its original size, the colors will intensify, and the plastic will become 1/16" thick. You can shape the piece while it's still warm or roll it up on a wooden dowel. If the plastic hardens before shaping is complete, just reheat it with the heat tool. Check the ideas below, and you'll see that there's no end to what you can do! Then, shrink your vast array of ideas.

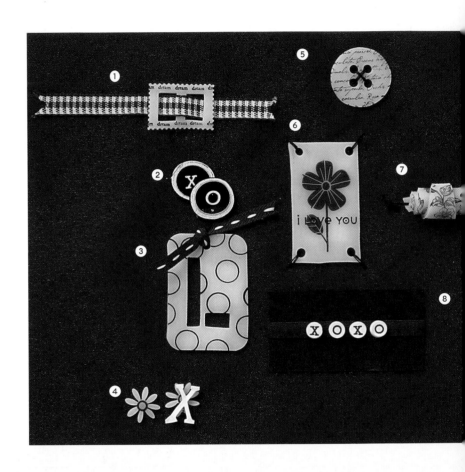

A VARIETY OF EMBELLISHMENTS

1 BUCKLE: Experiment with stamps and decorative-edge scissors.

2 TYPEWRITER LETTERS: Stamp circle and letter with white pigment ink on black shrink plastic. Let ink dry overnight.

3 STENCIL TAG: Cut, using a letter stencil.

4 CHARMS: Use punches, die-cuts, and templates to make shapes and letters.

5 BUTTON: Use a ¼" hole punch, because the holes shrink, too.

6 STITCHABLE LABEL: Punch holes before shrinking.

7 ROLLED BEAD: Cut triangle, stamp, shrink and roll while warm. Reheat to finish rolling.

8 FAUX ALPHABET BEADS: Stamp letters, punch out with ½" circle punch.

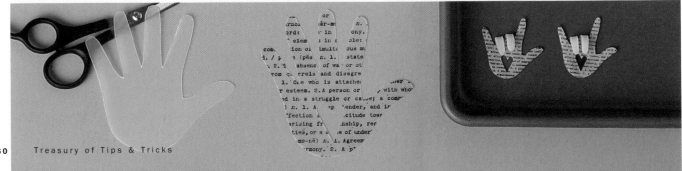

American Sign Language—
I Love You Card

Designer: Nichole Heady

SUPPLIES

All supplies from Stampin' Up! unless otherwise noted.

Cardstock: (Basic Black, Real Red, Ultrasmooth White)

Shrink plastic: (clear) PolyShrink, *Lucky Squirrel*

Rubber stamp: (By Definition)

Permanent ink: (Black) StazOn, *Tsukineko*

Dimensional glaze: (Crystal Effects)

Tools:
   (Folk Heart punch)
   (heat tool, pencil, scissors, wooden dowel) no source

Finished size: 4¼" x 5½"

INSTRUCTIONS

① Make card from Real Red cardstock.

② Cut Basic Black cardstock to 2" square. Double-mat with Real Red and Ultrasmooth White; adhere to card.

③ Trace hand pattern on shrink plastic and cut out.

④ Punch heart in palm; stamp.

⑤ Shrink with heat tool. While still warm, bend two central fingers forward over dowel.

⑥ Adhere small piece of Real Red behind heart opening. Adhere hand to card.

⑦ Fill heart with dimensional glaze.

DESIGNER TIPS

■ Pigment ink must be dried overnight before shrinking, or parts may touch one another and create an inky mess!

■ Use a heat tool and a casserole dish to shrink one piece. The dish keeps the piece from flying away.

■ Use the oven if you have several pieces to shrink at once. A baker's stone is perfect for shrinking in bulk.

■ Keep a large wood block (such as a good sized rubber stamp) nearby to flatten the warm plastic after it is done shrinking.

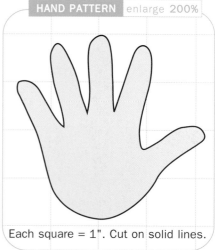

HAND PATTERN enlarge 200%

Each square = 1". Cut on solid lines.

Shades of Blue Card

Designer: Nichole Heady

SUPPLIES

All supplies by Stampin' Up! unless otherwise noted.

Cardstock: Brilliant Blue, Ultrasmooth White

Blue striped vellum

Rubber stamps: heart from Gentler Times set, script from Botanicals set, "congrats" from Good Times set

Silver metallic cord

Sterling Silver embossing powder

Watermark ink: VersaMark, *Tsukineko*

Azure solvent ink: StazOn, *Tsukineko*

Shrink plastic: PolyShrink, *Lucky Squirrel*

⅛" hole punch: *Fiskars*

Silver pen: ZIG Painty Pen, *EK Success*

Heat tool

Finished size: 5½" x 4¼"

HEART

1 Sand shrink plastic (see Figure a).

2 Stamp heart image with Azure ink (see Figure b).

3 Cut out image. Punch hole in top. Heat to shrink, following manufacturer's instructions (see Figure c).

4 Outline heart with silver pen and thread cord through hole.

CARD

1 Cut white cardstock square, and stamp script image with Azure. Rub watermark ink along edges and dip in embossing powder. Emboss with heat tool. Mat with blue cardstock; tear and curl edges.

2 Make card base from white cardstock. Cut and adhere striped vellum.

3 Adhere matted square and heart to card. Attach ends of cord to inside of card, then line inside with white cardstock.

4 Stamp "congrats."

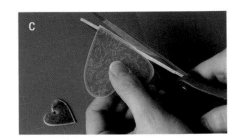

This shrink plastic heart image can be used to create a collection of wedding gifts that have a common look and theme. Stamp the script image on a candleholder, then tie the heart around the candle for a wonderful centerpiece. Accent place cards and favor boxes with hearts.

NICHOLE'S SHRINK PLASTIC TIPS

- Images and colors adhere better to shrink plastic if you sand it lightly before stamping, painting, or coloring.

- Create three-dimensional projects with shrink plastic. The shrink plastic is very pliable when it is still warm, and you can bend it around any object to replicate the shape. Create napkin rings, beads, and jewelry in this manner.

- Adhere shrink plastic objects to your projects with a strong adhesive such as UTB, E-6000, or jewelry adhesive, available in most craft stores.

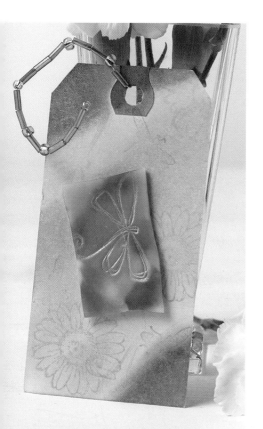

Dragonfly Tag

Designer: Christi Spadoni

SUPPLIES

Dragonfly stamp: *Magenta Rubber Stamps*

Bee stamp: *Stampendous!*

Flower stamp: *Inkadinkado*

Ink: (Royal Blue, Seaglass, Apple Green, Canary, Aqua) Cats Eye, ColorBox, *Clearsnap*

Metallic ink: silver, Encore Ultimate Metallic, *Tsukineko*

Gift tag: *Avery Dennison*

Bead mix: Blue Moon Beads, *Elizabeth Ward & Co.*

Other: shrink plastic, sandpaper, wire, liquid adhesive, pliers

Finished size: 2" x 4¼"

INSTRUCTIONS

1 Rub ink pads on tag starting with lightest ink.

2 Stamp flowers and bees with silver.

3 Sand shrink plastic lightly and cut to desired shape.

4 Apply various inks on shrink plastic. *Note: Touching inked areas will leave fingerprints.*

5 Heat shrink plastic in oven according to manufacturer's instructions.

6 Stamp dragonfly with silver on shrink plastic while soft and pliable. *Note: Firmly press stamp into plastic and leave in place until cool.*

7 Adhere shrink plastic to tag.

8 String wire on tag, fold both ends together and string beads. Twist ends of wire into loop with pliers.

Faux Molded Glass Jewelry

Designer: Vesta Abel

INSTRUCTIONS

Frosted shrinkable plastic sheet*
1" sun acrylic stamp*
Embossing heat tool
⅛" hole punch
Jewelry findings:
    3 silver head pins
    6 silver seed beads
    5 small clear frosted beads
    6 mm jump ring
    3 mm jump ring
    17" chip stone necklace or chain
    Lobster claw clasp
    2 French ear wires
Miscellaneous items: pen, scissors, needlenose pliers, wire cutters

*ArtSeeds.Com SeeGlass Shrink Plastic and Terry Medaris clear Wavy Sun stamp set were used in the sample project.

EMBOSS THE PLASTIC

① Transfer the earring and necklace pendant patterns onto a sheet of shrinkable plastic, being careful not to scratch the plastic. Cut out the shapes with scissors.

② Punch a hole in the top and bottom of each piece with the hole punch.

③ Shrink the shapes, one at a time, using the embossing heat tool. Note: As the shapes heat up, the corners will curl, but they will flatten as the plastic shrinks.

④ Turn the shapes frosted side down and concentrate the heat directly on the shiny sides. Heat the pieces for at least two minutes until they're extremely hot, then stamp each one immediately and firmly to leave a deep impression. Note: If the impression is not deep, it is because the plastic was not hot enough. Re-heat the piece until the impression disappears, and then stamp again.

ASSEMBLE THE NECKLACE

① Thread one silver seed bead, 3 frosted beads, and another silver seed bead onto a head pin.

② Trim the excess wire from the head pin, leaving approx. ¼" at the end. Bend the end into an eye loop.

③ Attach the loop to the bottom hole of the necklace pendant, and then close it with the pliers.

④ Open the 6 mm jump ring and feed it through the top hole of the pendant.

⑤ Attach the chip stone necklace or chain to the pendant, and close the jump ring with the pliers.

⑥ Add the lobster claw clasp on one end of the necklace and the 3 mm jump ring on the other.

ASSEMBLE THE EARRINGS

① Assemble the earrings following steps 1–2 of "Assemble the Necklace," using only one frosted bead for each.

② Insert the French ear wires in the top holes of the plastic shapes.

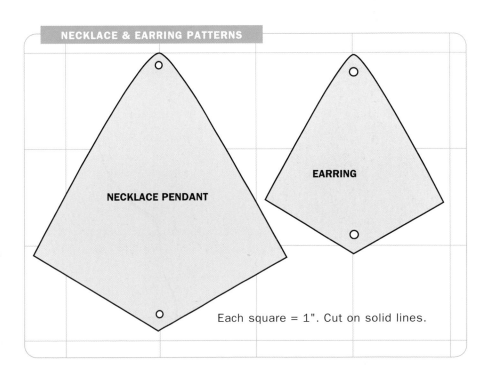

NECKLACE & EARRING PATTERNS

NECKLACE PENDANT

EARRING

Each square = 1". Cut on solid lines.

The Shaving Cream Secret

Discover a new use for shaving cream—it creates a fabulous marbled finish on paper!

Shaving Cream Marbling Technique

Designer: Denise Pauley

SUPPLIES

Cardstock
Shaving cream
Shallow pan or box frame
Ink pad refills (2–4 colors) or metallic pens that will drip ink
Stylus, chopstick, skewer, or other straight tool
Large piece of cardboard
Paper towels

① Smooth a thick layer of shaving cream into shallow pan or box frame.

② Add several drops of ink from ink pad refills or metallic pens, leaving space between each color.

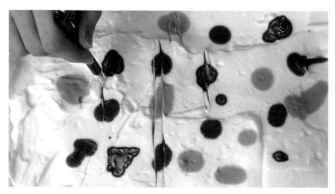

③ Pull ink across shaving cream to create a marbled look, using a straight tool. *Note: The pattern you create on the shaving cream will appear on the cardstock.*

④ Lay sheet of cardstock on shaving cream, smoothing lightly to make sure entire surface is in contact with shaving cream.

⑤ Lift cardstock off shaving cream.

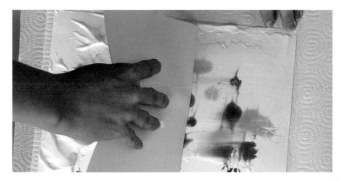

⑥ Scrape (do not rub) shaving cream off cardstock in a single motion, using piece of cardboard.

Note: If it takes more than one stroke to remove shaving cream, be sure to wipe shaving cream off cardboard between strokes.

Blot off remaining shaving cream with paper towel. Let dry.

Always My Friend Card

SUPPLIES

Cardstock: purple, red, white

Metallic pens: purple, red, silver; Metallic Brush, *Pentel*

"always my friend" sticker: Teri Martin, *Creative Imaginations*

Silver fiber: *Rubba Dub Dub*

Silver butterfly charm

Scissors

Finished size: 5½" x 3½"

INSTRUCTIONS

① Create marbled finish on white cardstock.

② Adhere sticker to marbled cardstock and trim edges. Double-mat with purple and red cardstock; run scissors along edges to curl.

③ Wrap fibers around matted piece; add butterfly charm and knot ends.

④ Make purple card base and adhere matted piece.

Bonus Ideas

Create different patterns with the ink:

- To make stars, pull the ink in several directions.

- To make spirals, swirl the ink outward.

- To create a more complex marbled design, swirl the ink with your fingers *Note: Do not mix colors.*

- Create smooth lines of ink, using a credit card.

- Draw images in the ink, using a paintbrush.

Chalk-Marbled Card

Designer: Denise Pauley

SUPPLIES

Cardstock: brown, caramel, cream

Chalk: *Craf-T Products*

Wood tile 1" x 1½": *Darice*

Embossing powder: Terra Cotta, *Ranger Industries*

Rubber stamps: little background bugs, small leaf impressions, *Hero Arts*

Black ink: StazOn, *Tsukineko*

Metal word: father; Charmed Words, *Making Memories*

Skeleton leaf

Other: brown acrylic paint, shallow container large enough for paper, water, brown and tan chalk, embossing ink, heat tool, sandpaper, embossing stylus or craft stick

Finished sizes:
  card 5" square,
  tag 3¼" x 5¼"

INSTRUCTIONS

❶ Make card base with caramel cardstock. Mat brown cardstock with card base.

❷ Cut four ¾" wide strips from chalk-marbled cardstock (See "How to Make Chalk-Marbled Paper).

❸ Weave and adhere strips, trimming ends so lengths vary (see photo).

❹ Adhere skeleton leaf.

❺ Apply embossing ink to wood tile, sprinkle with terra cotta powder and heat. Stamp dragonfly and leaves with black ink. Adhere to card.

❻ Apply brown acrylic paint to metal word, let dry. Sand slightly to age and adhere.

TASTEFUL TAGS

You can make wonderful tags using the chalk-marbled paper. Mat and accent with coordinating cardstock, and embellish with stamps, netting, and nailheads (see photo).

HOW TO MAKE CHALK-MARBLED PAPER

① Fill container with approx. 1" of water. Scrape a few colors of chalk onto water surface, using embossing stylus or craft stick.

② Swirl surface once to blend colors and create a marble pattern. *Note: Don't over-stir, or there will be no pattern.*

③ Place cardstock onto water surface.

④ Lift out immediately and check the pattern. If no color is visible, you may need to try again using darker colors or more chalk.

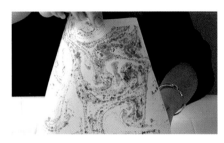

Note: Experiment with different chalk and cardstock colors. A single color of chalk will result in a subtle, textured pattern, while diverse colors can achieve a funky tie-dyed look.

⑤ Dry completely before use.

COOL COLOR STRIPS

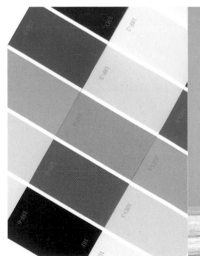

Most of us have pored over paint chips to select colors to paint a room. But more and more paper crafters are using these jazzy color strips to accent projects. Adding a paint chip is a quick, easy, and affordable way to create a color theme, or perk up a card or gift box. Traditional chips feature three or more monochromatic colors, but today's chips also imitate interesting faux finishes such as rag rolling, sponging, and color washing. You can even find metallic and woodgrain patterns. Paint chips are available at most paint and home improvement stores, and are usually free of charge.

Give Your Paper a Bubble Bath

Add a refreshing pattern to plain paper with a quick dip in a colorful burst of bubbles.

Designer: Denise Pauley

Bubble Background Technique

SUPPLIES

Cardstock: (white)
Shallow container

Drinking straw
Food coloring
Dishwashing liquid
Water

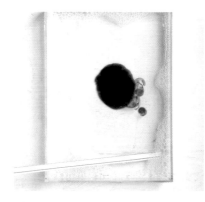

INSTRUCTIONS

① In shallow container, mix small amount of water with dishwashing liquid. Add one color of food coloring.

② Place end of drinking straw in water and blow until water is covered with layer of bubbles. *Note: For more bubbles, add more dishwashing liquid.*

③ Press piece of cardstock on bubbles. Bubbles will pop and tint cardstock.

④ Let dry.

⑤ Repeat steps 1–4 with different color(s) of food coloring, if desired.

Bonus Ideas

■ Dip the drinking straw or a bubble wand in the colored liquid and blow bubbles directly onto the cardstock. The result will be a slightly messier, splattered finish with deeper color.

■ Instead of food coloring, color the bubble water with dye-based re-inkers, ink pumped from metallic pens, or fabric dyes.

DESIGNER TIPS

■ If the color isn't transferring to the cardstock, or the color is too light, add more food coloring and repeat the technique.

■ The color will be richest from bubbles closest to the surface of the water. If you produce too many bubbles, the ones at the top may transfer little or no color.

Friendship Memories Bookmark

SUPPLIES

Cardstock: (light blue, lime green/white)

Fabric: (Pink from Girl Fabric set) Collectionz Swatchz, *Junkitz*

Stickers: (Label Word Strips, Word Circles Embossed) Studio K, *K&Company*

Fibers: (twill ribbon) Twill E Dee, *Creek Bank Creations*

Adhesive

Tools: ruler, scissors, hole punch

Other:
  (food coloring) DecACake, *Tone Brothers*

  shallow container, drinking straw, dishwashing liquid, water, sandpaper

Finished size: 3" x 6"

INSTRUCTIONS

❶ Apply bubble background finish to white cardstock, using blue, green, and pink (or red) food coloring (see "Bubble Background Technique"). Trim to 2¼" x 4½".

❷ Cut two flowers from bubble cardstock; mat one each with lime green and blue cardstock. Run fingernails along paper edges to add texture. Adhere to bubble piece.

❸ Cut lime green to finished size for bookmark; sand edges.

❹ Cut 2½" x 5½" piece of light blue; texture edges with fingernails and adhere to bookmark. Trim fabric to same size, fray edges, and adhere to bookmark.

❺ Adhere bubble piece and add label stickers.

❻ Adhere circle stickers to cardstock and trim. Adhere to top of bookmark (see photo). Punch hole through center of each circle and add ribbon.

Aging

Looking for the antique look? Try aging your paper with inks, dyes, crackles, and sanding.

High-Topped Greeting

Designer: Gretchen Schmidt

SUPPLIES

Burgundy cardstock: *Making Memories*

Tan tag: *DMD Industries*

Boot die cut: Fresh Cuts by Rebecca Sower, *EK Success*

Alphabet stickers: Nostalgiques, *EK Success*

White ink: Colorbox, *Clearsnap*

Sepia ink: *Ranger Industries*

Walnut ink crystals: *7gypsies*

Other: fibers (red, tan), cream trim, sandpaper, plastic bag

Finished size: 4¼" x 5½"

INSTRUCTIONS

❶ Make burgundy card base. Color edges with sepia and white ink.

❷ Distress boot die cut with sandpaper.

❸ Mix walnut ink crystals with water.

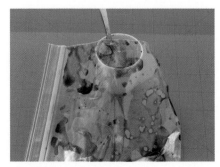

❹ Place small amount of walnut ink in plastic bag. Work with fingers to distribute ink

❺ Tear tag at one end. Place tag, cream trim, and boot, one at a time, in bag, and move around to absorb ink.

❻ Loop fibers through eyelet. Adhere tag, then boot to card.

❼ Spell "MOM" with stickers. Adhere two lengths of trim across boot.

Musical Collage

Designer: Stacy Mcfadden

SUPPLIES

Rubber stamps: *Hero Arts* (Printer's Type Alphabet); All Night Media, *Plaid* (Ransom Alphabet); Artee Stamps, *The Stamp Collection* (musical note)

Watermark ink: VersaMark, *Tsukineko* (gold, black)

Patterned music paper: *Rusty Pickle*

Wavy metal frame: *Making Memories*

Embossing powder: Currawong, Opals, *Pipe Dreamink, Australia*

Other: cardstock (red, brown), scissors, twine, envelope, small tag, embossing heat tool, adhesive, small cardboard disk

Finished size: 5" x 7"

PREPARE

① Cut strip of musical note paper and attach to card with brads. Cover small hanging tag with same paper.

② Tear one small and one large heart from red cardstock. Poke hole in small heart; thread with string and knot one end.

③ Thread second piece string through tag; knot one end. Tie together heart string and tag string and attach to second brad on top of card.

④ Ink envelope edges. Wrap torn strip of paper around center of envelope, then wrap with twine. Attach envelope to card.

⑤ Crumple and ink large heart. Attach to inside edge of envelope.

STAMP

① Stamp "Mothers Day" on brown cardstock. Cut into two separate strips and ink edges.

② Attach tags to envelope between layers of twine.

③ Heat metal frame plate with heat tool. Apply coat of embossing powder; melt. Apply two more coats until frame is thick and shiny. Attach frame over word "Mothers."

④ Stamp small cardboard disk using watermark ink. Apply coat of embossing powder. Heat and melt. Apply up to five coats to make thick and shiny.

⑤ While still wet, stamp using musical note inked with gold. Let dry. Attach to envelope.

⑥ Attach spiral clip.

⑦ Stamp "MOM" on music paper using Ransom alphabet. Cut and attach to card.

Crackled Bride & Groom Tags Card

Designer: Candi Gershon

SUPPLIES

Textured cardstock: sage, sand

Floral patterned paper: *Chatterbox*

Vellum: *Chatterbox*

Rubber stamp: heart from Heart & Posies set, *Stampin' Up!*

Pink polymer clay: Sculpey; *Polyform Products*

Ribbon: *Offray*

Bride and groom tags: *Chatterbox*

Nameplate sticker: Grand Adhesions, *K&Company*

Watermark Ink: VersaMark, *Tsukineko*

Ultra thick embossing powder: Suze Weinberg, *Ranger*

Font: Scrap Cursive, *Inspire Graphics*

Other: heat tool, piercing tool, sandpaper, craft knife

Finished size: 4" x 7½"

TAGS

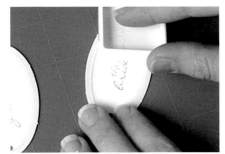

❶ Apply watermark ink to tags.

❷ Sprinkle liberally with embossing powder.

❸ Melt with heat tool. Repeat to achieve desired thickness. Clear holes.

❹ Place in freezer for 2 minutes; remove and bend slightly to create cracks. *Note: if you do not get the effect you desire, reheat and repeat the process.*

HEART

1 Roll out pink polymer clay. Stamp with heart image.

2 Cut out with craft knife and make holes with piercing tool.

3 Bake according to manufacturer's instructions.

CARD

1 Make card base from sage cardstock.

2 Tear strip of sand cardstock, distress lightly with sandpaper, and curl edges. Adhere to card.

3 Cut floral patterned paper to fit bottom ¾ of card. Tear top edge, sand lightly, and curl edges.

4 String ribbon through heart and tags and adhere to patterned paper. Attach ribbon ends to back of paper, and adhere patterned piece to card base.

5 Print names on cardstock; trim to fit nameplate and adhere to card.

You're So Sweet

Designer: Teri Anderson

SUPPLIES

Rubber stamps: (retro star from Tiny Circles set) *Hero Arts*; (Thank You) *Art After Dark*; (Antique Lowercase alphabet) PSX, *Duncan*

Dye ink: (Black) *Close To My Heart*

Watermark ink: VersaMark, *Tsukineko*

Chalk ink: (Burnt Sienna) ColorBox Petal Point Chalk, *Clearsnap*

Patterned paper: (Pink Speckle) Hippie Chick, *SEI*

Accents: (staples)

Stickers: (Frames, Saying Stickers) Hippie Chick, *SEI*

Fibers: (Hippie Chick ribbon card) *SEI*

Adhesive: foam squares, double-sided tape

Tools: stapler, scissors, craft knife, cutting mat, ruler

Other: sandpaper

Finished size: 3¾" x 4¾"

INSTRUCTIONS

1 Cut two rectangles of Pink Speckle patterned paper, adhere top ¾" of paper, pink sides together.

2 Stamp retro star at random on green side with watermark ink. Cut strip of patterned paper, adhere pink side up to card front. Stamp "thank you! You're so" with Black.

3 Adhere Frames sticker to front of card. Cut out inside of frame.

4 Adhere Sweet sticker to inside of card with foam squares.

5 Sand both stickers.

6 Staple four folded pieces of ribbon to top of card.

7 Ink edges of card with Burnt Sienna.

Bonus Idea

Use your paper scraps and leftover stickers to create variations on this fun design.

Decoupage

Decoupage adheres paper to itself and other objects, such as metal, wood, and glass. Create a seamless project using decoupage.

Bonus Idea

Use the same technique to create more shabby chic items from other tin home décor accents like vases, trays, or frames.

Shabby Chic Toile Watering Can

Designer: Tresa Black

SUPPLIES

Rubber stamps: (Toile set)
Close To My Heart

Dye ink: (Archival Black, Buttercup)
Close To My Heart

Small tin watering can

Paper: (white tissue paper)

Decoupage medium: (matte) Mod Podge, *Plaid*

Acrylic paint: (Antique White, Soft Black) *DecoArt*

Spray paint: (primer) *Krylon*

Tools: paintbrush, sandpaper,
toothbrush, scissors

Other: sponge, palette

Finished size: 10½" x 5"

INSTRUCTIONS

Let paint and ink dry between all coats and steps.

PAINT

1 Spray watering can with primer, inside and out.

2 Paint several thin coats on outside of watering can
with Antique White.

3 Sand paint in several spots. *Note: Pay special attention to
raised details, handles, and rims.*

STAMP

1 Stamp Toile images with Archival Black on tissue paper.

2 Tint stamped images as desired with Buttercup.

3 Cut stamped images from tissue paper.

4 Decoupage images onto watering can.

5 Splatter Soft Black paint on can with toothbrush.

Adventure Travel Trunk

Designer: Lori Bergmann

SUPPLIES

Rubber stamps: *Hampton Art Stamps* (Antique Texture, Chinese Handwriting, French Post, Journal Entry, Sail, Weathered Clock); *Limited Edition Rubberstamps* (European Mail Art set, Mail and Tag Art set, Exit Visa, London, London/Paris Block, Macau Passport Stamp, Paris, Sphinx, Women Trio); *Delta Rubber Stampede* (Chinese Dragon, Kokopelli, World Travel Kit); *Club Scrap* (Voyage Ticket); *PSX* (Antique Alphabet)

Dye ink: Ancient Page, *Clearsnap* (Chocolate, Henna, Sandalwood, Sienna)

Chalk ink: Creamy Brown, ColorBox, *Clearsnap*

Pigment ink: Gold, ColorBox, *Clearsnap*

Embossing powder: Queen's Gold, *Ranger Industries*

Acrylic paint: brown, Ceramcoat, *Delta*

Antiquing varnish: Instant Age Varnish, *Delta*

Gold tassel with cord: *Arnold Grummer*

Corner rounding punch: *Marvy Uchida*

Adhesive: *Xyron*

Patterned paper: Maps, Sonnets of the Sea, *Creative Imaginations*

Other: paper mache trunk, cream and teal cardstock, fine sandpaper, masking fluid, water in spray bottle, brayer, craft knife, paintbrush, embossing heat tool, stapler

Finished size: 10" x 8" x 6¼"

COVER TRUNK

❶ Lightly mist three sheets of patterned paper with water; crumple and dry flat.

❷ Lightly rub with Sandalwood.

❸ Stamp paper with desired images, using dye and chalk ink.

❹ Cut paper into strips slightly wider than each section of trunk. Apply adhesive to back (see "Glue Paper Smoothly").

❺ Cover sides of trunk and lid with paper, using brayer to flatten, and wrapping ¼" over edges (see Figures a–b). *Note: Clip paper at curve.*

❻ Cover front and back of trunk, slightly overlapping straps.

❼ Trim paper along edges (see Figure c).

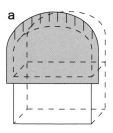

CLIP AT CURVE

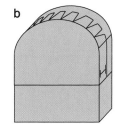

WRAP OVER EDGES

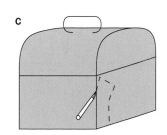

TRIM AT EDGES

EMBELLISH

❶ Coat trunk straps with brown acrylic paint; let dry.

❷ Stamp straps with Antique Texture and Sienna; sand edges to create aged leather look.

❸ For travel stickers, stamp a few images on cream cardstock. Cut out and adhere to trunk.

❹ Varnish entire trunk.

PASSPORT

❶ For passport cover, cut 3½" x 5½" piece teal cardstock; round corners. Fold in half widthwise.

❷ Stamp and emboss "PASSPORT" and compass (from World Travel Kit) with Gold.

❸ Ink edges with Creamy Brown and Sienna.

❹ For pages, cut cream cardstock slightly smaller than cover; round edges. Fold in half and staple to cover.

❺ Stamp each page with images representing a different country.

❻ Tie to trunk handle with tasseled cord.

GLUE PAPER SMOOTHLY

To adhere paper to a hard surface, use one of the following types of adhesive to keep the paper smooth:

- Adhesive machine
- Adhesive sheets
- Decoupage adhesive
- Glue stick
- Spray adhesive

Bonus Ideas

Use different styles of paper to create a variety of trunks:

- Floral tissue paper for a wedding keepsake box.
- Sports-themed paper for keeping awards, photos, and other sports memorabilia.
- Pastel paper for holding Baby's first shoes, hair from the first haircut, and favorite toys.

a Creative Outlet

Turning on the lights is more than routine in **Maya Opavska's** home with her jazzy decoupage switchplate and outlet covers! These are quick and easy to make, and with the great variety of papers available, you're sure to find the perfect look for any room in the house.

To make these fun covers, cut the paper 1½" larger than the plate. Mark and cut out the openings for the switch or outlets. Coat the back of the paper with decoupage adhesive and place the plate face down on the paper. Smooth the paper to the back along the edges, adding more adhesive if

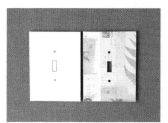

necessary. Turn the plate right side up, and smooth out any bubbles. Brush on a topcoat of decoupage adhesive.

Asian Influences Decoupage Box and Tray

Designer: Donna Bush

SUPPLIES

One 15" x 2⅞" x 11" wood tray*

One 12" x 4" x 8" wood box with lid*

Outdoor acrylic paint*:

  Daisy Cream

  Wrought Iron Black

  Natural Grey Grout

  Clear Coat

One package of 13" ultra-thin paper napkins, Oriental pattern*

One ¾" flat paintbrush

Clear polyurethane gloss varnish*

Miscellaneous items: disposable palette, water basin, paper towels, fine-point scissors, ruler

Walnut Hollow tray (3580), *Viking Woodcrafts* box (200-0639), and *DecoArt* Patio Paints, *Napkin Decor* paper napkins (N25), and *DuraClear* gloss varnish were used in the sample projects.

PAINT THE WOOD PIECES

Paint the inside bottom of the tray and the top of the box lid, excluding the curved edges, Daisy Cream. Let the paint dry completely.

CUT AND PREPARE THE NAPKINS

① Open the napkins as needed to display all four printed panels. Each panel consists of a gray background with black-frame focal block, wood-grain border, and ivory border.

② Cut out the napkin elements to fit the inside bottom of the tray, using the photo as a guide. Use four gray squares with black-frame blocks and separate them with wood-grain borders to cover approximately two-thirds of the tray bottom. Fill in the remaining end with a gray band and ivory border. *Note: Be sure the design lines of the gray band match the direction of the four gray squares.*

③ Cut out the napkin elements to fit the top of the box lid, using the photo as a guide. Use a gray background piece on one half, positioning the black-frame focal block in the bottom left corner 1" from the edges. Fill in the remaining half with a gray band, wood-grain border, and ivory border, piecing the gray band as necessary and matching the direction of the design lines.

④ Remove the napkin pieces, positioning them in an identical order on your work surface. Separate the napkin plies, keeping only the top imprinted pieces.

DECOUPAGE THE TRAY AND BOX

① Starting in a corner, apply Clear Coat paint on a small area of the inside bottom of the tray where the first napkin piece will be placed. Position the napkin in the wet paint and gently press flat. Apply more Clear Coat paint to the napkin, brushing from the center to the edges to eliminate any wrinkles or bubbles. *Note: Any napkin edges that stretch onto the sides of the tray will be covered up later with paint.* Repeat this process with the remaining napkin pieces until the inside of tray is covered. Let dry.

② Repeat step 1 to decoupage the top of the box lid.

FINISH THE ACCESSORIES

① Paint the inside of the box and lid Natural Grey Grout. Paint the remainder of the tray and box Wrought Iron Black. Let the paint dry completely after each color.

② Apply two or more coats of gloss varnish on each wood piece, letting each coat dry before proceeding. *Note: If you prefer a satin finish, use Clear Coat acrylic paint in place of the varnish.*

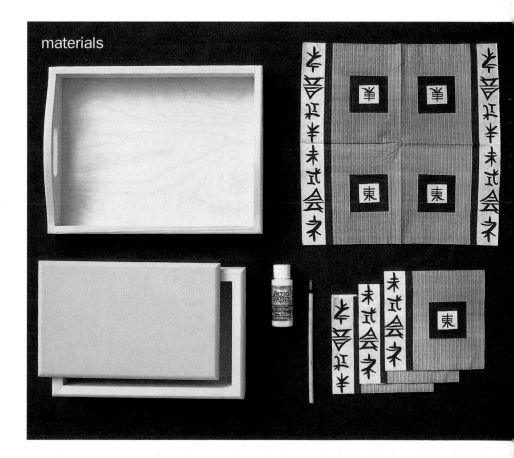

materials

Decoupage Suitcase

Design: Lori Jensen

SUPPLIES

Hard-shell suitcase or briefcase

Colored copies of old photos, documents, journal pages, etc.

Matte decoupage adhesive*

Brown craft paper

Two 2" sponge brushes

Antique decoupage finish*

Metal primer*

Glass surface conditioner*

Mocha Brown acrylic paint*

Spray adhesive*

3" x 6" rusty tin rectangle*

Tin cutters

6" length leather lacing, ribbon, or cording (to tie on the key)

Miscellaneous items: aluminum foil, three cotton rags, water, soap, small paintbrush, decorative-edged scissors (optional), straight-edged scissors, hammer, drill with large bit

*Plaid Enterprises Mod Podge decoupage adhesive; Delta Ceramcoat antique decoupage finish, metal primer, acrylic paint, and PermEnamel surface conditioner; Krylon spray adhesive; and Decorator & Craft Corp. Rusty Tin-Tiques tin rectangle (distributed by Cupboard Distributing) were used in the sample project.

Pretend you're Ernest Hemingway, who not only wrote books, but also documented his international adventures with journal entries and photos. Though your own life's adventures may not have spanned three continents, the memorabilia from your experiences are just as priceless and deserve to be cherished.

Rather than storing your keepsakes in a closet or attic, display them on the old suitcase that accompanied you on your adventures. Cover it with black and white photocopies of old letters, journal entries, photos, and even war medals. And don't forget copies of maps, postcards, napkins, and tickets. Then pack your suitcase with souvenirs for a trip down memory lane.

Own only what you can carry with you... Let your memory be your travel bag.
—Alexander Solzhenitsyn

INSTRUCTIONS

Work in a well-ventilated area and cover your work surface with aluminum foil.

PREPARATION

1 Clean the inside and outside of the suitcase with soap and water. Dry it thoroughly.

2 Basecoat the hard sides of the suitcase with glass surface conditioner.

3 Basecoat the metal parts with metal primer.

4 Apply two coats of Mocha Brown acrylic paint to the metal using the small paintbrush. Allow the paint to dry between coats. *Note: Do not paint the hinges or latch.*

DECOUPAGE THE FIRST LAYER

As you decoupage the suitcase, avoid the hinges, latch, and other unprimed metal areas.

1 Tear the brown craft paper into irregular shapes the size of your hand. *Note: Create some pieces with a straight edge on one side.*

2 Crumple each piece of paper into a ball, then smooth it out again.

3 Apply a small amount of matte decoupage adhesive to a small area on the suitcase and smooth it with a small foam paintbrush. Start along the straight edges and work your way toward the middle.

4 Apply a small amount of the adhesive to the back of a torn piece of brown paper, and smooth it with the paint-brush. Use the pieces of paper with straight edges along the straight edges of the suitcase.

5 Place the piece of paper on top of the freshly-glued area and smooth out any bubbles. Leave some wrinkles for texture.

6 Repeat steps 3–5 until the entire suitcase, including the handle, is covered with paper. Allow the adhesive to dry completely.

Before

7 Apply 1–2 coats of adhesive over the entire suitcase with the sponge brush, letting it dry between coats. Begin at the center of the suitcase and brush outwards, removing any bubbles or drips.

DECOUPAGE THE SECOND LAYER

1 Cut out the copies as desired, using decorative and/or straight-edged scissors.

2 Adhere the cutouts to the suitcase, using the same procedure as with the brown paper. Let the suitcase dry completely. *Note: To enhance the aged look of the cutouts, slightly crinkle, overlap, tear, or fold some of the corners.*

3 Apply 2–3 coats of adhesive over the entire suitcase, allowing it to dry between coats.

4 Apply a thin coat of antique de-coupage finish to the suitcase, using a damp rag.

MAKE THE KEY

1 Transfer the skeleton key pattern from the Pattern Section onto the rusty tin. Cut out the shape with tin snips. Drill holes in the top of the key.

2 Place the key on a flat surface and pound the edges with a hammer to flatten the sharp edges.

3 Tie the key onto the suitcase handle with leather lacing, ribbon, or cording.

CONTEMPORIZE YOUR SUITCASE

Instead of giving your suitcase an antique look, jazz it up with contemporary colors. Decoupage theme park brochures, color photos, maps, or postcards to the suitcase. Use glossy decoupage adhesive to add shine.

LINE THE SUITCASE

Line the inside of the suitcase with satin or other sturdy fabric. Secure the lining with fabric glue. Then, adhere matching ribbon around the inside edges of the suitcase and lid to cover the raw edges of the fabric.

Unraveling Collage

Although collages look like they take a long time, the best projects are usually quick and happen by chance.

BEFORE BEGINNING, CONSIDER YOUR BASE, ADHESIVE, AND MATERIALS:

Base: Use illustration boards, 300 lb. watercolor paper, wood, books, or canvas as a base. Although the classic base is paper, the base you choose will depend on how you use the collage. For example, one popular base is a blank book with heavy pages often referred to as an artist's journal. Artists use these books to record various ideas and thoughts.

Adhesive: The adhesives you use depend on the base. Paper-based projects use different glues than canvas and wood projects. Traditional glue sticks and gel glues (like UHU and Golden Regular Gel Matte) work well with paper, while acrylic gels (like Golden Acrylic Gel Matte) work well with canvas and decoupage glues are best for wood. All are available at your local art supply store.

Materials: Photographs, illustrations, text, handmade papers, napkins, advertisements, tulle, ribbons, metal mesh, washers, bottle caps, and game pieces are only a few of the interesting things found in collage pieces as well as an assortment of paper with different textures, colors, weights, and transparencies. As you collect your materials, create a theme or idea. The theme should develop around a single focal point like a photo or word.

Collage Journal

Designer: Beth Cote

SUPPLIES

Rubber stamp: Big Lavender, *Fred B. Mullett*

Chalk-finish ink: Yellow Ochre, ColorBox, *Clearsnap*

Eyelets and eyelet setter: *American Tag Co.*

Glass pebble: *Making Memories*

Adhesive dots and double-sided tape: *Therm O Web*

Paper: *Anna Griffin* (4¼" x 6¼" pink and 6½" x 4½" patterned)

Patterned paper: Legacy Paper by Beth Cote, *Design Originals*

Acrylic satin finish: Golden Artist Colors (Clear, Crimson, Gold, Sea Foam Green)

White acrylic liquid gesso: *Golden Artist Colors*

Art pencils: *Dick Blick* (Ochre, Raw Sienna)

Acrylic paint: Gold, *Jacquard Products*

Glue stick: *Saunders*

Matte finish: *Krylon*

Finishing spray: *Krylon*

Other: brown ink, journal, 4" x 6" mat board, tape measure piece, buttons, netting, 8" x 10" illustration board, transparent mulberry paper, text and bill paper, old photo, French and herb labels

JOURNAL

❶ Color-copy and reduce your collage to 3½" x 5¾". Tear collage in top right-hand corner. Apply finishing spray.

❷ Cover mat board with dictionary paper. Layer and adhere collage, mat board, pink paper, and patterned paper to journal.

❸ Embellish with tape measure, eyelets, buttons, and pebble.

Bonus Ideas

- Add contrast and texture to your design by tearing, burning, and cutting the edges of the papers for the collage.

- For a unique home accent, frame your collage.

DID YOU KNOW?

From its origins in the French word *coller*, which means "to paste or glue," collage was originally a favorite art form of famous artists Pablo Picasso and George Baque. Trying to add realism to their paintings, these artists glued paper, tickets, hair, sand, feathers, and other materials to their canvases. Today, collage has taken on new meaning as it is incorporated into not only canvases, but books, frames, and furniture.

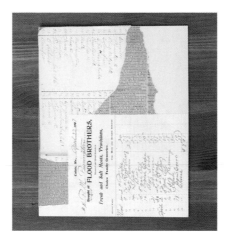

❶ Adhere pieces of dictionary and text patterned paper to illustration board, overlapping papers for contrast. Apply Sea Foam Green and Gold acrylic satin finishes with sponge. Let dry.

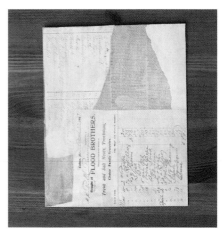

❷ Add gesso over colored background.

❸ Apply second layer of patterned paper. Add labels. Add half and half mixture of Crimson and Clear acrylic satin finishes to parts of background. *Note: If needed, blend hard edges with gesso.*

❹ Adhere photo. *Note: Burn edges of the photo to soften it.* Adhere transparent mulberry papers around the corners of the photo.

❺ Blend Ochre art pencil around the edge of the page with water. Add Raw Sienna at edge. Paint Gold acrylic paint over plastic netting around edge. Let dry. Apply matte finish spray.

INSTRUCTIONS

1 Remove back of shadow box; cover with gray patterned paper.

2 Cut 4½" x 5½" piece of black cardstock. Stamp with "love" definition; heat emboss. Adhere to patterned paper.

3 Adhere canvas piece to stamped piece.

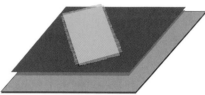

4 Print sentiment on upper left side of transparency, omitting the word "Mom" from the end; cut slightly smaller than shadow box.

5 Tear old photo along left side; place under transparency. Set antique brass eyelets in transparency, one on each side of photo. Insert ribbon through eyelets, wrap around photo; tie in front of transparency.

6 Print date that photo was taken on jewelry tag. Attach to transparency with silver eyelet.

7 Adhere transparency piece over the canvas piece and adhere to back of shadow box.

8 Adhere small photo under printed sentiment. Spell "MOM" on photo with charms, positioning it at end of sentiment.

9 Finish assembling shadow box as shown.

Memories of Mom Shadow Box

Designer: Kathleen Paneitz

SUPPLIES

Black cardstock

Gray vintage patterned paper: *Mustard Moon*

Transparency: *3M*

Shadow box: *EK Success*

"Love" definition stamp: By Definition background, *Stampin' Up!*

White ink: Versacolor, *Tsukineko*

White embossing powder: *Ranger Industries*

Jewelry tags: *Avery*

Alphabet circle charms: *Making Memories*

Metal photo corner: *Making Memories*

Silver watering can charm: *Giraffe Crafts*

Gold scissors charm: *Boutique Trims*

Antique brass square eyelets: *The Stamp Doctor*

Silver eyelet: *Doodlebug Design*

Black gingham ribbon: *Offray*

White fibers: *On the Surface*

Chalk: *Craf-T Products*

Mini adhesive dots: *Glue Dots International*

Font: Pepita, www.myfonts.com

Other: mini glass jar, mini glass vase, silver vintage button, 3" x 5" piece of canvas, pressed flower, 2 photos (approx. 4" x 5" and 3" square), heat embossing tool

Finished size: 6¾" square

A PERFECT WAY WITH PIGMENT

With pearlescent and iridescent pigments, the stamping possibilities are virtually endless. Try these tips and techniques for mixing, glazing, painting, and stamping with pigments.

PERFECT TECHNIQUES

■ Stamp an image using Perfect Medium and dust on Perfect Pearls with a small brush.

■ Add water to a Perfect Pearl color to make your own paint. Add more water for a transparent look. Splatter or sponge the paint on paper for a fun, funky look.

■ Mix Perfect Pearls with acrylic gloss or matte finishing medium for a lovely translucent glaze. Paint the glaze over watercolor designs to pearlize the colors.

■ Create cool resist designs by stamping an image on glossy paper with Perfect Medium. Use a brayer to apply dye ink over the top of the image. The stamped image will resist the ink.

■ Add Perfect Pearls to other mediums like polymer or air-dry clay, acrylic paint, and watercolors.

Collage Cigar Box

Designer: Julia Andrus

To make this easy collage box, create three different handmade papers and intersperse them throughout the design. Then stamp the desired images over your paper collage.

SUPPLIES

Roller stamp: seed packet, Jumbo Rollagraph, *Clearsnap*

Blank ink cartridge: Jumbo Rollagraph, *Clearsnap*

Permanent ink: Black, Archival Ink, *Ranger Industries*

Stamping medium: Perfect Medium, *Ranger Industries*

Powdered pigment: Sunflower Sparkle, Perfect Pearls, *Ranger Industries*

Thick embossing powder: Suze Weinberg's Ultra Thick Embossing Enamel, *Ranger Industries*

Other: assorted garden and bug stamps, script background stamp, cigar or paper mache box, assorted colors dye ink, gold pigment ink, white paint or gesso, decoupage adhesive, white copy paper, handmade paper, decorative chalk, two cardstock rectangles, paper towels, spray bottle with water, embossing heat tool

MAKE COLLAGE PAPERS

PAPER 1

1 Crumple paper and flatten out. Rub on dye ink.

2 Spritz; spread wet ink with paper towel.

3 Add more dye ink; spritz and spread.

PAPER 2

1 Stamp script background with dye ink.

2 Spritz; spread wet ink with paper towel.

PAPER 3

1 Fill blank roller ink cartridge with stamping medium.

2 Roll seed packet design on paper.

3 Apply chalk.

DECORATE BOX

1 Paint or spray box with white paint or gesso.

2 Tear collage papers into strips; decoupage to box. Let dry.

3 Mix powdered pigment with glue, water to form glaze; brush over box. Let dry.

4 Stamp bugs and garden images with black permanent ink.

5 Line box with handmade paper.

6 Apply gold pigment ink to larger cardstock rectangle and emboss with thick powder. Repeat several times.

7 Apply powdered pigment to smaller cardstock rectangle; apply chalk.

8 Apply powdered pigment to chalked piece. Emboss with thick powder. Add heavy layer of gold pigment ink and emboss with thick powder.

9 Ink garden saying stamp with black permanent ink; stamp rectangle while still warm. Let cool; lift stamp.

Reversible Collage Pendant

Designer: Laurie D'Ambrosio

SUPPLIES

Stamps: dragonfly*, mannequin*, schematics*, flower and sentiment*

Ceramic pendant*

Dye ink*: Sepia, Library Green, Black

Watercolor markers*

Copper pigment powder*

Black cord*

Matching beads

Matte spray sealer*

Silver glitter nail polish

Colored pencils

Black rhinestone

Miscellaneous items: white craft glue*, nail file, scissors

*Hampton Art Stamps Dragonfly, Dummy Row, and Figure 36 stamps; Penny Black Keepsake flower and sentiment stamp; Cridge pendant; Ranger Industries Archival inks; Tombow watercolor markers; Jacquard Products Pearl-Ex pigment powder; Darice cord; Plaid Enterprises matte spray sealer; and Duncan Enterprises Aleene's Clear Gel Tacky Glue were used in the sample project.

Finished size: 1⅜" x 2"

FRONT

❶ Color front of pendant with tan marker.

❷ Stamp mannequin with Sepia, half of dragonfly with Library Green, and schematic in Black on pendant, masking images as needed.

❸ Rub small amount of copper powder on pendant.

❹ Spray with sealer.

BACK

❶ Color back of pendant with purple marker.

❷ Stamp flower and sentiment stamp in Black on pendant.

❸ Color images with colored pencils.

❹ Apply glitter nail polish.

❺ Adhere rhinestone to flower center.

NECKLACE

❶ Smooth any rough edges of pendant

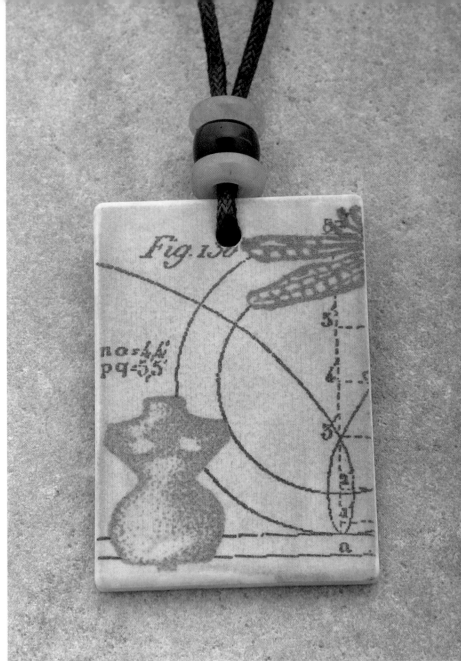

with file.

❷ Loop cord through pendant hole; string beads on both strands. Knot ends.

Travel Collage Trays

Designer: Allison Strine

SUPPLIES

Rubber stamps: *Above the Mark* (Globe); *Junque* (Ink Splats); *Rubber Baby Buggy Bumpers* (Travel Collage)

Dye ink: Sienna, Ancient Page, *Clearsnap*

Wood trays: *Michaels*

Patterned paper: Sonnets, *Creative Imaginations*

Acrylic paint: Raw Umber, *Plaid*

Other: decoupage adhesive; matte varnish; paintbrush; travel photos, postage stamps, other paper memorabilia

Finished sizes:
Large tray: 13¾" x 10½" x 2¾"
Small tray: 13" x 9½" x 2¾"

INSTRUCTIONS

❶ Dilute acrylic paint with water and brush over tray.

❷ Stamp images randomly on inside and outside of tray sides with Sienna.

❸ Adhere paper memorabilia inside tray with decoupage adhesive.

❹ Randomly stamp ink splats over memorabilia.

❺ Varnish tray, following manufacturer's instructions.

Merry Christmas Collage

Designer: Mary Lou Cacciatore

SUPPLIES

Rubber stamps: *Hero Arts* (Happy Holiday background, Snowman Postage Stamp, Seasons Peace, Must Be Christmas, Christmas Definition); *PrintWorks* (Wreath, Hollies and Berries); *Stamp Francisco* (Merry Christmas, Face); *Stampin' Up!* (Pine Sprig); *PSX* (Angel): *Limited Edition Rubberstamps* (Clock); *Impression Obsession* (Background Script); *Art Impressions* (Love Script); *Paper Inspirations* (Santa with Child)

Dye ink: *Stampin' Up!* (Creamy Caramel, Bordering Blue)

Pigment ink: Encore!, *Tsukineko* (Silver Metallic, Gold Metallic)

Solvent ink: Jet Black, StazOn, *Tsukineko*

Pen: gold, *Krylon*

Other: cardstock (cream, black), glossy paper, rubbing alcohol, cotton balls, gold cord, foam squares, scissors, adhesive

Finished size: 4¼" x 5½"

INSTRUCTIONS

① Make card from cream cardstock.

② Create marbleized stone technique with Creamy Caramel and Gold Metallic on glossy white.

③ Stamp images at random on marbleized paper; trim and mat with black; adhere to card.

④ Detail collage with pen.

⑤ Create marbleized stone technique on glossy white with Bordering Blue and Silver Metallic.

⑥ Stamp Santa with Child on blue marbleized square. Trim and mat with black; adhere to card front with foam squares.

⑦ Wrap cord around fold; tie knot.

HOW TO CREATE MARBLEIZED STONE LOOK

① Saturate cotton ball with rubbing alcohol.

② Blend with different colors of dye ink on glossy paper.

Music and Poinsettias

Designer: Holle Wiktorek

SUPPLIES

Rubber stamps: Anna Griffin, All Night Media, *Plaid* (Song Note); *Hero Arts* (Family, Celebrate); *Stamporium* (Persnickety Poinsettia)

Watermark ink: VersaMark, *Tsukineko*

Embossing powder: gold, Super Emboss, *PSX*

Clear tile: Perfect FX Mica Tiles, *USArtquest*

Rub-ons: *Craft-T Products* (maroon, green)

Other: cardstock (light green, burgundy, tan), black ink, postage stamp, black thread, needle, buttons, gold pen, scissors, adhesive, embossing heat tool

Finished size: 5¾" x 4"

INSTRUCTIONS

① Make card from light green cardstock.

② Stamp Song Note on tan and Family/Celebrate on burgundy with black; accent FAMILY and CELEBRATE with gold pen.

③ Stamp Poinsettia on light green cardstock with watermark ink; emboss and apply rub-ons.

④ Tear edges of stamped cardstock; ink with black.

⑤ Layer and adhere to card.

⑥ Cut clear tile to desired shape; adhere postage stamp and clear tile to card.

⑦ Stitch along card edges; sew on buttons.

Holiday Postage

Designer: Alisa Wolcott

SUPPLIES

Rubber stamps: Holiday Post De Luxe set, *Hero Arts*

Dye ink: Vintage, *Ranger Industries* (Christmas Tree, Seasons Greetings, Hot Cocoa)

Pigment ink: black, *Delta Rubber Stampede*

Embossing powder: Super Fine Clear, *Ranger Industries*

Adhesive: *Glue Dots International*

Mounting squares: *3L*

Patterned paper: *Rusty Pickle* (vintage music, marbled brown); *Creative Imaginations* (beige script)

Photo turns: black, Photo Anchors, *Making Memories*

Brads: black, *Making Memories*

Other: cardstock (dark brown, black), embossing heat tool, scissors

Finished size: 5½" x 4¼"

INSTRUCTIONS

❶ Make card from dark brown cardstock.

❷ Trim vintage music paper to fit card front; adhere.

❸ Crumple beige script paper. Stamp images on script paper at random with various inks; emboss. Mat with torn and inked marbled brown paper and torn black cardstock.

❹ Attach photo turns and brads to marbled brown paper and black cardstock. Adhere stamped block to card front.

Christmas Travels

Designer: Kathleen Wentz

SUPPLIES

Rubber stamps: *PSX* (Holly Spray, Heart Postage); *Stampington & Co.* (St. Nick's Greeting); *Stampin' Up!* (Pen Tip, 3 cent postage); *StampDiva.com* (Postcards); *Leavenworth Jackson* (Holiday Greetings); *Hero Arts* (Snowman Postage, Happy Holidays, Special Delivery); *Art Impressions* (Joy); *Just For Fun* (Your Friend); *Frantic Stamper* (Louvre Cancellation, Paris); *Close To My Heart* (Very Merry)

Dye ink: Archival, *Ranger Industries* (Coffee, red, Butterscotch)

Stickers: Christmas Fantasy, *Dover Publications*

Other: cream cardstock, Christmas Cancellation stamp, decorative-edge paper, colored pencils, double-sided tape, scissors

Finished size: 5¼" x 7¾"

INSTRUCTIONS

❶ Make card from cream cardstock.

❷ Stamp images at random with desired ink.

❸ Color holly and snowman postage with colored pencils.

❹ Adhere stickers.

❺ Ink card with Butterscotch.

❻ Insert folded decorative-edge paper and adhere.

Take advantage of coordinating patterned papers

Spring Blossom Trio

Designer: Heather D. White

SUPPLIES

All projects:

Cardstock: (white)

Fibers: (white ribbon) *Making Memories*

Tools: ruler, scissors, sandpaper

Pastel Palette card:

Paper: (Tangerine) Powder Room Collection, *Chatterbox*

Patterned paper: (Rosey Blossoms, Light Powder Plaid, Violet Dots, Violet Posie) Powder Room Collection, *Chatterbox*

Accent: (metal-rimmed tag) *Making Memories*

Fasteners: (silver eyelets) *Making Memories*

Font: (CBX Watson) *Chatterbox*

Adhesive

Tools: eyelet-setting tools, computer and printer

PASTEL PALETTE CARD

❶ Make card from cardstock.

❷ Print "Thanks!" on Tangerine paper; sand edges and adhere to tag. Set eyelet through hole.

❸ Cut patterned papers to fit card front. Adhere Light Powder Plaid to card. Tear approx. ¾" from right edge of Violet Posie and adhere to card. Tear right edge of Rosey Blossoms ¾" from previous paper and adhere.

❹ Tear right edge of Violet Dots ¾" from previous paper; set eyelet near torn edge and attach tag with ribbon. Adhere paper piece and tag to card.

❺ Sand edges of card.

POSIE CARD

❶ Make card from cardstock.

❷ Adhere Violet Posie side of paper to left side of card, and Spruce side of paper to right side. Adhere ribbon where papers meet. Adhere bow.

❸ Add tacks randomly to centers of flowers and green paper.

ROSEY CARD

❶ Make card from cardstock.

❷ Adhere 2" wide strip of Rosey Blossoms paper to top of card; adhere Light Powder Plaid paper to bottom.

❸ Adhere ribbon where papers meet.

❹ Cut 1¾" square of Tangerine paper and mat with cardstock; sand edges. Attach flower charm with eyelet. Adhere square to card with pop-up dots.

❺ Sand edges of card.

Posie card:

Patterned paper: (Violet Posie/Spruce) Powder Room Collection, *Chatterbox*

Fasteners: (Rosey Scrapbook Tacks) *Making Memories*

Adhesive

Tool: ⅛" hole punch

Rosey card:

Paper: (Tangerine) Powder Room Collection, *Chatterbox*

Patterned paper: (Rosey Blossoms, Light Powder Plaid) Powder Room Collection, *Chatterbox*

Accent: (silver flower Eyelet Charm) *Making Memories*

Fastener: (silver eyelet) *Making Memories*

Adhesive: pop-up dots, glue stick

Tools: eyelet-setting tools

Finished size: 3¾" x 5"

Raspberry Truffle Card

Designer: Alisa Wolcott

SUPPLIES

Textured cardstock: (cream)

Paper: (Brown) Cosmopolitan Collection, *Making Memories*

Patterned paper: (Floral Fishnet, Petite Paisley, Workweek Stripe) Cosmopolitan Collection, *Making Memories*

Fastener: (decorative brad) *Making Memories*

Fiber: (cream grosgrain ribbon) *May Arts*

Adhesive: (foam squares) *3L*

Tools: ruler, scissors, hole punch

Finished size: 5½" x 5"

INSTRUCTIONS

❶ Make card from cardstock.

❷ Cut tag from Workweek Stripe paper; attach brad. Punch hole through top.

❸ Adhere 2½" square of Petite Paisley to 3½" square of Floral Fishnet paper. Adhere to 4" square of Workweek Stripes paper. Mat with brown paper.

❹ Wrap ribbon twice around piece to form crisscross; knot ribbon and attach tag. Tie bow over tag. Secure tag with foam squares.

❺ Adhere piece to card.

COMPLETE THE CARD SET

Experiment with different designs, using the same line of patterned paper, to create a set of unique cards. The patterned paper collections from Making Memories make it so easy. The solid colors on the back of the patterned sheets make perfect complementary accents.

Eat Cake!

Designer: Linda Beeson

SUPPLIES

Rubber stamps:
Rubbermoon Stamp Company (Cake); *A Muse Artstamps* (Eat Cake sentiment

Watermark ink: VersaMark, *Tsukineko*

Embossing powder: white, Enchanted Creations, *Eclipse Cards & Crafts*

Patterned paper: black/silver stripe, *Pixie Press*

Fibers: Fun Fur, *Lion Brand Yarn*

Rectangle tag: black, *Making Memories*

Other: ink (black, silver, white), cardstock (black, white), adhesive foam squares, adhesive, embossing heat tool, scissors

Finished size: 4¼" x 5½"

INSTRUCTIONS

1 Make black card.

2 Stamp cake with watermark ink on black tag; emboss.

3 Stamp sentiment on black cardstock with white. Mat on white cardstock.

4 Cut out rectangle of patterned paper, mat on white cardstock; trim to fit front of card.

5 Stamp sentiment randomly on white cardstock with black and silver ink. Tear long edges and adhere to card.

6 Secure fibers on tag; adhere tag and sentiment to card with adhesive foam squares.

Black Toile

Designer: Linda Beeson

SUPPLIES

Rubber stamps: *Impression Obsession* (Happy Birthday); *Stampa Barbara* (Wild Rose Spray)

Patterned paper: Shabby Chic, *me & my BIG ideas*

Plaid ribbon: *Michaels*

Other: black ink, cardstock (black and tan), silver heart button, clear embossing powder, embossing heat tool, adhesive, scissors

Finished size: 5½" square

INSTRUCTIONS

1 Make black card.

2 Stamp sentiment with black on tan cardstock; emboss with clear.

3 Cut rectangle out of black, adhere ribbon around center. Adhere stamped sentiment on rectangle.

4 Stamp rose spray with black on tan cardstock. Cut square, mat with black; adhere to patterned paper and trim to fit front of card.

5 Adhere sentiment to stamped rose paper; adhere all to front of card.

6 Knot ribbon and adhere to corners. Thread ribbon through heart button; adhere to sentiment.

Charmed Birthday Wish

Designer: Melissa Caligiuri

SUPPLIES

Cardstock: light pink, pink, *Bazzill Basics Paper*

Striped paper: *KI Memories*

Color block accent: *KI Memories*

"happy birthday" stamp: *Impress Rubber Stamps*

Ribbon: *Offray*

Other: black ink, heart charm

Finished size: 4" x 5½"

INSTRUCTIONS

1 Make pink card base.

2 Adhere striped paper across top.

3 Adhere narrow strip of light pink cardstock along bottom of striped piece.

4 Adhere color block accent.

5 Tie ribbon through charm; adhere to block.

6 Stamp "happy birthday."

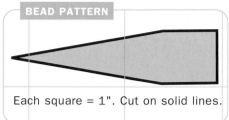

Each square = 1". Cut on solid lines.

Transfer pattern to paper.

Paper Bead Bracelets

Designer: Lori Bergmann

SUPPLIES

FOR BOTH:

Clear dimensional adhesive: Aleene's Paper Glaze, *Duncan*

Craft glue: Aleene's Fast Grab Tacky Glue, *Duncan*

Round nose pliers: NSI

Other: cotton swabs, paintbrush (for applying adhesive)

FOR BLUE BRACELET:

Blue toile patterned paper: Laura Ashley, *EK Success*

Silver washed rings: *The Beadery*

Silver wire: *Artistic Wire*

Silver barrel clasp

FOR VIOLET BRACELET:

Violet patterned paper: *Design Originals*

Amethyst beads: *JewelCraft*

Gold wire: *Artistic Wire*

Gold barrel clasp

INSTRUCTIONS

① Transfer pattern to back of patterned paper and cut 9–12 bead pieces (see Figures a and b). *Note: The number of beads depends on desired size of bracelet.*

② Brush thin layer of craft glue on back of each bead piece, starting about ¼" from wide end. Cut one tip off a cotton swab. Roll bead on swab, starting with wide end (see Figure c). Carefully remove swab and let bead dry. *Note: If you leave swab in place, it may stick to bead.*

③ To glaze beads, apply two or three coats of clear dimensional adhesive. Let dry between coats.

④ Attach half of clasp to wire end. String beads on wire, alternating with amethyst beads or silver washed rings. Attach other half of clasp.

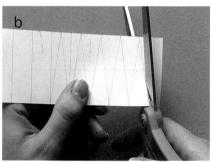

Cut shapes.

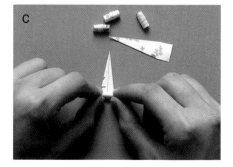

Apply glue and roll.

Bonus Ideas

- To make textured beads, use textured paper and/or cut out the bead pieces with decorative-edge scissors.

- For a weathered look, lightly sand the beads before or after rolling them. Coat the beads with antiquing gel and matte lacquer.

Gingham Card Gift Set

Designer: Alisa Bangerter

SUPPLIES

FOR CARD:

Cardstock: purple, white

Square punch: *Marvy Uchida*

Colored eyelets: *Doodlebug Design*

Other: eyelet setter

FOR BOX:

Alphabet stamps: *Stampin' Up!*

Blue embossing powder, embossing fluid: *Stampin' Up!*

Other: white gift box, small tag, chalk, heat embossing tool

FOR BAG:

White cardstock

Colored eyelets: *Doodlebug Design*

"Happy Birthday" stamp: *Stampin' Up!*

Other: white gift bag, eyelet setter, heat embossing tool

FOR ALL:

Patterned paper: Green, Pink, Purple, Yellow, *Pebbles In My Pocket*

Gingham ribbons: *Offray*

Colored wires: *Making Memories*

Finished sizes:
   card 5¼" square
   box 3½" cube
   bag 8½" x 5¼" x 3¼"

CARD

❶ Cut 5" square of white cardstock; set eyelets at corners. Lace four different colors of wire through eyelets and along sides.

❷ Punch one square from each color of patterned paper . Wrap matching ribbon around each and tie with bow; adhere to cardstock square.

❸ Make a 5¼" square card from purple cardstock. Adhere embellished white square to card.

GIFT BOX

❶ Cut five 3¼" squares from patterned paper and glue to box sides and top.

❷ Emboss "Happy Birthday" on tag; color edges with chalk. Loop ribbon through hole; adhere to box top.

❸ Place gift in box. Adhere a piece of matching gingham ribbon to the bottom of each side of box. Bring opposing pairs together and tie in two bows on box top. Thread wires under bows. Wrap ends around pencil to curl.

GIFT BAG

❶ Cut four 4" x 2½" rectangles from patterned paper and adhere to bag front.

❷ Cut a 2¾" purple square and mat on white. Emboss "Happy Birthday" in center. Set eyelets at corners and attach wire as for card.

❸ Tie several strands of ribbon together in a bow; trim and knot ends. Adhere to top of bag.

TYING IT UP

You're creating your own gifts and gift wrap—now top things off with a handmade bow. **Heather Melzer** contributed this wonderful way to coordinate all elements of your gift giving so that the whole package looks great!

❶ Cut seventeen 1" x 8" strips of paper. Create a loop by overlapping the front side of one end over the back side of the other end, and adhere (see photo). (For a different look, adhere the back sides of the ends of a strip together.)

❷ Once you've made all the loops, create the bow. Starting at the bottom, work in a circle to layer the loops until the bow looks full. Hold the center of the bow tightly and puncture it with a craft knife. Push a large brad through the hole and secure it. Cover the brad with a tag or another loop.

The key to creating a beautiful bow is to use double-sided patterned paper, because both sides of the completed bow are visible. Using a heftier paper ensures that the loops keep their shapes.

Welcome Baby

Designer: Bonnie Lotz

SUPPLIES

Rubber stamps: (Baby's Hand Left, Antique UC Alphabet, Antique LC Alphabet, Buttons Alphabet) PSX, *Duncan*

Dye ink: (Indigo) Raised Dye, PSX, *Duncan*

Watermark ink: VersaMark, *Tsukineko*

Cardstock: (light blue, medium blue, navy blue, white)

Patterned paper: (Blue Raspberry Lines) *The Scrapbook Wizard*

Accents: (cream, navy buttons) *Making Memories*

Fibers: (white rickrack) *Carolace*; (blue gingham ribbon, white floss, white thread)

Adhesive: pop-up dots

Tools: scissors, sewing machine

Finished size: 5¼" x 4¼"

INSTRUCTIONS

1 Make card from navy blue cardstock.

2 Trim white cardstock slightly smaller than card front; adhere. Trim rectangle from Blue Raspberry Lines paper; adhere.

3 Thread white floss through buttons; tie knot. Adhere.

4 Trim square from medium blue cardstock; stamp hand with watermark ink and machine-stitch to card.

5 Trim square from light blue cardstock. Stamp "Welcome" with Indigo. Adhere to card.

6 Stamp "Baby" on light blue with Indigo. Trim letters into squares; ink edges. Adhere with pop-up dots.

7 Adhere rickrack and ribbon to card.

Peekaboo

Designer: Sara Horton

SUPPLIES

Rubber stamps: (Baby's Hand Right, Baby Pixie Expressions) PSX, *Duncan*

Dye ink: (Turquoise, Neptune, Saffron) Ancient Page, *Clearsnap*

Card: (white) *Halcraft*

Patterned paper: (My Guy Simple Stripe) Collection IV, *KI Memories*

Fibers: (light green ribbon) *Offray*

Adhesive

Tools: scissors

Finished size: 5½" x 4"

INSTRUCTIONS

1 Trim strip of My Guy Simple Stripe paper; adhere to card.

2 Stamp sentiment twice with Turquoise.

3 Stamp handprint with Neptune.

4 Ink card edges with Saffron.

5 Tie ribbon in bow; adhere to card.

Bonus Ideas

- Personalize the card by replacing the striped paper with a favorite ribbon or using your baby's foot or hand to stamp the card.

- Use alphabet stamps and coordinating inks to adapt the card for use as a birth announcement or shower invitation.

- Emboss the stamped handprint to add texture to the card.

All Boy

Designer: Linda Beeson

SUPPLIES

White cardstock

Textured cardstock: dark blue, red, *Bazzill Basics Paper*

Denim patterned paper: *Frances Meyer*

Red bandana patterned paper: *Colors by Design*

Red gingham patterned paper: *Keeping Memories Alive*

Jeans pocket and button cut-outs: *This & That, My Mind's Eye*

Word stickers: *Creative Imaginations*

Red pearle cotton embroidery floss: *DMC*

Other: silver eyelets

Finished size: 5½" square
(card does not open)

CARD

❶ Attach jean pocket to red gingham paper square, using eyelets (see photo). Mat with red cardstock. Adhere button cutouts to corners.

❷ Mat with denim patterned paper; adhere to blue card base.

❸ Press "all" and "boy" stickers on white cardstock. Cut into tag shapes. Attach to pocket with floss.

BANDANA INSERT

❶ Print birth announcement on back of bandana patterned paper, and trim to 5½" square.

❷ Fold announcement in quarters, patterned side out.

❸ Fold sides in back.

❹ Tuck in jean pocket.

Wine Tasting Party Invitation

Designer: Jennifer Fish

SUPPLIES

Textured cardstock: (black)

Patterned paper: (Fleur De Lis, French Poetry Print, Plum & Moss Damask) Sonnets, *Creative Imaginations*

Rubber stamps: (Evolution Magnetic Alphabet Stamps and Base Set) *Making Memories*

Dye ink: (Coal) Ancient Page, *Clearsnap*

Fasteners: (Lilac Matte Finish Brads) *Lasting Impressions for Paper*

Fonts: (Arial, Arial Black) *Microsoft*

Adhesive: mini dots

Tools:
(Euro Personal Paper Trimmer) *Fiskars*

⅜" hole punch, computer and printer, ruler, scissors

Finished size: 4½" x 6½"

INSTRUCTIONS

❶ Print invitation on Fleur De Lis paper. Trim to 4½" x 6½".

❷ Cut Plum & Moss Damask and French Poetry Print paper to 1½" x 4½". Tear along bottoms, making French Poetry paper narrower.

❸ Stamp "Wine Tasting" on French Poetry, mixing capital and lower case letters randomly. Adhere to Plum & Moss Damask piece. Attach to top of invitation with brads.

❹ Cut French Poetry Print to 2¼" x 4½". Stamp wine name and tear top.

❺ Cut Plum & Moss Damask 2¼" x 4½". Tear along top. Adhere, overlapping French Print piece, to invitation bottom. Attach brads.

❻ Mat invitation with cardstock.

Bonus Idea

Create an entire ensemble with matching wine tasting notes, bottle label covers, food identifiers, and wine glass tags.

Latest & Greatest

MOSAIC IN MINUTES

Now anyone can create mosaic-look frames, clocks, birdhouses, gift boxes and bags, journal covers, and scrapbook pages. It's as simple as grouting the surface, cutting out and adhering paper tiles, and glazing. Tera Leigh's **Faux Mosaic Kit** from **Ranger Industries** includes grout, glue, and tile glaze; you provide the surface and the inspiration. Retail $12.99. 800/244-2211, *www.rangerink.com.*

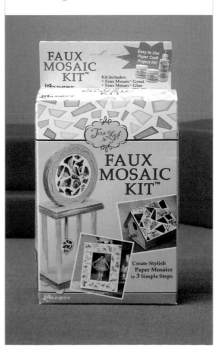

Faux Mosaic Frame

Designer: Alisa Bangerter

SUPPLIES

Maroon cardstock

Patterned paper:

Green plaid, green stripe, green vine: Summer Sage, *Bo-Bunny Press*

Green Gold Dot: *K&Company*

Faux Mosaic Kit: *Ranger Industries*

Wood frame: *Provo Craft*

Lettering template: ABC Tracers Block Upper, *EK Success*

Burgundy buttons: *Making Memories*

Fiber: *On the Surface*

Silver metallic rub-on: *Craf-T Products*

Light ivory acrylic paint: *Delta*

Paintbrush

Finished size: 8½" x 6¼"

INSTRUCTIONS

Follow kit manufacturer's instructions for grout, tile adhesion, and tile glazing. Let project dry between coats and steps.

① Paint frame.

② Grout frame front.

③ Paint grout.

④ Trace and cut letters from cardstock.

⑤ Cut holly leaves from Green Gold Dot paper and tile pieces from all patterned papers. *Note: Cut irregular tile pieces; avoid perfect triangles or squares.*

⑥ Arrange tiles and leaves on frame; adhere.

⑦ Glaze tiles and leaves with several coats.

⑧ Thread buttons with fiber and adhere to frame.

⑨ Use metallic rub-on around frame edge for a worn, antique look.

Happily Ever After

Designer: Kathleen Paneitz

SUPPLIES

Rubber stamp: (Dress) *Stampabilities*

Dye ink: (Coal Black) *PrintWorks*

Cardstock: (cream)

Textured cardstock: (cream) *Lasting Impressions for Paper*

Specialty paper: (cream ribbed)

Rub-on: (happily ever after from Wedding) Simply Stated, *Making Memories*

Accent: (silver oval concho) *Scrapworks*

Fibers: (black twill ribbon) Wrights; (cream thread)

Adhesive

Tools: scissors, sewing machine, ruler

Finished size: 4" x 5¼"

INSTRUCTIONS

❶ Make card from cream cardstock.

❷ Cut 4" x 2" rectangle of cream textured paper, 2½" x 3¼" rectangle of cream cardstock, and 1½" x 3¼" rectangle of cream ribbed paper. Zigzag-stitch papers together to fit card front.

❸ Stamp Dress in upper left corner of stitched papers.

❹ Apply rub-on to bottom right corner.

❺ Adhere ribbons around stitched papers; thread through accent and trim.

❻ Adhere stitched papers to card front.

Forever

Designer: Tracie Smith

SUPPLIES

Rubber stamps: *Hero Arts*
Green cardstock: *Bazzill Basics Paper*
Confetti cream cardstock: *Stampin' Up!*
Floral and quilted patterned paper: *K&Company*
French script patterned paper: *7gypsies*
Decorative chalk: *Stampin' Up!*
Acrylic paint: Americana, *DecoArt*

(Black, Fawn)
Ribbon: *Stampin' Up!*
Fine-tip pen: ZIG Millennium, *EK Success*
Transparency film: *3M*

EMBELLISH WITH ACRYLIC

Add variety and a fresh look to your layouts by stamping with acrylic paint. The lettering on this wedding layout was stamped in acrylic paint for a soft, romantic look.

Sheer Delight

The versatility of vellum is transparent.

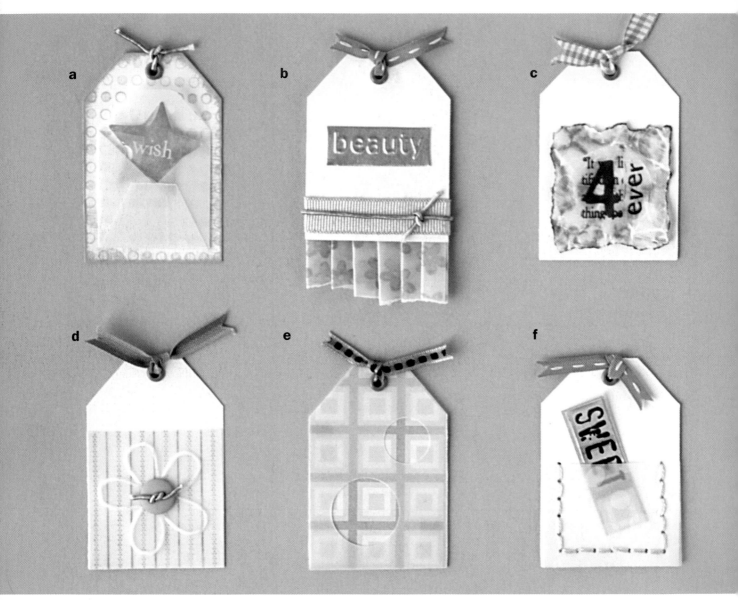

Anything paper can do, vellum can do better! It's a translucent paper that can be punched, folded, torn, stitched, crumpled, dry embossed, or stamped. The bonus of being see-through gives vellum its charm. Layering vellum softens and brings an air of mystery to the paper behind it. Every paper crafter should explore the lovely effects that can be created.

TECHNIQUES TO TRY WITH VELLUM

a FOLD INTO ENVELOPE: The paper shows a tempting hint of what's inside.

b TEAR, FOLD, PLEAT: Adds softness as well as dimension.

c CRUMPLE, INK, LAYER: Creates an instant focal point with texture.

d DRY EMBOSS: Creates a lacy white-on-white raised pattern.

e PUNCH, LAYER: The punched areas show the pattern clearly while the solid areas mute the design.

f STITCH POCKET: Sews easily and lets you peek into the pocket.

Vellum Envelope
Birthday Card

Designer: Nichole Heady

SUPPLIES

Cardstock: (Almost Amethyst, Pale Plum) *Stampin' Up!*

Patterned paper: (Slumber Party) *Stampin' Up!*

Vellum: (clear) *Stampin' Up!*

Rubber stamps: (happy, birthday from Everyday Flexible Phrases set) *Stampin' Up!*

Solvent ink: (Black) StazOn, *Tsukineko*

Accents:
 (clear flower charm from hair barrette) *Goody*

 small white candles

Fibers: (lavender gingham ribbon) *Making Memories*

Adhesive:
 (clear mounting squares) *3L*

 (Crystal Effects) *Stampin' Up!*

 (Glue Dots) *Glue Dots International*

Tools:
 (¼" circle punch) *Fiskars*

 craft knife, scissors, wire brush, ruler

Finished size: 3½" x 5"

INSTRUCTIONS

➊ Make card from Almost Amethyst cardstock.

➋ Cut Slumber Party paper to 3" x 4½" and roughen edges with wire brush. Mat with Pale Plum cardstock and adhere to card.

➌ Make envelope, using pattern. Assemble with mounting squares and adhere to card with adhesive dots.

➍ Tie five candles together with ribbon. Stamp happy and birthday on ribbon ends (see "Ribbon Stamping Tip").

➎ Cut tabs off barrette with craft knife. Punch circle from Almost Amethyst and adhere to back of flower's center with Crystal Effects. Adhere flower to envelope.

RIBBON STAMPING TIP

Tie the candles before you try to stamp the ribbon. Hold the ribbon ends flat on a table edge and allow the candles to dangle. The ribbon will remain perfectly flat and you can successfully stamp it.

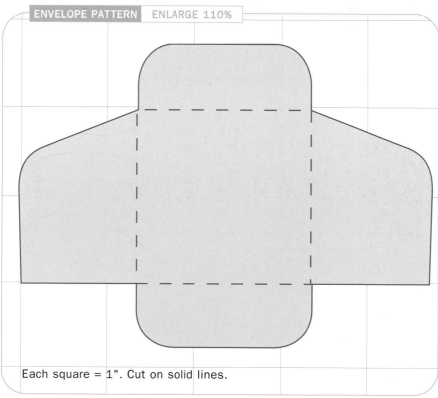

ENVELOPE PATTERN ENLARGE 110%

Each square = 1". Cut on solid lines.

Cherish Happy Memories

Designer: Sande Krieger

SUPPLIES

Rubber stamp: (Gown of Dreams) *Stampendous!*; (cherish, happy, memories) *Making Memories*

Dye ink: (Basic Black) *Stampin' Up!*

Pigment ink: (Petal Pink) VersaColor, *Tsukineko*

Embossing powder: (clear, clear Ultra Thick Embossing Enamel) *Ranger Industries*

Cardstock: (white, cream)

Patterned paper: (Coral Splash) *Scenic Route Paper Company*

Vellum

Paint: (Galaxy Blue, Sapphire on Ice, Passion Flower) Radiant Pearls, *LuminArte*

Sticker: (Cherish) Defined, *Making Memories*

Fibers: (blue ribbon) *Making Memories*; (pink ribbon) *Offray*

Tools: scissors, heat tool

TIPS FOR THICK EMBOSSING

Rub edges of paper or cardstock with ink and then dip them in thick embossing powder and heat set from underneath. This way, the powder will not blow off while embossing. Use the same color embossing powder as your paper for a dramatic and glamorous monochromatic effect.

Flower Girl

Designer: Lori Bergmann

SUPPLIES

Flower rubber stamps: *Delta Rubber Stampede* (Leaves, Rose Blossom)

Alphabet rubber stamp set: *Wordsworth*

Dye ink: Ancient Page, *Clearsnap* (Leaf Green, Sage, Bordeaux)

Patterned paper: Green Damask, *Creative Imaginations*

Rose nail head: *JewelCraft*

Embossing pen: ZIG, *EK Success*

Embossing powder: Adirondack, *Ranger Industries* (Cranberry, Moss)

Clear vellum tape: *3M*

Roller adhesives: *Henkel Consumer*

CREATE A 3-D ROSE BORDER

1. Stamp rose image lightly on vellum. *Note: Stamp first on scrap paper, then vellum for a lighter application. Let dry.*

2. Stamp two roses on scrap paper. Cut out.

3. Cover back of each image with repositionable adhesive. Align vellum.

4. Stamp leaf image around masked roses.

5. Peel off mask. Lay over third rose. Repeat process.

6. Restamp roses; heat set.

Lovely Leaf Necklace

Design: Chera Sands

SUPPLIES

Small leaf rubber stamp

Black ink pad*

1" x 2" metal-rimmed vellum tag*

Silver eyelet*

9 mm jump ring*

24" silver ball chain necklace*

Decorative chalk: green, yellow

Eyelet setter and hole punch

Miscellaneous items: hammer, self-healing mat, needlenose pliers, cotton swab or make-up applicator

*Stewart Superior Corporation Memories acid-free ink pad; Making Memories Details tag; Impress Rubber Stamps eyelet; and Westrim Crafts Crafting Expressions jump ring and ball chain necklace were used in the sample project.

INSTRUCTIONS

❶ Stamp leaves on the tag with black ink and let them dry.

❷ Apply green and yellow chalk to the tag with a cotton swab or make-up applicator.

❸ Set the eyelet near the top of the tag.

❹ Open the jump ring with the pliers, and attach the tag to it. Close the jump ring, and place the tag on the necklace.

Bonus Ideas

- Attach the tag to a key chain ring.

- Create personalized tags with names, themes, or favorite colors.

- Use part of a large stamp instead of smaller ones. Simply apply black ink to the desired section and stamp the tag.

Joy

Designer: Linda Beeson

SUPPLIES

Rubber stamps: *PrintWorks* (Joy); *Hero Arts* (manuscript background); *Delta Rubber Stampede* (Redwood)

Brads: black, Nails, *Chatterbox*

Other: black ink pad, cardstock (black, white, textured white) scissors, clear embossing powder, embossing heat tool, ink-jet transparency, green craft paint, foam squares

Finished size: 5" square

INSTRUCTIONS

❶ Make white textured card.

❷ Trim transparency to fit card. Apply green paint to back of transparency; let dry.

❸ Stamp script and branches with black, some on front of transparency and some on back.

❹ Stamp "Joy" on white cardstock square with black; emboss. Mat with black cardstock.

❺ Attach transparency to white cardstock; mat with black. Adhere to card using brads.

❻ Adhere "Joy" block to transparency.

Moments

Designer: Kathleen Paneitz

SUPPLIES

Rubber stamps: *Paper Inspirations* (large pocket watch face); *Stampin' Up!* (small pocket watches); *Wordsworth* (Pointillism alphabet); *PSX* (antique alphabet)

Pigment ink: VersaColor, *Tsukineko* (blue); Page Craft, *Clearsnap* (brown); ColorBox, *Clearsnap* (gold)

Computer font: Typewriter, downloaded from Internet

Metal plaque: *Scrapworks*

Metal numbers: *Making Memories*

Square punch: *Marvy Uchida*

Circle punch: Whale of a Punch, *EK Success*

Eyelet: silver, *ScrapArts*

Transparency: *3M*

Other: blue fiber, cardstock (tan, navy), sponge dauber, adhesive, scissors, eyelet-setting tools

Finished size: 4" x 7¼"

CARD POCKET

① Transfer pocket pattern onto tan cardstock; cut out.

② Sponge edges with brown; assemble pocket.

③ Punch half of circle punch through top of pocket; sponge brown on edges.

④ Randomly stamp watch images on front and back of pocket with gold, and messages on front and back of envelope with blue and brown.

⑤ Thread metal numbers through blue fiber; tie around card.

CARD

① Cut navy cardstock slightly smaller than width of pocket.

② Stamp large pocket watch using Gold.

③ Print message on transparency. Transfer pattern onto transparency and cut. Fold transparency according to pattern and adhere to back of navy cardstock.

④ Adhere metal plaque to navy cardstock.

⑤ Set eyelet through top of card; tie on blue fiber.

⑥ Insert card into pocket.

Insert

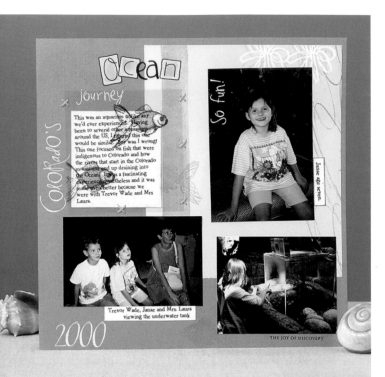

Ocean Journey

Designer: Kathleen Paneitz

SUPPLIES

Rubber stamp: (Goldfish) *Magenta Rubber Stamps*

Pigment ink: (Black, Marigold, Smoke Blue) VersaColor, *Tsukineko*

Cardstock: (cream, orange)

Patterned paper: (Tangerine/Blue) *Scrappy Cat Creations*

Transparency: *3M*

Rub-on letters: (Heidi White) Simply Stated Alphabet, *Making Memories*

Stickers: (Snorkle Alphablocks, Fancy Pants) *Doodlebug Design*

Fibers: (aqua floss) *DMC*

Font: (CK Constitution) "CK Fresh Fonts" CD, *Creating Keepsakes*

Tools: scissors, computer and printer, needle

CREATE ILLUSIONS

In this layout, the designer created the illusion of depth by stamping and embossing images on a transparency. She placed the transparency stamped side down on the layout, for a great visual effect on the reverse side. Experiment with transparencies on your next layout to create a look that will make your pages unique.

Starting School

Design: Shimelle Laine

SUPPLIES

Rubber stamps: alphabet*, apple*

Brown chalk finish ink pad*

Gold pigment ink*

12" x 12" cardstock*:

Brown

Celery

Hunter green

Red

Lettering template*

Gold glitter embossing powder*

Brush markers*: green, red

Transparency film

PSX Antique Lowercase alphabet stamps; *A Stamp in the Hand* apple stamp; *Stampa Rosa* Fresco chalk finish ink pad; *Clearsnap* ColorBox pigment ink pad; *Bazzill Basics Paper* cardstock; *Provo Craft* lettering template; *JudiKins* gold embossing powder; and *EK Success* brush markers were used in the sample project.

TRANSPARENT WINDOW BORDER

Apply the brush marker ink directly to the apple stamp and press the stamp on transparency film three times. Cut or punch three squares in a strip of hunter green cardstock to frame the stamped apples. Place the green strip over the background paper and stamp "a is for apple" with brown ink inside the squares. Embellish the border as desired with gold ink, glitter powder, and torn cardstock. Adhere the stamped transparency film to the back of the hunter strip, and then adhere the border with adhesive pop-up dots over the stamped background.

MONEY-SAVING TIP

Invest in versatile stamps that you can use throughout an album or season, such as an apple stamp for a school album or sun stamp for summer.

Irreplaceable Mom

Designer: Kathleen Paneitz

SUPPLIES

Rubber stamp: Spiral Frame, All Night Media, *Plaid*

Pigment ink: black, VersaColor, *Tsukineko*

Embossing powder: clear, *Ranger Industries*

Patterned paper: Pink Lemonade Script, *Mustard Moon*

Computer font: Freestyle Script, downloaded from the Web

Transparency: *3M*

Other: scissors, silver thread, adhesive, embossing heat tool

Finished size: 5¼" x 4¾"

INSTRUCTIONS

1 Make black card.

2 Stamp spiral frame stamp on transparency with black ink; emboss. Trim around image.

3 Cut patterned paper to fit transparency; adhere to transparency and to card.

4 Stamp quote on patterned paper scrap. Trim and mat with black cardstock. Adhere to transparency.

5 Tie bow using silver thread; adhere to transparency above quote.

transparency trick$

¢ Money Saver

Looking for a real deal on transparency sheets? Popular 3-D accents, such as those from Meri Meri, JoLee's Boutiques by EK Success, and Paper Bliss by Westrim, come on sturdy plastic sheets that most people throw away. **Nancy Church**, a talented and thrifty paper crafter, uses them like regular transparency sheets. She prints journaling or greetings on them, stamps them with permanent ink, or places them in slide mounts or shaker boxes. You can't beat the price!

Beginning Handmade Paper

Create beautifully textured paper using items from around the house

Basic Handmade Paper

Design: Sharon Lewis

SUPPLIES

About 50 sheets of paper (not newspaper) cut into 2" squares

Large plastic vat or container

Liquid starch (for sizing)

Two 10" x 12" wood boards

4 disposable dishcloths

Bricks

Mold and deckle (or two finished wood picture frames and fine-gauge aluminum mesh or screening)

Miscellaneous items: scissors, saucepan, water, strainer, blender, wooden spoon or stick, sponge, clothespins, staple gun, paintbrush

MAKE A MOLD AND DECKLE

First, remove the glass and backing insert from the two wood picture frames. Set one frame aside as the deckle. (The deckle gives shape to the wet pulp and determines the size of the paper sheet.) To make the mold, cut a piece of fine-gauge aluminum mesh or screening (found at any hardware or building supply store) ½" longer than the inside edges of the frame. Staple the mesh to the back of the frame, making sure that it is tight and smooth.

INSTRUCTIONS

Half fill the saucepan with water. Add the paper pieces and simmer on medium-low heat for 30 minutes. Pour the paper into the strainer and rinse it thoroughly with cold water.

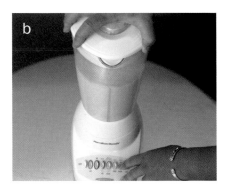

Half fill the blender with water. Add the strained paper to the blender and blend until smooth.

Half fill the vat with water. Add 2–3 tbsp. of liquid starch and the blended pulp. Stir the contents briskly with the wooden spoon. Add more pulp as needed. *Note: The contents should be about 90% liquid. More pulp will yield thicker paper. More water will yield thinner paper.*

Position the deckle over the mold and dip it vertically into the vat of pulpy water, leveling it out under the water.

Pull the mold and deckle up horizontally from the pulpy water, gently shaking them back and forth to evenly distribute the pulp. Let as much water as possible drain over the vat.

Carefully remove the deckle from the mold.

Stack three damp disposable dishcloths on top of a piece of wood. Place the mold face down onto the dishcloth-covered wood, pressing a sponge onto the back of the mesh to help remove the paper.

Lay a dry disposable dishcloth on top of the molded paper, and place the other piece of wood on top. Place the bricks on top of the wood to press the water out of the paper. Let them press for several hours.

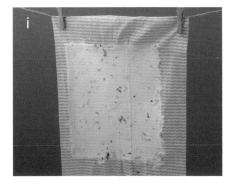

Remove the bricks, wood, and disposable dishcloth from the top of the molded paper. Hang the dishtowel with the paper attached to it from a clothesline to dry. *Note: You can also lay the paper facedown on a flat, heat-safe surface and iron it dry.* Peel the dry paper from the dishtowel.

Handmade Paper Valentine

Design: Sharon Lewis

SUPPLIES

Handmade paper supplies from p. 214, except paper

3 sheets cream-colored paper cut into 2" squares

1/4 c. crushed dried rose leaves

2 dried pink rose petals

8½" x 11" cardstock:
  Cream speckled
  Sage

Forest Green mulberry paper*

Lowercase alphabet stamps*

Champagne ink pad*

Silver grommet

Grommet setting tool

19" lengths fibers: Green*, Silver*

Adhesive pop-up dot*

Miscellaneous items: handful of white dryer lint, scissors, cotton swab, hammer

*Stampin' Up! mulberry paper; PSX Antique Alphabet stamp set; Tsukineko Champagne Dauber Duo mini stamp pad; On the Surface Green fiber; DMC Silver fiber; and Glue Dots International Pop Up Glue Dot were used in the sample project.

MAKE THE PAPER

❶ Make the paper as described in "Basic handmade paper," substituting cream paper squares. Add the dried rose leaves and a handful of white dryer lint to the vat in Step c.

❷ Place two dried rose petals in the shape of a heart on the paper before beginning Step h. Press as indicated and dry the paper.

MAKE THE CARD

❶ Cut the sage cardstock in half widthwise, and fold one piece in half to make a card.

❷ Tear the handmade paper to fit the card front, placing the petal heart slightly above the center.

❸ Mat the handmade paper with torn mulberry paper, and adhere it to the front of the card. *Note: To tear the mulberry paper, moisten where you plan to tear with a damp cotton swab, then slowly pull the paper apart with both hands.*

MAKE THE TAG

❶ Cut a tag shape from the cream speckled cardstock (see photo).

❷ Stamp "i love you" on the tag. Shade the edges with the ink pad.

❸ Attach the grommet to the top of the tag, using the grommet-setting tool and hammer.

❹ Tie Silver and Green fibers around the front of the card (see photo). Trim the ends.

❺ Slip the tag onto the tail of the bow, and adhere it in place with an adhesive pop-up dot.

HANDMADE PAPER FOR THE SENSES

You don't need to be a writer to capture nature's beauty and fragrance on paper. In *Scented Herb Papers,* Polly Pinder shows you how to make your own paper using herbs, flowers, fruit, and essential oil. Accent your paper with inlaid flowers and leaves, or impress shapes into it for dimension. Your handmade stationery, drawer liners, candle shades, and place mats will be a real treat for the senses. (Search Press, 64 pages.)

Blossom Box

Designer: Vee Kelsey-McKee

SUPPLIES

Box: (paper maché) *Darice*; (or wood)

Vellum: (Radiant White) *Neenah Paper*

Walnut ink

Paint:
(Cameo Pink acrylic spray)
American Tradition, *Valspar*

(Cashmere Pink texture) Paper
Perfect, *DecoArt*

Font: (your choice)

Tools:
(palette knife) *DecoArt*

power drill and small drill bit or
needle tool, computer and printer,
paintbrush

Other: dried flower petals, twig, raffia,
pencil

Finished size: 4¼" x 4¼" x 2½"

INSTRUCTIONS

1 Paint inside of box and lid Cameo
Pink; let dry. Turn box over and paint bottom and lip that will be covered by lid; let
dry. *Note: Repeat if needed.*

2 To make sentiment piece, print text on
vellum. Tear out, crumple, flatten, and
age with diluted walnut ink. Roll edges
while still wet.

3 Place lid on box and lightly mark with a
pencil where lid ends. Remove lid and
spread texture paint on box sides with
palette knife, ending at pencil mark.
Spread texture paint on outside of lid.
*Note: Paper Perfect has the appearance
of handmade paper when dry. You can
make the finish smooth or more heavily
textured.*

4 While paint is wet, press vellum sentiment into box front. Press flower petals
randomly into paint. Let dry overnight.

5 To add handle, position twig on box
lid. Drill or pierce small holes on each
side of twig at both ends. Tie twig in
place with raffia.

Bonus Idea

To make a matching gift tag or
bookmark, spread a thin layer of
Paper Perfect texture paint on
waxed paper, embed flower
petals, and let dry. Peel off, and
punch or cut the dry material
into the desired shape. Embellish
as you wish.

Weeds are flowers too,
once you get to know them.
--Eeyore

With hope, kindness and
love used in their tending
May your seeds of joy
blossom sweet and unending

Place cardstock in blender.

Pour pulp on cookie sheet.

Remove from cookie sheet.

Grow-a-Seed Card

Design: Cheryl McMurray

SUPPLIES

3–4 sheets varying shades of tan cardstock, torn into 1" squares

Off-white mulberry paper

Blender

1 pkg. herb or flowering seeds

1 tsp. cornstarch

Green chalk*

Green ink pad*

Foliage rubber stamp*

Fine green twine

⅛" hole punch*

Miscellaneous items: water, cooking spray, cookie sheet, paper towel, water, cotton swab or make-up sponge, computer with printer, a twig

*Craf-T Products Moss Green decorative chalk; Stampin' Up! Moss Green ink pad; Provo Craft rubber stamp; and EK Success hole punch were used in the sample project.

MAKE THE SEEDED PAPER

① Place about 3–4" of the torn cardstock into the blender. Add enough water to cover the top of your cardstock pieces.

② Add 1 tsp. cornstarch to the paper and water mixture and blend at a high speed until well mixed (see Figure a). *Note: Cornstarch will make the handmade paper more pliable.*

③ Lightly spray a cookie sheet with cooking spray and then wipe it clean with a paper towel. *Note: The film left from the spray will allow you to remove your paper easily when dry, but won't leave any oily residue.*

④ Pour the paper mixture onto the cookie sheet and add the seeds. Gently hand-mix the seeds into the mixture and spread across the cookie sheet until it is approx. ⅛" thick (see Figure b). *Note: Make sure there are no holes in the layer.*

⑤ Soak up any excess water with a paper towel. *Note: Drying time depends on room temperature.*

⑥ When the paper is completely dry, remove it carefully from the cookie sheet (see Figure c).

CREATE THE CARD

① Cut a 3½" x 4" piece from the seeded paper.

② Apply the chalk to the paper edges with a cotton swab or make-up sponge.

③ Using your favorite computer font, print a message onto the mulberry paper.

④ Apply the ink to the rubber stamp and stamp it underneath the printed message.

⑤ Trim around the message and the stamped image, leaving about a ⅜" border at the top.

⑥ Punch two holes above the message. Punch four more holes through the seeded paper so that two each are in line vertically with the holes on the message.

⑦ Tie the twig to the seeded paper with the green twine, knotting it on the backside. Cut off any excess twine.

⑧ Tie the printed note to the twig holders with more twine. *Note: Leave a little slack so the message appears to hang from the twig.*

VARIATION

If you would like to add more texture to your paper, add very small scraps of contrasting color to the initial paper mixture and fold in with a spoon.

Book Review

CREATIVE PAPERMAKING

Adding seeds to paper is just one way to enjoy your garden's harvest. In *300 Papermaking Recipes*, authors Mary Reimer and Heidi Reimer-Epp present hundreds of ideas for creating unique, homemade paper. Even if you've never made paper before, you'll learn all you need to know from the complete instructions and the guides to the best tools. For the more experienced paper maker, the inventive recipes in this book will stimulate your creativity. You'll learn how to incorporate herbs, petals, and even spices into paper pulp for different textures, colors, and scents. So collect your favorite herbs and plants, and create cards, books, and even scrapbook pages, fresh from your garden. (Martingale & Company, 96 pages)

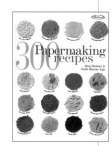

Creative Card Swap Ideas

Get inspired to join the world of online card swaps with helpful suggestions and innovative card designs

By Susan Neal

It doesn't matter what I'm in the middle of during the day—I stop when the mail arrives! It started years ago when I got my first pen pal, and the sweet anticipation hasn't dimmed over the years. No matter how many bills, ads, and junk mailers seem to take over my mailbox, I'm thrilled whenever I spot a little handwritten envelope and open it immediately. And I've found a way to keep a steady stream of "fun" mail coming to my mailbox—online swaps!

Online or Web swaps are almost exactly like traditional card swaps where members exchange handmade cards.
The difference is that an online swap is organized on the Web within rubber stamping communities. Instead of swapping with neighbors and friends, you might end up in a swap with stampers from six different states or countries. I've swapped cards with stampers from Australia, England, Finland, Germany, South Africa, Canada, and the United States.

Even if you've never attempted to start an online swap, you'll be ready to start within minutes. Review these online swap tips, browse through our gallery of creative card designs, and start stamping for impressive results any swap member will appreciate.

WHERE TO FIND RUBBER STAMPING COMMUNITIES

Perform a simple search on the Web using a search engine and keywords such as "rubber stamping", "communities", and "swaps." Yahoo! has listings for hundreds of rubber stamping groups and MSN has over 75 such groups. You might also look for communities or message boards affiliated with Web sites or magazines, such as *www.rubberstampinglinks.com.*

ONLINE SWAP HOSTING TIPS

Once you find a community that fits your style and needs, ask the moderator for permission to host a swap. Then:

- Determine the number of group members. I recommend 12 or fewer members.

- Pick a theme. You might try a holiday, color scheme, or design technique.

- Learn mailing terms so you can quickly communicate swap details with group members. A few basic terms include SAML (self-addressed mailing label), SASE (self-addressed stamped envelope), and SAE (self-addressed envelope).

- Establish a deadline.

- Extend an invitation that includes all the necessary info, including the number of cards participants need to make. Most swaps are one card per person in the group, including an extra card for the hostess as a thank you for coordinating the swap.

- Send a reminder to participants as the deadline approaches.

- Collect the submissions and distribute the cards.

Online Swap Participation tips

- Do your best! No one expects prize-winning cards, but neatness and thoughtfulness will be appreciated.

- Be reliable and 100% committed. Submit your cards by the swap deadline.

- Label the back of your cards with your name and e-mail address, so recipients can contact you if they have questions. Include a small printed page that lists the materials you used.

- Mail your cards in a plastic bag inserted in a bubble mailer to protect them from water and other damage.

- Include a return address label and postage.

- Write the swap name on the outside of your package to assist the hostess in sorting.

Join your friends - or make new friends- with a local swap group

I remember buying my first rubber stamp about 12 years ago. I made stationery, embossed images, and decorated some invitations, but that's about it. I felt like I'd reached a dead end and wasn't really satisfied with how I'd used my stamps.

Then a friend invited me to join a card swap four and a half years ago. It was a new concept to me, getting together monthly with other stampers to swap card ideas, but I soon learned card swaps are very popular all over the U.S. and even in other countries.

I remember the first card I made to swap. Although it was elementary by my standards today, I was so excited to make a real card. It was even more fun to receive the other cards (or "swaps") from the members in my group, and to realize the potential of card making beyond my own ideas.

My rubber stamp collection has grown dramatically over the last four years and so has my understanding of this hobby and art form. But my real enjoyment has come from sharing my hobby with others.

In a swap group you'll find the inspiration, ideas, and knowledge you need to fully enjoy your new hobby. You'll also enjoy new friendships and possibly a little break every month. My swap group is the only extracurricular activity I do, and despite being tempted to drop it a few times due to my busy schedule, I have held on. I just can't drop it—it's the one thing I do just for me!

Participating in swaps will also enhance your skills. Stamping for other people challenges and refines your abilities. In the long run, you'll improve your stamping and artistic skills, like choice of color, composition, and technique, and have fun doing it. And you'll save money on cards as well, since store-bought cards range in price from $2–$8! That's the average price of a stamp, which can be used over and over again.

HOW TO START A LOCAL SWAP GROUP

Make a list of people you know who already stamp or may have some inclination to stamp. You may be starting with a small group, but it will grow, I assure you. If you can't find any stampers, then introduce your hobby to some friends and get started that way.

CREATE AN INVITATION—STAMP IT!

Indicate how many members your group will have. I would recommend 12 or fewer. This number works well with pre-packaged materials that often come in sixes or twelves. Also, doing more than 12 cards can be a chore, and this is supposed to be fun!

After you've received your replies you can then give instructions for how many cards to make and where you're meeting for the first time.

MEETING OPTIONS

Meet in a restaurant, a park, or in member's homes, or don't meet at all, just swap. (Meeting is much more fun, though!)

Meet to swap, but you can also take turns teaching new techniques or doing a make-and-take.

Swap cards with no restrictions, or create themes for the month, like birthdays, weddings, babies, Christmas, etc.

Swap cards or anything you can stamp: scrapbook pages, bookmarks, candles, or anything else you can think of!

One Card, Three Recipients

Create sophisticated cards with a trendy Asian stamp, patterned papers, and hot techniques.

Asian Love Symbols

Designer: Sande Krieger

Mosaic Squares

SUPPLIES

Rubber stamp: (Asian Love) *Ducks in a Row*

Dye ink: (Cappuccino Delight) Kaleidacolor, *Tsukineko*; (Vermillion Lacquer) Nick Bantock, *Ranger Industries*

Cardstock: (cream, black)

Patterned paper: (California Poppies) *Scenic Route Paper Company*

Specialty paper: (Black handmade) Jennifer's Handmade Paper, *Sakar*

Fasteners: (red brads) *Making Memories*

Dimensional glaze: Diamond Glaze, *JudiKins*

Adhesive

Tools: (ColorToolBox Stylus Handle & Blender Tip), ColorBox, *Clearsnap*; scissors, paintbrush, ruler

Finished size: 5" x 7"

INSTRUCTIONS

1 Make card from black cardstock.

2 Cut California Poppies paper slightly smaller than card front; cut Black textured paper slightly smaller than California Poppies. Adhere papers to card.

3 Cut cream cardstock to 4" x 6". Stamp Asian Love with Vermillion Lacquer.

4 Brush Cappuccino Delight over stamped cardstock with blender tool.

5 Cut stamped cardstock into 2" squares; paint with dimensional glaze.

6 Adhere squares to card. Attach brads to bottom of card.

Burnished Metal

SUPPLIES

Rubber stamp: (Asian Love) *Ducks in a Row*

Solvent ink: (Jet Black) StazOn, *Tsukineko*

Cardstock: (Raven) *Bazzill Basics Paper;* (black)

Patterned paper: (Stage Diamonds) *Scenic Route Paper Company*

Accents: (Light Copper metal sheet) ArtEmboss, *American Art Clay Co.;* (safety pin) *Li'l Davis Designs*

Fasteners: (silver brads) *Creative Impressions*

Fibers: (black gingham ribbon) *Offray;* (black grosgrain ribbon) *May Arts*

Adhesive

Tools: scissors, lighter, tweezers, hole punch, ruler

Finished size: 5" x 7"

INSTRUCTIONS

❶ Make card from black cardstock.

❷ Cut Stage Diamonds paper slightly smaller than card front; adhere.

❸ Cut Raven cardstock to 5¾" x 4" and adhere to card.

❹ Cut metal sheet slightly smaller than Raven. Stamp Asian Love on metal.

❺ Hold metal sheet with tweezers; hold lighter under metal, dragging flame across sheet to burnish. Let cool.

❻ Punch hole in bottom center of metal; attach ribbons with safety pin.

❼ Attach brads to metal; adhere to card.

Unique Clay

SUPPLIES

Rubber stamps: (Asian Love) *Ducks in a Row;* (Background Script) *Limited Edition Rubberstamps*

Solvent ink: (Jet Black) StazOn, *Tsukineko*

Pigment ink: (Gold) Anna Griffin, All Night Media, *Plaid*

Cardstock: (Raven) *Bazzill Basics Paper*

Patterned paper: (Sun Spot) *Scenic Route Paper Company*

Specialty paper: (Black handmade) Jennifer's Handmade Paper, *Sakar*

Fasteners: (small copper brads) *American Label & Tag Co.;* (large copper brads) *Creative Impressions*

Polymer clay: (Terra Cotta) Premo! Sculpey, *Polyform Products*

Adhesive

Tools: (shape template) Shapelets, *Polyform Products;* clay slicing blade, acrylic roller, oven, baking sheet, scissors, eyelet-setting tools

Other: index cards

Finished size: 4" x 8"

CLAY ACCENT

❶ Roll out clay to ⅛" thickness on index cards.

❷ Stamp Background Script with Gold; let dry. Stamp Asian Love with Jet Black over script.

❸ Cut top and bottom edges of clay using template and slicing blade.

❹ Punch three holes in one side of clay with eyelet-setting tool.

❺ Bake clay according to manufacturer's instructions.

❻ Attach small brads to clay accent; mat with Black handmade paper.

CARD

❶ Make card from Raven cardstock.

❷ Cut Sun Spot paper slightly smaller than card front.

❸ Adhere clay accent to card.

❹ Attach large brads in corners of card.

Make a statement with three classic looks that will suit anyone on your Valentine's Day list.

L-O-V-E

Designer: Linda Beeson

Floral Elegance

SUPPLIES

Rubber stamps: (Collage Lower & Numbers) *My Sentiments Exactly*

Chalk ink: (Deep Green, Yellow Citrus) ColorBox, *Clearsnap*

Cardstock: (moss green, white)

Patterned paper: (Red floral, Cream floral) *Daisy D's*

Specialty paper: (Green textured) *Hero Arts*

Accents: (white photo corners, heart locket charm)

Fibers: (green satin ribbon)

Adhesive

Tools: scissors, 1" square punch

Finished size: 4¼" x 5½"

PREPARE & STAMP

1 Make card from moss green cardstock.

2 Cut Cream floral paper slightly smaller than card front. Ink edges with Yellow Citrus.

3 Ink photo corners with Deep Green; attach to corners of Cream floral. Adhere to card.

4 Stamp "love" on white with Deep Green. Punch out each letter with square punch.

FINISH

1 Adhere squares to Green textured paper. Mat with Red floral and tear bottom edge.

2 Ink torn edge with Yellow Citrus.

3 Tie ribbon around love accent, tying on charm.

4 Adhere love accent to card.

Classic Black & White

SUPPLIES

Rubber stamps: (Collage Lower & Numbers) *My Sentiments Exactly*

Dye ink: (Black) Memories, *Stewart Superior Corp.*

Embossing powder: (clear)

Cardstock: (Raven, White) *Bazzill Basics Paper*

Patterned paper:
  (Black/Gray striped) *Pixie Press*

  (Black swirl, Red swirl) Heritage, *Making Memories*

Rub-ons: (Rummage White) Simply Stated Alphabets, *Making Memories*

Fibers: (black gingham ribbon)

Adhesive

Tools: scissors, 1" square punch, heat tool, hole punch, ruler

Finished size: 4¼" x 5½"

INSTRUCTIONS

1 Stamp "love" on White cardstock; emboss.

2 Punch out each letter with square punch and mat with Red swirl paper.

3 Make card from Raven cardstock.

4 Cut Black/Gray striped paper slightly smaller than card front; adhere.

5 Cut Black swirl paper to 3¾" x 3½"; tear top edge. Ink all edges.

6 Adhere letters to black swirl; punch two holes in left-hand edge and add ribbon.

7 Adhere Black swirl to card. Spell out "you & me" with rub-ons.

Chalkboard Fun

SUPPLIES

Rubber stamps:
  (Collage Lower & Numbers) *My Sentiments Exactly*

  (Antique Typewriter alphabet) *EK Success*

Dye ink:
  (Black) Memories, *Stewart Superior Corp.*

  (silver)

Embossing powder: (clear)

Cardstock: (red, white, black)

Patterned paper:
  (Chalkboard) *Karen Foster Design*

  (Red swirl) *Provo Craft*

Paper accent: (tiny white tag) Cardstock Tags, *Making Memories*

Fastener: (heart eyelet)

Adhesive

Tools: scissors, eyelet-setting tools, 1" square punch, heat tool

Other: plastic wrap

Finished size: 4¼" x 5½"

INSTRUCTIONS

1 Stamp "love" on white cardstock with Black; emboss.

2 Punch out each letter with square punch and mat with Red swirl paper.

3 Make card from red cardstock.

4 Cut black cardstock slightly smaller than card front. Ink cardstock with silver using wadded plastic wrap.

5 Cut Chalkboard paper slightly smaller than black cardstock. Adhere both to card.

6 Adhere letters to card.

7 Stamp "YOU" on tag with Black; attach to card with eyelet.

Surprise your sweetheart, a good friend, or a dear child with this Valentine that's a card and a gift in one!

Valentine Hearts

Designer: Vickie Clontz

Amour

SUPPLIES

Rubber stamps: (Kiss, Amour) *Stampabilities*; (Old French Writing) *Hero Arts*; (Antique Lowercase alphabet) *Duncan*

Dye ink: (Black) *Stampabilities*

Chalk ink: (Blush Rose, Rose Coral, Pink Pastel) ColorBox, *Clearsnap*

Cardstock: (dark pink, dark purple, cream)

Specialty paper: (uncoated parchment)

Fibers: (pink, purple) Fiber Accents, *AIC*

Reinforcement labels: *Avery Dennison*

Adhesive: (glue) Aleene's Memory Glue, *Duncan*

Tools: (Ripple decorative-edge scissors) Paper Edgers, *Fiskars*; craft knife, ruler, ¼" hole punch, sponge paintbrush

Other: pencil

Finished size: 5½" x 6½"

MAKE CARD

❶ Fold dark pink cardstock in half and transfer large heart pattern, placing edge of heart at fold in cardstock. Cut out card.

❷ Cut two 2¾" horizontal slits, 1" apart, in center of card back (for inserting bookmark).

DECORATE CARD

❶ Transfer small heart pattern to dark purple cardstock and cut out with decorative-edge scissors.

❷ Tear slightly smaller heart from parchment paper.

❸ Stamp Old French Writing on card with Black.

❹ Stamp Kiss on parchment heart with Blush Rose, Rose Coral, and Pink Pastel.

❺ Stamp Amour inside card between slits with Black.

❻ Stamp Amour on parchment heart with Black.

❼ Adhere hearts to front of card.

MAKE BOOKMARK

❶ Cut 2½" x 6½" dark pink bookmark. Punch hole in top.

❷ Sponge reinforcement label with Blush Rose; attach to hole in bookmark.

❸ Stamp Old French Writing on bookmark with Black.

❹ Stamp "you hold a special place in my heart" on cream rectangle with Black. Stamp Kiss around sentiment with Blush Rose, Rose Coral, and Pink Pastel; tear edges.

❺ Cut rectangle from dark purple cardstock with decorative-edge scissors; adhere both rectangles to bookmark.

❻ Tie fibers through hole; slide bookmark through slits inside card.

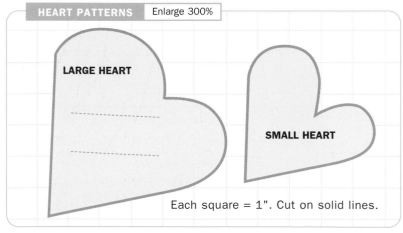

HEART PATTERNS | Enlarge 300%

LARGE HEART

SMALL HEART

Each square = 1". Cut on solid lines.

Bee Happy!

SUPPLIES

Rubber stamps:
(sun, bee, dragonfly, boy, girl, Bee happy! from Design set) *Nicole Industries*

(Antique Lowercase alphabet) *Duncan*

Chalk ink: (Wisteria, Blush Rose) ColorBox, *Clearsnap*

Dye ink: (Black) *Stampabilities*

Cardstock: (light pink, medium purple, cream)

Fibers: (pink, purple) Fiber Accents, *AIC*

Paper accent: (small white tag)

Accent: (dried pressed flower)

Reinforcement labels: *Avery Dennison*

Adhesive: (glue) Aleene's Memory Glue, *Duncan*

Tools: (Ripple decorative-edge scissors) Paper Edgers, *Fiskars*; craft knife, ruler, ¼" hole punch, sponge paintbrush

Other: pencil

Finished size: 5½" x 6½"

MAKE CARD

Repeat "Make Card" from Amour, substituting light pink cardstock.

DECORATE CARD

① Transfer small heart pattern to medium purple cardstock and cut out using decorative-edge scissors.

② Tear cream cardstock heart slightly smaller than purple heart.

③ Stamp images on card front with Wisteria.

④ Stamp Bee happy! inside card between slits; and bee, sun, boy, and girl in corners of slits with Wisteria.

⑤ Stamp girl and boy on cream heart with Wisteria; adhere flower between boy and girl.

⑥ Sponge Wisteria and Blush Rose onto tag; stamp Bee happy! in center and bees in corners with Black.

⑦ Tie fibers on tag and adhere tag below boy and girl.

⑧ Adhere hearts to card front.

MAKE BOOKMARK

① Repeat step 1 of "Make Bookmark" from Amour, substituting light pink cardstock for bookmark.

② Sponge reinforcement label with Blush Rose; attach to hole in top of bookmark.

③ Stamp Bee happy!, boy, girl, sun, bee, and dragonfly on bookmark with Wisteria.

④ Stamp "you hold a special place in my heart" on cream with Black; tear edges and mat with medium purple. Trim with decorative-edge scissors.

⑤ Adhere sentiment rectangle to bookmark; tie fibers through top.

⑥ Slide bookmark through slits inside card.

Laugh, Trust, Friend

SUPPLIES

Rubber stamps:
(Pixie Friendship set) *Duncan*

(Fresh Flowers) *Stampabilities*

(Floral Background) *Savvy Stamps*

(Antique Lowercase alphabet) *Duncan*

Dye ink: (Black) *Stampabilities*; (Magenta, Purple from Spectrum) Kaleidacolor, *Tsukineko*

Cardstock: (medium purple, lavender)

Specialty paper: (magenta mulberry)

Accents: (Roses buttons) Dress It Up, *Jesse James Button Co.*

Fibers: (pink, purple) Fiber Accents, *AIC*

Color medium: (colored pencils)

Reinforcement labels: *Avery Dennison*

Color media: (desired shades colored pencils)

Adhesive: (Memory Glue, Glass & Bead Adhesive) Aleene's, *Duncan*

Tools: (Ripple decorative-edge scissors) Paper Edgers, *Fiskars*; (sponges) Tulip, *Duncan*; craft knife, ruler, paintbrush, ¼" hole punch

Other: pencil

Finished size: 5½" x 6½"

MAKE CARD

Repeat "Make Card" from Amour, substituting medium purple cardstock.

DECORATE CARD

① Transfer small heart pattern onto mulberry paper; tear out. *Note: Outline heart with wet paintbrush to make tearing easier.*

② Stamp Floral Background on card front with Black.

③ Sponge edges of card with Magenta and Purple.

④ Adhere mulberry heart to card front.

⑤ Stamp Fresh Flowers and Pixie Friendship words on lavender cardstock with Black. Cut out stamped flowers; tear around stamped words.

⑥ Color flowers with colored pencils.

⑦ Adhere stamped images to mulberry heart with glue and buttons with glass adhesive.

⑧ Stamp "You are my friend" between slits inside card with Black.

MAKE BOOKMARK

① Repeat step 1 of "Make Bookmark" from Amour, substituting medium purple cardstock for bookmark.

② Sponge Magenta and Purple ink on reinforcement label; attach to hole in bookmark top.

③ Stamp Floral Background on bookmark with Black; sponge edges with Magenta and Purple.

④ Stamp same sentiment from "Make Bookmark" from Amour, substituting lavender cardstock for cream.

⑤ Trim stamped lavender cardstock with decorative-edge scissors; mat with torn mulberry paper.

⑥ Adhere sentiment rectangle to bookmark; tie fibers through top.

⑦ Slide bookmark through slits inside card.

COMPOSITION BOOKS:
WHAT YOU DIDN'T LEARN IN SCHOOL

Here's an assignment you'll enjoy—turn an ordinary composition book into a fun journal, record keeper, or inspirational treasure. Add interest to an old, used book or start something new.

BIRTHDAYS
DESIGNER: ERIN TENNEY

SUPPLIES

Cardstock: Petunia, Walnut, *Bazzill Basics Paper*

Dotted paper: Eye Candy Rhinestone; Collection III, *KI Memories*

Striped paper: Eye Candy Runway; Collection III, *KI Memories*

Composition book

Alphabet stamps: Fun Type, *Delta Rubber Stampede*

Brown dye ink: Walnut Stain; Distress Ink, *Ranger Industries*

Circle brad: *Making Memories*

Letters:

Eyelet Alphabet: *Making Memories*

Scrap Essentials: *JoAnn Stores*

Bubble Type: Li'l Trinkets and Treasures, *Li'l Davis Designs*

Stencil: It's My Type, *Colorbök*

Black tile: Paper Bliss, *Westrim Crafts*

Adhesive: Mono Multi Liquid, *Tombow*

White thread: *Coats & Clark*

Brown gingham ribbon: *Offray*

Other: sewing machine, double-sided tape, adhesive tape, metal adhesive

Finished size: 9¾" x 7½"

PAPER PIECES

❶ Cut striped paper and dotted paper to fit cover front.

❷ For cover front and divider pages, cut 13 strips brown or pink cardstock 2" wide.

❸ For spine and back cover, cut brown cardstock 9¾" x 8¾".

❹ Use inside cover as template and cut 12 brown or pink cardstock dividers.

COVER

Refer to photo for placement.

❶ To prepare pieces for sewing, tape striped and dotted papers together. *Note: Use only enough tape to keep papers in place. If you sew over a lot of tape, your needle will get sticky.*

❷ Crumple, smooth, and ink pink cardstock strip. Adhere over seam with double-sided tape and zigzag-stitch to paper.

❸ Slightly overlap and adhere brown cardstock to left of front cover. Zigzag-stitch over seam.

❹ Adhere cover to book and trim to fit.

❺ Line inside covers with patterned paper of your choice; ink cover edges.

❻ Spell "Birthdays" with assorted letters.

DIVIDERS

❶ Count every 10–12 pages and adhere a ribbon loop tab for each month.

❷ Crumple, smooth, and ink cardstock strips. Adhere strips to cardstock dividers near ribbon loops and zigzag-stitch in place. Stamp month on strips.

❸ Adhere cardstock dividers over ribbon looped pages.

Create a divider page for each month

EXPECTING YOU

DESIGNER:
HEATHER D. WHITE

SUPPLIES

All supplies from Pebbles Inc. unless otherwise noted.

Composition book: Black and White Marble, *American Scholar*

Patterned paper:
   Licorice Mini Gingham
   Licorice Stripes
   Numbers: Type Count, *Rusty Pickle*

Black and white stickers:
   Photo: Baby Classic; Real Life Snapshots
   Alphabet: Ransom, Real Life Snapshots
   Alphabet label: ABC's; Real Life Labels

Adhesive dots: 3D-Dots, *EK Success*

Double-sided tape: *3M*

Other: black chalk, wedge sponge, sandpaper, craft knife

Finished size: 9¾" x 7½"

INSTRUCTIONS

Leave spine binding undecorated. Chalk torn edges as desired.

❶ Cut gingham paper for front and striped paper for back cover; adhere and trim. Sand surface and edges.

❷ Tear "9" for upper left corner and strip for bottom of cover from number paper. Sand paper surfaces and edges, and adhere pieces to cover (see photo).

❸ Sand photo sticker edges. Adhere three small photo stickers to paper strip. Mat large photo sticker with number paper and sand edges. Adhere to cover with adhesive dots. *Note: For correct placement, lay out photos and stickers before adhering to cover.*

❹ Spell "EXPECTING" with alphabet stickers. Spell "MONTHS" and "YOU" with label stickers.

TIPS FROM HEATHER

▪ To achieve a more interesting look, tear paper edges in varying widths.

▪ Sand paper from the edges toward the center. This will make the wider edges curl, creating a shabby look that adds character to the project. Try sanding in circles and up and down to create a more natural look.

▪ Change the paper to more traditional boy and girl colors for a different look. The trendy black and white look works for either a boy or girl, and is great if you don't know the baby's gender.

VARIATIONS

▪ Add photos, footprints, and other memorabilia after your baby is born.

▪ Keep a pet journal with photos of your pets, important documents, mini envelopes with hair clippings, and ID tags.

▪ Teachers can keep a class journal to remember each year of teaching.

WEIGHT LOSS JOURNAL

Keep your weight loss notes and motivational ideas in this creative journal.

DESIGNER:
MELISSA FORTENBERRY

SUPPLIES

Cardstock: Black, Chili, Peach, *Bazzill Basics Paper*

Crinkled gray paper: Rebecca Sower Paper, *EK Success*

Black ribbed paper: Metropolis Lined Embossed, *Evergreen-Packaging*

Composition notebook: Mead Square Deal, *Meadwestvaco*

Black fibers: Adornments, *EK Success*

Silver pen: *Sanford*

Alphabet stamps: Pixie Antique, PSX, *Duncan Enterprises*

Black pigment ink: VersaColor, *Tsukineko*

Double-sided tape: Scotch, *3M*

Other: square silver eyelet, dark peach chalk, chalk applicator, eyelet-setting tools, craft knife

Finished size: 9¾" x 7½"

INSTRUCTIONS

❶ Align gray paper with binding and adhere to front, back, and inside covers. Trim edges with craft knife.

❷ Cut pattern pieces. Adhere to cover, leaving opening for bookmark (see photo). Chalk body edges. Draw clothing details with pen.

❸ Cut gray bookmark and mat with black cardstock. Stamp phrase. Set eyelet and tie on fibers. Slide in opening (see photo).

MELISSA'S TIPS

▪ Write motivational quotes on the journal's inside cover.

▪ Create a measurement chart with a word processor and adhere to the inside back cover.

▪ Include beneficial recipes that you have collected.

▪ Write a menu for each week.

▪ Create a visual progress report by adding photos of you getting thinner.

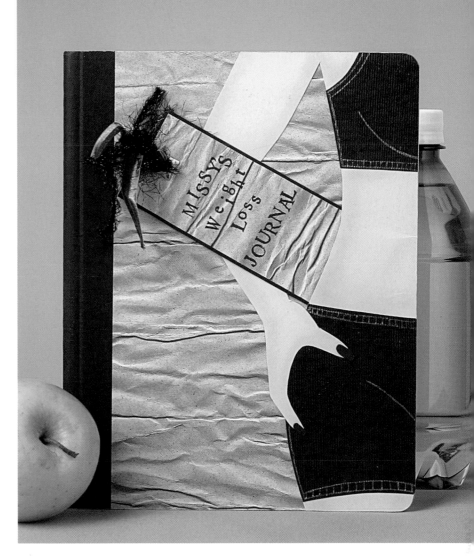

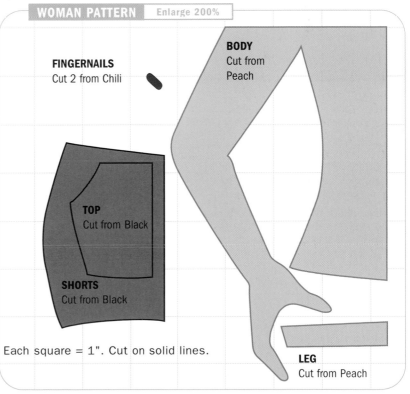

WOMAN PATTERN   Enlarge 200%

FINGERNAILS
Cut 2 from Chili

BODY
Cut from Peach

TOP
Cut from Black

SHORTS
Cut from Black

LEG
Cut from Peach

Each square = 1". Cut on solid lines.

HOPES & DREAMS JOURNAL
DESIGNER: NICHOLE HEADY

SUPPLIES

All supplies from Stampin' Up! unless otherwise noted.

Cardstock: Blush Blossom, Pale Plum; Soft Subtles

Confetti White cardstock

Composition book

Transparency film: Window Sheet

Flower parts stamp set: Tropical Blossoms

Alphabet stamp set: Classic

Pigment ink: Mauve Mist, Pale Plum, Pretty in Pink; Soft Subtles

Black solvent ink: StazOn, *Tsukineko*

Fonts:
    Palace Script, www.fonts.com

    Schindler Small Caps, www.searchfreefonts.com

Small corner punch: Corner Rounder

Hole punches: ¼", ⅛", *Fiskars*

White organdy ribbon

Clear shrink plastic: PolyShrink, *Lucky Squirrel*

Clear adhesive dots: Zots, *Therm O Web*

Other: white feather, craft knife, oven or heat tool, computer and printer

Finished size: 9¾" x 7½"

FRONT COVER

① Cut 2" x 3" window in front cover. Cut two pieces Blush Blossom cardstock, for front cover and one for back cover. Cut windows from front pieces.

② Cut two 3" x 4" window panes from transparency film. Adhere one pane over window on inside of front cover. Close book.

③ Place feather in window and adhere other clear pane over window. *Note: The feather will be sandwiched between the two panes.*

④ Adhere equal lengths of ribbon to outside front and back covers for tie closure. Adhere back cover piece over ribbons.

⑤ Adhere Blush Blossom cardstock to front and inside front cover; trim to fit. Cut 2" x 3" window from Pale Plum cardstock. Tear around edges to create frame and adhere around window.

⑥ Stamp "hopes & dreams" on shrink plastic and trim. Punch to round corners. Heat to shrink, following manufacturer's instructions. Adhere below window.

FIRST PAGE

① Adhere white cardstock to first page. Stamp flowers with mauve, pink, and plum inks. Punch flower centers from cardstock scraps with ¼" and ⅛" hole punches. Adhere centers to flowers.

② Print quotation on plum cardstock, using script for "Hope" and the author's signature and small caps for the text. Cut into strips and adhere to page.

Quotation:

"Hope is the thing with feathers
That perches in the soul
And sings the tune without the words."
—Emily Dickinson

First page

Bonus Idea

MATCHING PEN

You can make a quick, inexpensive, coordinating pen for this pretty journal. Just cut a piece of paper to the same length as the barrel of a clear pen and about 3/4" wide. Use coordinating patterned paper or stamp your own design. Add initials or a name for a personal touch! Unscrew the tip of the pen, roll the paper around the ink cartridge, and reinsert the tip.

QUOTES & RANDOM ADVICE

DESIGNER: LINDA BEESON

SUPPLIES

Pastel striped paper: Groovy Pants; Retrospect, *SEI*

Pastel polka dot paper: Groovy Mini Dots; Retrospect, *SEI*

Little composition book: Marble Memo; Mead Square Deal, *Meadwestvaco*

Accents:
  Oval metal frame: Antique Silver; Li'l Trinkets and Treasures, *Li'l Davis Designs*

  Alphabet rub-ons: Providence, *Making Memories*

  "Wisdom" embossed sticker: Black Label Words; Life's Journey, *K&Company*

  Pink polka dot ribbon: *Offray*

Oval word pebble

Miscellaneous ribbons

Other: sewing machine, white thread, craft knife

Finished size: 4½" x 3¼"

INSTRUCTIONS

❶ Cut dot paper 4½" x 1¾" for spine. Adhere lengths of miscellaneous ribbons across paper (see photo).

❷ Cut two pieces of striped paper for covers. Lightly adhere dot paper spine between striped paper covers. *Note: See if cover fits book properly and adjust as necessary before sewing. Zigzag-stitch where papers meet and trim excess. Adhere to book.*

❸ Spell "& random advice" with rub-ons and apply "Wisdom" sticker. Fold 18" length ribbon in half for bookmark and adhere to cover with framed word pebble.

Resolutions Journal

Designer: Wendy Sue Anderson

SUPPLIES

Rubber stamps: *Making Memories* (Rummage alphabet, date)

Foam stamps: *Making Memories* (Philadelphia alphabet, Corner, Misunderstood numbers)

Dye ink: Sand, Memories, *Stewart Superior Corp.*

Acrylic paint: Evergreen, *Making Memories*

Patterned paper: Sand Flower, *KI Memories*

Brads: Willow, *Lasting Impressions for Paper*

Other: twill ribbon, scissors, adhesive, cardstock (light green, cream)

Finished size: 9½" x 5½"

INSTRUCTIONS

❶ Cut 14 pieces of cream cardstock 9½" x 5½"; ink edges with Sand.

❷ Cover one piece of cream cardstock with light green cardstock. Adhere slightly smaller patterned paper to light green cardstock to create cover.

❸ Stamp "RESOLUTIONS" on cover with Philadelphia alphabet and Evergreen. Stamp year with Misunderstood numbers and Corner with Evergreen.

❹ Stamp "GOALS," "HOPES," "PROGRESS," and "WORK" with Rummage on twill ribbon with Sand; attach to cover with brads.

❺ Stamp months with date stamp on cream cardstock with Sand; cut out to create tabs. Ink edges and adhere one to each page of cream cardstock.

❻ Bind pages together at local copy center.

Gratitude Journal

Designer: Linda Beeson

SUPPLIES

Rubber stamps: *American Art Stamp* (Blessings); *Postmodern Design* (key, ruler); *A Stamp in the Hand Co.* (pen nibs); *Peddler's Pack* (Thank You); *PSX* (alphabet); *Art Impressions* (script); *A Country Welcome* (ABC, Postage Cancellations)

Chalk ink: ColorBox Fluid Chalk, *Clearsnap* (Chestnut Roan); Fresco, *Gary M. Burlin* (Tuscan Earth)

Other: journal, black ink, adhesive, ribbon, buttons, eyelets, eyelet-setting tools, white printer paper, brown handmade paper, black card-stock, scissors, ruler

Finished size: 5¾" x 8½"

ASSEMBLE JOURNAL

❶ Randomly stamp 11" x 17" printer paper with all stamps using Chestnut Roan, Tuscan Earth, and black ink.

❷ Randomly smear ink pads on stamped paper.

❸ Adhere paper to journal cover, making sure to crease paper at binding.

❹ Trim excess paper, leaving ¾" border. Set excess paper aside. Fold border and adhere to inside back and cover of journal.

❺ Cut 2½" x 8½" strip of handmade paper. Adhere around journal binding.

EMBELLISH JOURNAL

❶ Stamp Blessings with black ink on excess printing paper. Set eyelets through bottom corners; thread ribbon through eyelets and mat with handmade paper. Adhere to journal front.

❷ Stamp "gratitude" on excess printer paper. Mat with handmade paper and black cardstock; adhere to journal front.

MAKE PAGE MARKER

❶ Fold 24" ribbon in half.

❷ Thread folded ribbon through large button, leaving 1" loop.

❸ Tie two smaller buttons on loose ends of ribbon; secure with knot.

Count Your Blessings

Designer: Janelle Clark

SUPPLIES

Rubber stamps: *Hero Arts* (Rose Leaf); *Close To My Heart* (alphabet)

Dye ink: Adirondack, *Ranger Industries* (Cabin Fever); Vivid!, *Clearsnap* (Coffee Bean)

Journal: *Canson*

Other: adhesive, handmade paper, brown cardstock

Finished size: 5½" x 8½"

INSTRUCTIONS

❶ Stamp Rose Leaf on handmade paper with Cabin Fever.

❷ Stamp "count your blessings" with Coffee Bean.

❸ Trim around image; tear top and bottom.

❹ Mat image with brown cardsotck; adhere to journal front.

Flower Garden Journal

Designer: Diane Anthony

SUPPLIES

Rubber stamps: *Stampin' Up!* (Watercolor Garden set); *Stamps by Judith* (Flowers; Grater Bouquet; Stubby Stamp, Dots); *Close To My Heart* (Calendar, Flower Medley background)

Watermark ink: VersaMark, *Tsukineko*

Dye ink: Exclusive Ink, *Close To My Heart* (New England Ivy, Oak Brown, Olive, Desert Sand); *Stampin' Up!* (Summer Sun)

Cardstock: *Close To My Heart* (White, Green, Yellow, Naturals)

Vellum: *Close To My Heart*

5 brown mini buttons: *Magic Scraps*

6" x 6" page protectors: *Close To My Heart*

Font: Little Ladybug, *Two Peas in a Bucket*

Eyelets: *Making Memories*

Markers: Many Marvelous Markers, *Stampin' Up!*

Other: black ink, black pen, jute, sponge, tape, scissors, cream thread, sewing machine, adhesive, computer and printer, eyelet-setting tools

Finished sizes:
  Journal: 7½" x 6½"
  Layouts: 6" x 6"

JOURNAL

❶ Cut 5½" x 6⅜" rectangle from Natural cardstock. Stamp Flower Medley background with Desert Sand. Tear short edges.

❷ Score line 1¾" in from each side and every ½" in between; accordion-fold.

❸ Punch two holes through folded layers using page protector as guide. Set eyelets on front and back of binding.

❹ Print title on medium Natural cardstock. Cut two 6" squares from lightest shade of Natural cardstock; cut 2¼" x 6" rectangle of dark Natural cardstock and title to 1¾" x 5½ rectangle.

❺ Adhere small rectangle in center of large rectangle; adhere large rectangle to left edge of one cardstock square. Straight-stitch around edges of small rectangle; zigzag stitch along edge of large rectangle.

❻ Stamp Grater Bouquet with black and color with markers. Sew mini brown buttons to daisy centers.

❼ Place both squares in page protectors for front and back covers. Thread jute through back side of binding, pages, front cover, and front side of binding and tie bow.

RUDBICKEA PAGES

❶ Cut two 6" squares of Natural cardstock for spread. Stamp three and a half daisies with Summer Sun on White cardstock. Stamp flower center with Oak Brown on three daisies; cut out flowers.

❷ Tear Yellow cardstock and trim Green cardstock. Adhere to left and right sides of spread.

❸ Make Green cardstock tag. Set eyelet through half daisy at top of tag.

Inside

4. Write journaling and title of page with black pen and accent with brown marker on Natural cardstock; tear edges.

5. Adhere journaling to tag, and tag to right page of spread.

6. Set eyelets at top corners of title; adhere to top of left page of spread. Adhere photo of flowers below title.

7. Stamp leaves and stems with New England Ivy on Green borders; adhere flowers to tops of stems.

CALENDAR PAGES

1. Stamp Calendar with black on vellum; let dry.

2. Print journaling and month title on vellum; let dry.

3. Cut Natural cardstock in half; tear long edge. Lay torn edge over bottom straight edge of second rectangle and secure both to work surface.

4. Stamp wildflower stems along top of torn edge. *Note: Stamped image border will be wavy.* Remove torn edge; stamp wildflowers on stems using markers to ink stamps. Cut stamped page into two 6" squares for spread.

5. Cut out journaling and calendar; tear bottom edge of each. Tear edges around month title.

6. Attach month title to calendar and stamped cardstock with eyelets; repeat for journaling on right page to complete spread.

7. Number days of month and add year to calendar with black pen. Stamp flowers on journaling and stamp corresponding flowers on calendar.

Inside

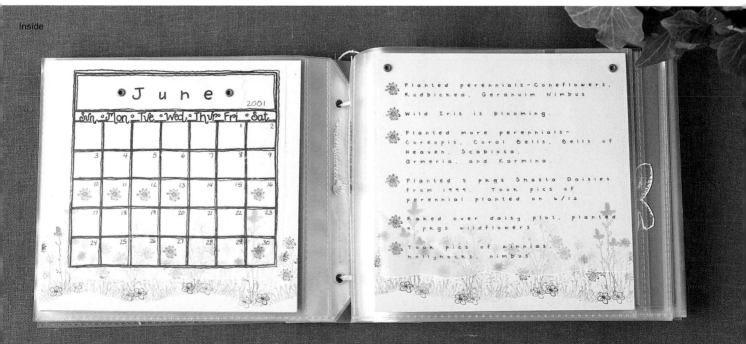

My Favorite Recipes Album

Designer: Ticee Moore

SUPPLIES

Patterned paper: (Tangerine Posie/Tangerine Weave) Powder Room, *Chatterbox*

Photo flip album

Paper accents: (Ivory Vinca flowers) Jolee's By You, *EK Success*

Stickers: (Flea Market alphabet) Sonnets, *Creative Imaginations*

Adhesive: clear craft glue

Tools: scissors

Finished size: 6¼" x 5¼"

INSTRUCTIONS

❶ Remove cover from album, if possible.

❷ Cut Tangerine Posie paper slightly larger than cover. Adhere paper to front, cut an X through window, and wrap paper back to expose window. Wrap and adhere paper around edges, as though wrapping a gift.

❸ Cut another piece of Tangerine Posie slightly smaller than backside of cover and adhere, hiding paper edges. *Note: Tangerine Weave side of paper will show through window.* Embellish window with flowers and stickers (see photo). *Note: If your photo flip album has no window, adhere square of Tangerine Weave to cover to create focal point.*

❹ Pierce holes through paper and replace cover on stand.

Bonus Idea

Choose paper and accents to match your kitchen.

Mom's Recipes

Designer: Sande Krieger

SUPPLIES

Rubber stamp: (Pear) *Delta Rubber Stampede*; (Old French Writing, Tiny Friendship alphabet) *Hero Arts*

Dye ink: (Vermillion Lacquer, Chartreuse Leaf) Nick Bantock, *Ranger Industries*

Cardstock: (Leapfrog) *Bazzill Basics Paper*; (white textured)

Spiral-bound notebook: *Rusty Pickle*

Paint: (Mayan Gold, Solar Bronze, Marigold, Fandango Green, Warm Cinnamon) Radiant Pearls, *LuminArte*

Dimensional glaze: (Diamond Glaze) *JudiKins*

Accents: (gold charm, cork)

Fibers: (Red ribbon) *Jo-Ann Stores*; (white yarn)

Adhesive: (craft glue)

Tools: scissors, ruler, paintbrush, foam paintbrush, needlenose pliers, ¼" hole punch

Finished size: 6¼" x 6¾"

INSTRUCTIONS

❶ Remove spiral from notebook; cut two rectangles of Leapfrog, 1" larger than cover all around.

❷ Stamp Old French Writing with Vermillion Lacquer on Leapfrog; adhere to front cover, folding excess over to inside. Adhere unstamped Leapfrog to back cover, using same process. *Note: Use patterned paper or cardstock, cut slightly smaller than cover to finish inside front and back covers.*

❸ Paint Pear with assorted colors and stamp on white textured cardstock.

❹ Stamp "MOM'S RECIPES" around Pear with Chartreuse Leaf.

❺ Mat Pear with cork, tearing edges; adhere to cover.

❻ Apply dimensional glaze to both sides of front and back covers; let dry and repeat.

❼ Replace spiral in book; attach ribbon and charm with fibers.

SANDE'S TIPS

■ Practice stamping the Pear image several times on white cardstock to get a feel for the amount of paint needed.

■ Apply thin coats of dimensional glaze; tiny bubbles will smooth out as the paper dries. Use a bone folder or brayer to smooth out big bubbles or wrinkles.

"10 Things I Love About You" Mini Book

Design: Sharon Lewis

SUPPLIES

8½" x 11" paper:
  2 sheets gold decorative paper
  Dark brown cardstock
  Red cardstock
  Several sheets gray cardstock
  Several sheets oatmeal cardstock

Two 4½" x 6" pieces mat board

1 yd. sheer organza ribbon

Rubber stamps: heart locket*, script*, square*

Watermark ink pad*

Gold embossing powder*

Embossing heat tool

Brown decorative chalk*

Miscellaneous items: scissors, craft knife, self-healing mat, glue stick, cotton swab or make-up applicator

*Plaid Enterprises All Night Media Posh Impressions Open Heart stamp; PSX Designs Antique Alphabet; Stampington & Company Print Blocks stamp; Clearsnap Top Boss watermark clear embossing pad; Ranger Industries embossing powder; and Craf-T Products decorative chalk were used in the sample project.

MAKE THE BOOK

Use the craft knife and self-healing mat to cut the mat board pieces.

① Cut a window in one mat board piece large enough to display your stamped image.

② To assemble the book, cover both mat board pieces with the gold decorative paper.

③ Cut the paper out of the window in the mat board, leaving enough paper to tuck inside the window and secure on the back of the cover.

④ Trim the oatmeal and gray cardstocks in half to make 12 pieces. Fold the pieces in half and adhere them back to back to make the pages of the book.

⑤ Wrap the ribbon around the pages and adhere them inside the book with the ribbon ends facing out.

EMBELLISH THE BOOK

① Stamp the script, square, and heart locket images layered on red cardstock with watermark ink and heat emboss them with gold.

② Tear around the stamped image. Apply brown chalk to the torn edges with a cotton swab or make-up applicator. Mat with dark brown cardstock.

③ Adhere the stamped image to the inside of the front cover, showing through the window.

④ Stamp and embellish the pages of the book as desired .

Believe Mini Photo Album

Designer: Katie Hacker

SUPPLIES

Rubber stamps: Believe, Dawn Hauser, *Inkadinkado*

Other: photo album, cardstock (white, purple), scissors, pencil, adhesive, scrap paper, blue ink, blue handmade paper, flower sticker

Finished size: 5" x 6½"

PREPARE

① Remove cardboard cover from mini photo album to use as template.

② Place template on white cardstock; trace with pencil and cut out.

③ Place cardstock rectangle on piece of scrap paper.

STAMP AND DETAIL

① Stamp Believe multiple times on white cardstock with blue. *Note: Turn stamp frequently for variation. Let dry.*

② Cut purple cardstock rectangle slightly larger than flower sticker.

③ Adhere sticker to center of rectangle.

④ Tear handmade paper rectangle at least ½" wider and 1" longer than cardstock rectangle.

⑤ Adhere matted flower to center of handmade paper.

FINISH ASSEMBLY

① Adhere handmade paper rectangle to center of stamped cardstock.

② Place stamped cover inside front flap of album.

③ Replace back cover with coordinating cardstock.

Bonus Ideas

- Use this technique to make a checkbook or pocket calendar cover. They're easy to carry in a purse or backpack!

- Experiment with different color combinations and motivational sayings to personalize the album.

Christmas Through The Years Album

Designer: Julie Scattaregia

SUPPLIES

Rubber stamps: *Postmodern Design* (Large Romantic Swirl, Large Plain Jane Alphas alphabet set); *EK Success* (Antique Typewriter Alphabet); *PSX* (script); *Stampendous!* (Crackle)

Dye ink: Sepia, Archival Ink, *Ranger Industries*

Pigment ink: black, VersaColor, *Tsukineko*

Solvent ink: Jet Black, StazOn, *Tsukineko*

Patterned paper: *Daisy D's Paper Co.* (brown canvas, red floral); *Karen Foster Design* (green crackle); *7gypsies* (musical)

Tags: *Rusty Pickle*

Metal frame: *Making Memories*

Star eyelet: *Making Memories*

Metal letters: *Making Memories*

Brads: black, *Making Memories*

Photo turns: black, *7gypsies*

Ribbon: *Me & My Big Ideas* (decorative black); *Offray* (gingham, black, brown); *Anna Griffin* (light green)

Other: scissors, eyelet-setting tools, adhesive, sewing machine, white thread, metal photo corner, twine, spiral album, paintbrush, walnut ink

Finished size: 8" x 6"

1 Cut, tear, and layer patterned paper to fit album cover; stitch together.

2 Stamp script on metal letters as desired with Jet Black.

3 Stamp Crackle on tags with Sepia; brush with walnut ink and let dry. Attach metal letters "MERRY" to paper, first attaching "Y" to stamped tag.

4 Stamp "JOY," "LOVE," "believe," and "HOPE" on metal frame with alphabet stamps and Jet Black. Insert patterned paper behind frame; adhere to patterned paper block.

5 Stamp "christmas" on tag with black; adhere to patterned paper block. Adhere photo corner and turns; adhere to album cover.

6 Tie ribbons to spiral rings.

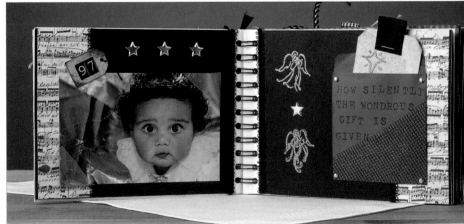

Bonus Idea

Use the album to record special Christmas memories. Add journaling and photos to the album each year.

Holiday Card List Booklet

Designer: Kathleen Paneitz

SUPPLIES

Rubber stamps: *PSX* (Evergreen Bough, Pinecone)

Watermark ink: VersaMark, *Tsukineko*

Fonts: "Fresh Fonts" CD, *Creating Keepsakes* (CK Elusive); *fonts.com* (Rage Italic)

Chalk: *Craf-T Products* (green, brown)

Rub-ons: *Craf-T Products*

Staples: red, *Making Memories*

Floss: brown, *DMC*

Other: raffia, button, bleach, cardstock (green textured, red), white linen paper, scissors, cotton swab or make-up applicator, plastic plate, paper towels, green pen

Finished size: 4¼" x 7¾"

INSTRUCTIONS

1. Make booklet cover from red cardstock.

2. Stamp Evergreen Bough on textured green cardstock with bleach.

3. Fold and adhere stamped green cardstock to red cardstock cover.

4. Print card list information on white linen paper; fold. Staple inside red cardstock.

5. Cut strip of cream cardstock to fit around booklet. Tie raffia in bow around strip.

6. Print "Holiday Card List" on cream cardstock. Stamp Pinecone; chalk. Draw green border around image.

7. Adhere threaded button to strip of green cardstock; adhere to stamped image.

8. Mat stamped image with red; adhere to cream strip and slide around booklet.

INSIDE

TAG, YOU'RE IT!

Tags are more than mere accents—
they're **FUNCTIONAL!**
Discover the exciting and practical uses
for this **HOT** item.

Thankful Album

Designer: Carolyn Peeler,
courtesy of Rusty Pickle

SUPPLIES

Tag album: *Rusty Pickle*

For cover:

Vanilla textured cardstock: *Bazzill Basics Paper*

Patterned paper: Grey Argyle, *Rusty Pickle*

Brown polka dot organdy ribbon: *May Arts*

Pigment ink: Chocolate Chip, Creamy Caramel, *Stampin' Up!*

Fonts:
GF Ordner Inverted, *www.gfonts.com*

Harting, *www.dafont.com*

Hulkbusters, *www.iconian.com*

P22 Cezanne Regular, *www.p22.com/products*

Selfish, *www.dafont.com*

Trebuchet MS, *Microsoft*

2Ps Frazzled Stencil Negative, *www.twopeasinabucket.com*

Other assorted fonts

For Art spread:

Patterned paper:
Pink Argyle, Pink Paisley, Pink Flowers, *Rusty Pickle*

Antique Dots, Antique Graph, Powder Linen, Sand Flower, *KI Memories*

Button, Script, *K&Company*

Manila tag: *Avery*

Transparency film: *Avery*

Accents:
Pink grosgrain ribbon: *May Arts*

Other assorted ribbon

Pink flower, decorative brad: *Making Memories*

Photo of someone or something you're thankful for

Fonts:
DS VTCorona Cyr, *www.abstractfonts.com*

Hannibal Lecter, *www.dafont.com*

Misproject, *www.dafont.com*

Other assorted fonts

Binding square hole punch

Finished size: 3¼" x 6¾"

ALBUM COVER

❶ Remove binding from album. Wrap cover with patterned paper.

❷ Print dictionary definitions on cardstock to create background, using Trebuchet MS font and tan ink (see "Easy Background Design"). Place cardstock in printer again and print Thanksgiving words or phrases in assorted fonts and bright colors.

❸ Tear left edge of cardstock and wrap around cover, leaving approx. 1½" of patterned paper showing on left side.

❹ Rub both shades of ink on cover for aged look. Re-punch binding holes through paper and replace cover.

EASY BACKGROUND DESIGN

Create a background of dictionary definitions in minutes:

❶ Go to Merriam-Webster's Web site: *www.m-w.com*.

❷ Look up words related to thanksgiving such as "thankful," "grateful," "gratitude," and "blessings."

❸ Copy and paste the definitions in a blank document until it is completely covered.

Create text boxes and type Thanksgiving phrases vertically and horizontally (see "Thanksgiving Phrases" for ideas). *Note: Be sure text boxes are transparent (select "No Fill" and "No Line" in the Format Text Box menu).*

THANKSGIVING PHRASES

Bountiful blessings.

Blessed beyond measure.

We give thanks.

Appreciate.

Glad.

May the Lord make us truly thankful.

Count your blessings.

Circle of Friends Flip Book

Designers: Shannon Tidwell,
Nichol Magouirk, Margie Scherschligt,
and friends

SUPPLIES

For cover tag:

Patterned paper: black polka dot, black and white checked, pink floral, pink striped, *Kangaroo & Joey*

Kraft tag

Green mini book: *Kolo*

Adhesive: Gloo, *KI Memories*

Accents:
  Acrylic "S": Icicles, *KI Memories*
  Assorted ribbon
  Black and white cord
  Sweet pea charm

Black dye ink: Memories, *Stewart Superior*

Other: staples, stapler, large jump ring, hole punch

Finished size: 5" x 3"

COVER TAG

1 Cut 2" wide strip of striped paper. Ink edges and adhere to tag bottom.

2 Cut flower from floral paper and adhere to bottom corner of tag; trim edges.

3 Staple ½" wide strip of polka dot paper over other paper pieces.

4 Adhere acrylic initial (see photo).

5 Ink tag edges. Punch holes across bottom and add ribbon.

6 Replace ribbon on mini book with black and white cord. Adhere checked paper behind window. Tie sweet pea charm to top of book with ribbon. Adhere book to tag.

7 Connect tags with large jump ring; accent ring with ribbon.

Bonus Ideas

■ Create a Circle of Friends album in which each of your friends decorates one page.

■ Create a Family Circle tag book. Bring craft supplies to a family gathering so each member can decorate a tag. Compile the tags into a book or create a family tree wall hanging with each person's tag hanging on a branch.

TAG SWAPPING TIPS

- Hold a tag-making party where you and your friends make a tag for each person. Decorate your tag to match your personality—include your favorite colors, images, quotes, and photos. List your favorite things, hobbies, responsibilities, and personal attributes.

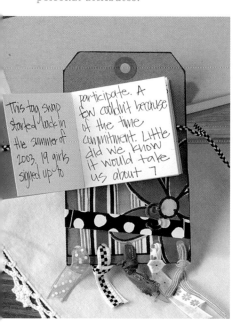

- Inside the mini book on the cover tag, write about your experience creating the tag book with your friends. Describe how you swapped tags—did you hold a tag-making party or send the completed tags to one another via mail? Include the date of the tag swap and the names of the participants.

Friendship Quotes Flip Book

Designer: Amber Crosby

SUPPLIES

For all:

Cardstock: Aloe Vera textured, Natural, Sandstone, Walnut textured, *Bazzill Basics Paper*

Accents:
  Silver eyelets: *Making Memories*
  Jump rings: *Darice*
  Gingham ribbon: brown, light blue, light green, *Impress Rubber Stamps*
  Silk ribbon: light blue, light green, *7gypsies*

Font: Garamond, *Microsoft*

Other: hole punch, eyelet-setting tools

For cover tag:

Patterned paper: Den Big Stripes, *Chatterbox*

Accents:
  "Friendship" transparency film: *7gypsies*
  Label holder, "F" charm, ribbon charm, silver brads: *Making Memories*

Font: Antique Type, *www.scrapvillage.com*

Metal adhesive

For friends spread:

Patterned paper:
  Dictionary Heritage, *K&Company*
  Gray

Small photo

Accents:
  "friends" sticker: *Pebbles Inc.*
  Gold photo corners

Finished size: 4½" x 2¾"

COVER TAG

Adhere metal accents with metal adhesive.

① Cut tag from Walnut textured cardstock.

② Cut small rectangle from Sandstone cardstock and adhere to top of tag. Set eyelet and add ribbon.

③ Cut piece of Den Big Stripes paper; adhere to center of tag. Adhere smaller piece of Aloe Vera cardstock.

④ Print "Quotes" on Natural cardstock; trim and adhere to tag. Adhere label holder.

⑤ Thread brown gingham ribbon through ribbon charm; adhere to tag.

⑥ Trim "Friendship" transparency film and attach to tag with brads. Adhere "F" charm over "F" on transparency.

⑦ Punch three holes in left side of tag. Attach additional tags with jump rings. Decorate with gingham ribbon.

TIPS FROM AMBER

- Keep metal and other bulky accents away from photos so they won't scratch the photos when the book is closed.

- Maintain the same color scheme throughout the tag book.

- As you embellish the tags, the book will become thicker so you can display it upright on a table. What a great conversation piece it will make!

Bonus Ideas

Make a quote tag book as a wedding, graduation, or baby shower gift.

Inside

One Fall Day Fold-Out Book

Designer: Kathleen Paneitz

SUPPLIES

Cardstock: black, cream, orange textured

Patterned paper: Shopping Series, *Scrappy Cat Creations*

Cardstock tag stickers: Shopping Series, *Scrappy Cat Creations*

Alphabet rubber stamps:
Antique uppercase ("FALL"), *PSX*

Versals ("ONE"), *Wordsworth*

Ink:
White pigment; Versacolor, *Tsukineko*

Black dye, *PrintWorks*

White embossing powder: *Ranger Industries*

Font: CK Stenography, "Fresh Fonts" CD, *Creating Keepsakes*

Label maker and black tape: *Dymo*

3/4" square punch, *EK Success*

Accents:
Orange flat eyelets: Dotlets, *Doodlebug Design*

Eyelets: orange, yellow, *Creative Impressions*

Orange brad and mini buttons: *Karen Foster Design*

Epoxy alphabet stickers, silver square eyelet: *Creative Imaginations*

White alphabet stickers: Dee's Pointed Brush, *Paper Adventures*

Jewelry tags: *Avery*

"2003" metal tag, black photo anchors, rub-on words ("foliage," "nature"), *Making Memories*

Gold leaf charm: *PSX*

Black slide mount: *Design Originals*

Assorted ribbon: orange, white, yellow

Other: chipboard, eyelet-setting tools, fine sandpaper, heat tool, scoring tool, sewing machine, orange thread

Finished sizes:
Book 5½" x 3½" (closed),
5½" x 20" (opened)
Tags 4¾" x 2¾"

ASSEMBLE

❶ Cut two 5½" x 3½" pieces of chipboard for covers; cover with patterned paper. Adhere 22" length of white ribbon, centered, to inside of back cover (see Figure a).

❷ Create 5¼" x 19½" strip of orange textured cardstock. Score every 3¼" and fold accordion-style into six sections (see Figure b).

Inside

3. Create 2¾" x 19¼" strip of patterned paper. Place on cardstock strip; score along same lines and fold accordion-style. Stitch to bottom of cardstock strip to form six pockets (see Figure c).

4. Adhere end sections of cardstock strip to inside of covers.

a Adhere ribbon to inside back cover.

b Score and fold strip.

c Stitch pockets, add covers.

EMBELLISH

1. Stamp "ONE" on front cover with white ink; heat emboss.

2. Stamp jewelry tags with "FALL," using black ink. Set flat eyelets through holes. Adhere to cover.

3. Spell "DAY" with epoxy stickers.

4. Print "photo shoot" with label maker and adhere to cover.

5. Distress edges of covers with sandpaper.

6. Cut six tags from cream cardstock. Cover with patterned paper, photos, and text as desired. Punch six squares from black cardstock; adhere to tops of tags. Set eyelets and add ribbon.

7. Embellish tags, pockets, and reverse side of book as desired.

8. Tie book closed with white ribbon.

Four tags make a quick box

Tag—You're a Box!

Never underestimate the versatility of a tag! Just look what **Cindy Knowles** has done with a few coordinated tags. To create a quick gift box, adhere two tags end to end, then repeat. Fold to create a box, and accent with ribbon, metal-rimmed tags, or other embellishments as desired. This fun and easy favor box works well for any occasion.

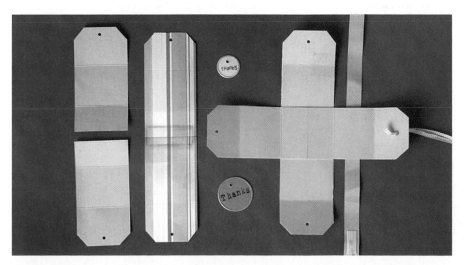

For Your Graduation Tag Booklet

Designer: Lisa Schmitt

SUPPLIES

Black cardstock

Vellum: *Making Memories*

Stardust paper: gold, silver, *Making Memories*

Patterned paper: number, word, *7gypsies*

Laser cuts: Graduation Simplicities white, *Deluxe Cuts*

Metal hole reinforcers: Tag Tops, *Deluxe Cuts*

Pocket template: 1P, *Deluxe Cuts*

Alphabet stickers

"Graduation" sticker

Vellum graduation quotes:
   Quotes, *Memories Complete*
   Quote Stacks, *DieCuts with a View*

Tag template: Coluzzle, *Provo Craft*

Eyelets, mini brads, star charm, shaped clips: *Making Memories*

Tinker pin, elastic cord: *7gypsies*

Alphabet stamps: *PSX*

Ink: Black, Gold, Platinum, White; Brilliance, *Tsukineko*

Pens:
   Gold Leaf, *Krylon*
   Silver; Sharpie, *Sanford Corp.*

Black embossing powder: *Ranger Industries*

Embossing ink: *Ranger Industries*

Fibers: *On the Surface*

Adhesive: *Xyron*

1¼" circle punch: *Family Treasures*

Other: gold charms (heart, year numerals) gold star nail head, jump ring, ribbon (black, white), embroidery floss (white, gold) or 1" mini tassel, heat tool, ⅛" hole punch

Finished size:
   closed 2½" x 4¼"
   opened 4¼" x 11"

ACCORDION BOOK

① Fold 8½" x 11" cardstock in half lengthwise. *Note: Fold is card bottom. Fold card into four equal sections to form accordion. Note: Inside of folded sections will be torn, folded over, punched, etc. Back of folded sections are left intact.*

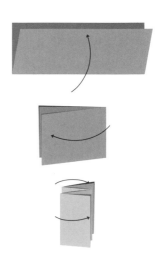

Inside

② Create cover by layering vellum over silver and gold stardust paper (see photo). Apply stickers for message. Attach with black eyelets.

③ Tear diagonal strip off first section from right to left. Attach star nail head.

④ Punch semi-circle in top of second section.

⑤ Cut slit between sections 3 and 4. Cut diagonal piece off section 3, fold over edge and secure with mini brads.

⑥ Make mini tassel.

⑦ Fold down top edge of section four and secure; punch ⅛" hole and add mini tassel.

⑧ Attach year numeral charms with jump ring.

⑨ Decorate inner sections with metallic ink, pens, and patterned paper.

⑩ Use template to create vellum pocket. Edge with black ink. Insert card stamped "Words of Wisdom" in white ink.

⑪ Create closure for book with elastic cord and tinker pin.

TAGS

① Cut vellum quotes into tags using template.

② Layer and adhere laser cuts between vellum quotes and Stardust paper. Trim Stardust paper, leaving ¼" border.

③ Edge each tag with embossing ink and emboss with black powder.

④ Decorate tags with metal hole reinforcers, eyelets, shaped clips, and charms.

⑤ Stamp "congrats" on white ribbon with black ink.

⑥ Tie each tag with coordinating ribbon.

DESIGNER TIPS

■ This project is a variation of the "Accordion Pocket Book" project featured in *The Art of Collage* book from PineCone Press. The designer adapted the project for a formal look with black, gold and silver materials.

■ Use a Xyron machine, Helmar Vellum Adhesive spray, or 3M Scotch Vellum Adhesive tape for vellum and you won't have to worry about ugly adhesive showing through.

■ Express sentiments with famous quotes and sayings.

POCKETS OF PLENTY

Here are some adaptations that will add delight to the commemorations:

■ Use school colors for the mini tassel and ribbons.

■ Add photos to tags for a mini-scrapbook.

■ Replace tags with gift cards or money.

■ Insert movie, concert, or sporting event tickets for an added surprise.

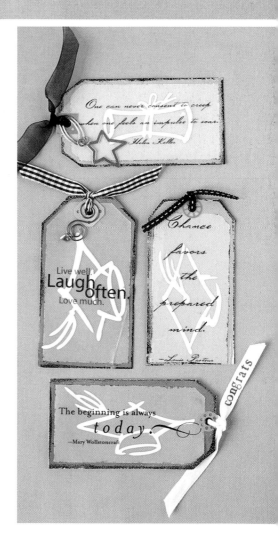

Favorite Author Bookmark (Mark Twain)

Designer: Janelle Clark

SUPPLIES

Cardstock: cream textured, oatmeal, olive green

Patterned paper:
  Shabby Parchment, *Karen Foster Design*
  Aged letter, *Design Originals*
  Tan striped, *Ever After Scrapbook Co.*

Tan vellum: *Club Scrap*

Alphabet rubber stamps: Image Tree, *EK Success*

Fern stamp: Mother Fern Leaf Impression, *Hero Arts*

Dye ink:
  Chocolate; Ancient Page, *Clearsnap*
  Olive; Memories, *Stewart Superior*

Copper embossing powder

Font: Harting, *www.dafont.com*

Accents:
  "laugh" definition sticker: Nostalgiques, *EK Success*
  Gold organza ribbon: *Europa Imports*
  Green jute

Other: rectangle punch, heat tool, laminating machine or clear contact paper, photo of author (see "Tip from Janelle")

Finished size: 6" x 2¾"

INSTRUCTIONS

❶ Cut tag from oatmeal cardstock.

❷ Stamp author's name on Shabby Parchment paper with Chocolate ink.

❸ Stamp fern image on cream cardstock with Olive ink; cut out.

❹ Print quote from author on vellum. While ink is still wet, sprinkle embossing powder and emboss with heat tool.

❺ Cut or tear paper pieces and sticker; adhere to bookmark as desired.

❻ Mat author photo with olive green cardstock and adhere to bookmark.

❼ Run bookmark through laminating machine, or seal between two pieces of contact paper. Trim edges.

❽ Punch hole through top. Add ribbon and jute.

TIP FROM JANELLE

To find a photo of your favorite author, visit an Internet search engine such as *www.google.com* and type "image" and the author's name. Save the image, adjust the size as needed, and print it on glossy photo paper.

Bonus Ideas

■ Create a series of bookmarks featuring your favorite authors, decorated with motifs, titles, and/or quotes from the author's literature. A great source of literary quotes is *www.bartleby.com/100*.

■ Make bookmarks for kids who love to read, featuring authors of favorite children's literature. Embellish the bookmarks with illustrations from the books.

Mini Luggage Tags

Designer: Dawn Brookey

SUPPLIES

For both:

Laminate sample chips (from home improvement store)

Alphabet rubber stamps: Playful, *Hero Arts*

Jet Black solvent ink: StazOn, *Tsukineko*

Fine sandpaper

Hole punch

For Journey tag:

Yellow cardstock

Patterned paper: Travel Stickers, *K&Company*

Patterned vellum: Dictionary, *K&Company*

Ochre pigment ink: ColorBox, *Clearsnap*

Accents:
  Label sticker: "Journey," *Pebbles Inc.*
  Gold eyelet: *Creative Imaginations*
  Brown grosgrain ribbon\

Spray adhesive: *Krylon*

Eyelet-setting tools

For Escape tag:

Accents:
  Stickers: Hydrangeas, Hydrangea Borders & Corners, Garden Treasures Journal Tags sheet, *K&Company*
  "escape" rub-on word, cream ribbon: *Making Memories*

Finished size: 2½" x 1½"

JOURNEY TAG

❶ Lightly sand laminate chip to roughen surface.

❷ Cover back of laminate chip with patterned vellum, using spray adhesive.

❸ Adhere travel stickers to front of laminate chip, folding edges of some stickers to back side. Add "Journey" label sticker.

❹ Stamp name and address on cardstock with Jet Black. Trim, ink edges with Ochre, and adhere to back of laminate chip.

❺ Set eyelet through hole and add ribbon.

ESCAPE TAG

❶ Lightly sand laminate chip to roughen surface.

❷ Adhere stickers as desired. Add rub-on word to front.

❸ Stamp name and address on label sticker and adhere to back of laminate chip.

❹ Punch hole through stickers; add ribbon.

Back

Backpack Shaker Tag

Designer: Lori Bergmann

SUPPLIES

Light green two-tone card-stock: *Paper Adventures*

Patterned paper: Pink Flowers; Pink & Green Plaid, *The Scrapbook Wizard*

White square shaker box kit: *Idea Toolbox*

Tag die: Super Crescent Tag (38-0948); Sizzix, *Provo Craft*

Die-cutting machine: Sizzix, *Provo Craft*

Alphabet rubber stamps: Funky Brush, *Wordsworth*

Chalk ink: Lime Pastel, Rouge; ColorBox, *Clearsnap*

Tracing and cutting tool: Magic Matter, *PM Designs*

Small adhesive dots: Zots, *Therm O Web*

Accents:
   White flower eyelet: *Creative Impressions*

   Seed beads: clear, white, *JewelCraft*

   Flower buttons: green, pink; Dress It Up, Jesse, *James & Co.*

   Pink variegated ribbon

Other: sandpaper, eyelet-setting tools

Finished size: 4¾" x 3¼"

INSTRUCTIONS

❶ Cut tag from flowered paper, using die-cutting machine.

❷ To make larger tag from cardstock, trace and cut around flower tag, using tracing and cutting tool. Lightly sand edges of cardstock tag to expose white layer.

❸ Tear bottom edge of flowered tag and adhere to cardstock tag.

❹ Adhere acetate cover over shaker box base.

❺ Adhere flowered paper to shaker box cover. Trim and adhere over acetate cover.

❻ Adhere 2" square of plaid paper to center of tag. Place beads and buttons on square and adhere shaker box on top. Ink edges of shaker box with Lime Pastel.

❼ Stamp child's name on bottom of tag with Rouge ink. Adhere flower button next to it with adhesive dot.

❽ Add eyelet and ribbon to top of tag.

Favorite Recipes Flip Book

Designer: Gretchen Schmidt

SUPPLIES

For all:

Cardstock: red, tan, *Making Memories*

White paper

Tag template: downloaded from *www.red-castle.com*

Silver washer eyelet: *Creative Impressions*

For cover tag:

Patterned paper: cooking and recipe motifs, *MPR Paberbilities*

Vellum: *MPR Paperbilities*

Ink:
   Black embossing: *Ranger Industries*

   Watermark: Versamark, *Tsukineko*

Walnut ink: *7gypsies*

Font: Rust, *Chatterbox*

Accents:
   Black gingham ribbon: *Scrap by Design*

   Silver brads: *Magic Scraps*

For recipe pages:

Font: Ancient Script, *www.elliestreasures.com/fontsabnum/fontsabnum.html*

Hole punch: *McGill*

Other: adhesive dots, vellum adhesive, eyelet-setting tools, heat tool, silver jump ring, stencil paintbrush, sewing machine, repositionable tape, cream thread, water

Finished size: 5¼" x 2½"

TAG BASES

Print tags for cover and recipes on tan cardstock, using template; cut out.

COVER TAG

❶ Adhere patterned paper to front of tag.

❷ Print "Favorite Recipes" on vellum; sprinkle embossing powder on words and heat-emboss. Trim and adhere to cover tag with vellum adhesive.

❸ Adhere ribbon around vellum piece. Punch holes in corners of ribbon and add brads.

❹ Cover back of tag with patterned paper to hide prongs of brads (see Tip from Gretchen).

RECIPE TAGS

❶ To print recipe on each tag, create text box the same size as tag in word processing program. Print recipe on white paper. Center tag over recipe and secure with repositionable tape. Run through printer again.

❷ Cover back of tags with patterned paper.

❸ Randomly daub front of tags with diluted walnut ink, using stencil paintbrush.

BOOK ASSEMBLY

❶ Adhere small rectangle of red cardstock to top of each tag.

❷ Stitch edges of each tag and red rectangle. Set eyelet through top. Tie ribbon through eyelet in cover tag.

❸ Place tags on jump ring.

TIP FROM GRETCHEN

Bend the prongs of the brad so they run vertically. That way your sewing machine needle won't catch them when you sew around the edges. Apply the brads and then the back cover so the brads are hidden.

Bonus Ideas

To give the recipe tags an aged look:

- Coat each tag completely with walnut ink before you print the recipes. Iron the tags with a warm iron to dry the ink.

- Rub a brown ink pad along the tag edges.

Papa Bill's Salsa

5–6 plum or Roma tomatoes

1 medium white onion, chopped

1 jalapeno pepper

1 lemon

2 Tbsp. cilantro

2 garlic cloves, minced

1 tsp. salt

Chop tomatoes until chunky, transfer to bowl. Finely chop onions and pepper and add to tomatoes. Stir in juice of one lemon, cilantro, garlic, and salt. Let stand covered for 30 minutes. Makes 2–3 cups.

Note: To make the salsa milder, add more chopped tomatoes and a little lemon juice.

It's a Girl Shaker Tag

Designer: Dee Gallimore-Perry

SUPPLIES

Rubber stamp: (Onesie) *Stampin' Up!*

Dye ink: (Basic Black) *Stampin' Up!*

Cardstock: (White) *Bazzill Basics Paper*

Patterned paper: (Lipstick Disco, Lipstick Flower) Collection I, *KI Memories*

Paper accent: (small tag) *Avery Dennison*

Accents: (acrylic heart) Icicles, *KI Memories*; (mini glass beads)

Fibers: (pink gingham ribbon, black gingham ribbon) *Offray*

Font: (CK Handprint) "The Best of Creative Lettering" CD, *Creating Keepsakes*

Adhesive: (foam tape, glue stick)

Color medium: (pink pencil) *EK Success*

Tools: (hole punch) Fiskars; craft knife, scissors, computer and printer, ruler

Other: (transparency) *Hammermill*

Finished size: 3" x 5"

PREPARE

1 Cut 3" x 5" rectangle from White cardstock; adhere to Lipstick Disco paper; cut out. Trim two adjacent edges at an angle.

2 Cut 2" x 3½" rectangle from center of tag.

3 Cut transparency to cover window; adhere to back of tag.

4 Cut Lipstick Flower paper slightly smaller than tag; adhere to White cardstock and cut out.

5 Print "yeah, baby" three times and "It's a girl!" five times on White card-stock.

STAMP, COLOR, AND CUT

1 Stamp Onesie above "yeah, baby" phrases; color images pink and cut out.

2 Stamp Onesie on small tag and color pink.

3 Cut out "It's a girl!" phrases; set two aside.

MAKE SHAKER

1 Apply foam tape along edges of window on back of tag. *Note: Apply two layers to increase depth.*

2 Place stamped images, word phrases, small heart, and glass beads inside foam tape square. *Note: Place stamped images and word phrases face down.*

3 Adhere Lipstick Flower piece face down to back of tag.

EMBELLISH

1 Punch hole at top of tag.

2 Thread gingham ribbons through hole; knot and trim excess.

3 Adhere "It's a girl!" to bottom right corner of tag.

4 Punch hole in remaining phrase and attach to small tag.

5 Thread string through hole at top of tag; adhere small tag to upper right corner of tag.

Snowman Shaker Tag

Designer: Tracy Kyle

SUPPLIES

Patterned paper: *Paper Patch*
Cardstock: *Bazzill Basics Paper*
Holly trim: *Westrim Crafts*
Star eyelet: *The Eyelet Factory*

Foam tape: Mounting Tape, *3M*
Page protector: *C-Line Products*
Black pen: ZIG Millennium, *EK Success*
Glitter: Shaved Ice, *Magic Scraps*
Adhesive: Mono Aqua, *Tombow*
Other: jute, iridescent fiber

Finished size: 3" x 5"

INSTRUCTIONS

❶ To create shaker, attach circle of page protector to white cardstock circle outline.

❷ Adhere small pieces of foam tape to page protector.

❸ Pour glitter inside taped area.

❹ Adhere blue cardstock circle to back of shaker.

Winter Shaker Tag

Designer: Tracy Kyle

SUPPLIES

Vellum: *Paper Adventures*
Font: Wonderful, *Two Peas in a Bucket*

Star eyelets: *The Eyelet Factory*
Silver paper: *Petersen-Arne*
White cardstock: *Bazzill Basics Paper*
Foam tape: *3M*
Page protector: *C-Line Products*
Beads, flowers, and stars: *Westrim Crafts*

Other: iridescent and silver fibers, wire

Finished size: 2½" x 5"

Note: Create shaker similar to "Snowman Shaker Tag"; fill with beads, flowers, and stars.

Shaker Gift Bag

Designer: Anne Heyen

SUPPLIES

8½" x 11" cardstock:
  Teal blue
  White

Star of David die cut

Clear page protector

Foam tape*

Blue, clear, and white beads*

Miscellaneous items: scissors, computer with printer, double-sided tape, ruler

*3M foam tape; and Darice beads were used in the sample project.

INSTRUCTIONS

① Print "Happy Hanukah" onto white cardstock, leaving about 4" between the two words using your favorite font (the designer used Glitter Girl, *Two Peas in a Bucket*) or your own handwriting (see photo).

② Trim to 6" x 3" and mat with teal cardstock.

③ Mount the cardstock on the bag front.

④ Trace the die cut onto teal and white cardstock and the page protector. Cut out the three stars, trimming the teal one to form a frame.

⑤ Adhere the white star to the bag. Completely edge the star with foam tape. *Note: This will create a seal to prevent the beads from coming out.*

⑥ Carefully pour some beads into the star shape.

⑦ Adhere the teal frame to the page protector star, and press it down on the foam tape. *Note: Apply pressure along the edges to ensure a tight closure.*

I Love Snowmen Shaker Box

Designer: Alice Golden

SUPPLIES

Cardstock:
  Light blue, *Bazzill Basics Paper*
  White glossy

Patterned paper: Lacy Blue Dots, *Carolee's Creations*

Transparency film

Snowman Block stamp: *DeNami Design*

Dye ink: Coal Black; Ancient Page, *Clearsnap*

Accents:
  Woven label: "I Love Snowmen";
  Threads, *Me & My Big Ideas*
  "Love" sticker: Real Life, *Pebbles Inc.*
  Snow confetti: Shaved Ice, *Magic Scraps*
  Silver 1/16" eyelet: *Hyglo Crafts*
  Purple fibers: *On the Surface*

Foam tape: Black Sticky Strips, *Therm O Web*

Other: eyelet-setting tools, craft knife, cutting mat

Finished size: 4" x 2½"

INSTRUCTIONS

1 Stamp snowman on white glossy cardstock. Cut away background around snowman with craft knife. Trim.

2 Adhere transparency film behind snowman piece to create window. Mat with frame of light blue cardstock. *Note: Cardstock should not show through window.*

3 Set eyelet through top and add fiber.

4 Adhere foam tape to back edges of window to create box, making sure tape doesn't show through window.

5 Place confetti in box, remove backing from foam tape, and adhere patterned paper face-down. Trim to size. Adhere light blue cardstock over paper for stability.

6 Cut "I" and "snowmen" from woven label and adhere to front. *Note: Adhere "I" label reverse side up.* Add "Love" sticker.

TIPS FROM ALICE

■ Substitute scraps of glossy photo paper for white glossy cardstock—it works well with dye ink!

■ Practice cutting around the snowman on a scrap of glossy cardstock. Be sure to use a craft knife with a sharp blade, cut slowly, and cut the most detailed areas first. For example, I first cut around the snowman's nose and hat brim.

Bonus Ideas

■ Adhere the ornament to a card with repositionable adhesive. Or, use magnetic tape so the ornament can double as a magnet!

■ Look for other stamps that would make great shaker boxes. Make sure the design has a section that can be cut out for a window. A snow globe stamp would make a fun shaker ornament!

■ Make your own shaker box scene by first cutting out a window and then decorating around it with stickers, die cuts, or punch-outs. The window can be any shape you'd like.

■ Use transparency film on both sides of the shaker box so that you can see through it. Hang in front of Christmas tree lights or a sunny window.

Card is covered with Water Mosaic paper from KI Memories.

BASIC SHAKER BOX DIAGRAM

Frame

Acetate

Vellum lined
with foam squares

Shaved ice and
glass marbles, etc.

Light pink
cardstock

White cardstock

Folded pink card

Autumn Leaf Shaker Tag

Designer: Dee Gallimore-Perry

SUPPLIES

8½" x 11" paper:
  Rusty Kettle plaid print*
  Off-white cardstock
  Terra cotta cardstock

Leaf template*

Silver eyelet

Eyelet setter

⅛" hole punch*

Foam tape

8½" x 11" transparency film or page protector

Mini leaf punch

Small orange beads

Mini brads

Metallic embroidery floss

Miscellaneous items: white craft glue, computer with printer, glue pen*, hammer, scissors

*Mustard Moon paper; Provo Craft template; McGill, hole punch; and EK Success ZIG Memory System 2-Way glue pen were used in the sample project.

MAKE THE LARGE TAG

1 Cut a large tag pattern from terra cotta cardstock. Mat it with off-white cardstock.

2 Punch a hole at the top using a small hole punch. Tie several strands of metallic floss through the hole.

3 Using the leaf template, draw and cut out a leaf from the tag.

4 Cut a piece of page protector or transparency film large enough to cover the entire leaf. Adhere it securely to the back of the tag.

5 Create the back of the shaker box by cutting a piece of off-white cardstock to 2¼" x 2¾". Edge the cardstock with narrow strips of foam tape. For better shaking, make the shaker box deeper by doubling the layer of foam tape.

6 Fill the shaker box with leaf punches and beads.

7 Center the shaker box behind the leaf cutout window and adhere.

8 Tear a small strip of plaid paper and attach it to the tag using glue and mini brads (see photo). *Note: See p. 129 for tearing instructions.*

O, Christmas Tree Shaker Tag

Designer: Marla Bird

SUPPLIES

Tree punch: Punchkins, *EK Success*
Hole and star punches: *McGill*
Snowflake punch: *Family Treasures*
Font: P22 Garamouche, *Impress Rubber Stamps*

Transparency sheet: *3M*
Other: tag; red, light and dark green, yellow, speckled white, and brown cardstock

Finished size: 4⅞" x 2½"

Vintage Santa

Designer: Alice Golden

SUPPLIES

Wood tags: *Lara's Crafts*

Vintage Santa stickers

Acrylic paint:
Cranberry, Evergreen, Nutmeg, *Making Memories*

Antique White; Apple Barrel, *Plaid*

Crackle medium: Folk Art, *Plaid*

Gold metallic rub-on finish: *Craf-T Products*

Glitter glue: Gold Ice; Ice Stickles, *Ranger Industries*

Accents:

Metal labels: Christmas tree, Joy, Noel, *Lasting Impressions for Paper*

Metal charms: Christmas tree, sled, stocking, *Making Memories*

Gold satin ribbon: *Anna Griffin*

Gold organza ribbon: *May Arts*

Other: fine sandpaper, paintbrushes, paper towels, metal adhesive

Finished size: 5¼" x 2¾"

INSTRUCTIONS

❶ Lightly sand tags. Paint one each with Cranberry, Evergreen, and Nutmeg. Paint metal charm to match each tag. Let dry.

❷ Apply crackle medium and thin coat of Antique White to tags, following crackle medium manufacturer's instructions. Let dry.

❸ When paint starts to crackle, sand to distress; let dry. Apply rub-on finish to edges.

❹ Drybrush Santa stickers with Antique White; apply rub-on finish to edges. Adhere to tags. Highlight Santas with glitter glue.

❺ Rub Antique White into crevices of metal charms; blot excess with paper towel. Highlight with rub-on finish.

❻ Apply rub-on finish to crevices of metal label to highlight words. Use sparingly—it's easier to add more than to remove excess.

❼ Adhere satin ribbon and metal accents to tags. Loop organza ribbon through hole.

Noel Tag

Designer: Kathleen Paneitz

SUPPLIES

Rubber stamps: *Stampabilities* (Holly); *Wordsworth* (Boxed alphabet)

Watermark ink: Versamark, *Tsukineko*

Pigment ink: Sage, VersaColor, *Tsukineko*

Embossing powder: gold, *Ranger Industries*

Cardstock: *Bazzill Basics Paper* (Aloe Vera, Chiffon)

Mesh: red, Maruyama Paper, *Magenta Rubber Stamps*

Eyelet: red, *Creative Impressions*

Sequins: red, *Sulyn Industries*

Other: cardstock (light green, red), eyelet-setting tools, embossing heat tool, adhesive, scissors, ruler, ribbon

Finished size: 2½" x 4¾"

INSTRUCTIONS

❶ Cut tag from Chiffon cardstock.

❷ Stamp "NOEL" on tag with Sage.

❸ Adhere strip of mesh to right side of tag.

❹ Stamp holly on light green cardstock with watermark ink; emboss. Cut out and adhere sequins; adhere to tag.

❺ Adhere thin strip of Aloe Vera to tag bottom; adhere sequins.

❻ Cut red cardstock to fit top of tag; tear bottom edge and adhere to tag. Cut strip of Aloe Vera and fold over top of tag; set eyelet and add ribbon.

Joy Tag

Designer: Kathleen Paneitz

SUPPLIES

Rubber stamps: *PSX* (Antique Uppercase alphabet); *Stampin' Up!* (Musical Score)

Dye ink: Coal Black, *PrintWorks*

Pigment ink: Gold Rush, ColorBox, *Clearsnap*

Embossing powder: gold, *Ranger Industries*

Paper: Gold Metallic, Canford, *Daler-Rowney*

Patterned paper: Holiday Poinsettias, *Magenta Rubber Stamps*

Stickers: round epoxy, Page Pebbles, *Making Memories*

Eyelet: gold, Extreme Eyelet, *Creative Imaginations*

Punches: Paper Shapers, *EK Success* (rectangle tag); *Family Treasures* (½" and ⅝" circle)

Other: cardstock (cream, red), poinsettia stamp, fine gold cord, black eyelet, scissors, ruler, adhesive, embossing heat tool, eyelet-setting tools, cosmetic sponge

Finished size: 2½" x 4¾"

INSTRUCTIONS

❶ Stamp Musical Score on cream cardstock with Gold Rush; emboss with gold. Cut into tag; ink edges with Gold Rush.

❷ Tear strip of patterned paper; adhere to center of tag. Tear small pieces of patterned paper; adhere to top and bottom edges.

❸ Punch mini tag from Gold Metallic paper; set black eyelet in top and add cord. Adhere to large tag.

❹ Stamp poinsettia on red cardstock with Gold Rush; emboss. Cut out and adhere to tag.

❺ Set eyelet in top of tag.

❻ Punch ⅝" circles from red cardstock. Stamp "JOY" on cream cardstock with Coal Black. Punch letters with ½" circle punch; mat with red circles. Adhere stickers over letters; adhere to tag.

World's Best Dad Map Tags

Designer: Lucy Marino

SUPPLIES

Rubber stamps: *Close To My Heart* (gift tag, map background)

Dye ink: Exclusive Inks, *Close To My Heart* (black, brown)

Chalk: *Close To My Heart* (blue, yellow, lavender)

Mini tags: *Avery Dennison*

Floss: *DMC* (blue, yellow)

Other: cream cardstock, cotton swab or make-up applicator, scissors, stamp aligner, hole punch, fibers, adhesive

Finished size: 2" x 3"

INSTRUCTIONS

❶ Stamp map background on cardstock with brown ink.

❷ Color image with chalk.

❸ Using stamp aligner, stamp gift tags over map image with black ink; cut out tags.

❹ Write message on mini tags; wrap around stamped tags with floss.

❺ Punch holes in tags; add fibers.

STAMPING LARGE IMAGES

To achieve a clear impression from a large stamp, set the stamp on your work surface with the rubber side facing up, and then apply ink. Align the cardstock on the stamp and apply pressure to the cardstock with your fingers. Carefully lift the cardstock off the stamp.

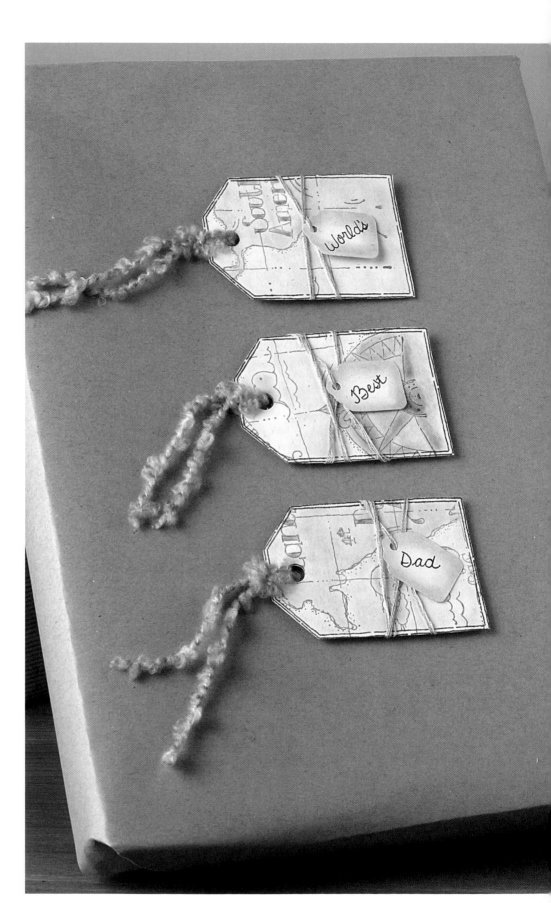

Autumn: Captured On Paper

Nature Wrapping Paper & Tag

Designer: Kathleen Paneitz

SUPPLIES

Rubber stamps: *Delta Rubber Stampede* (Rose Leaves); *Hero Arts* (2" square shadow background); *PSX* (Evergreen, Maple, Oak Leaf); *Stampabilities* (Gerbera Daisy, Monarch Butterfly, Swirl Frame)

Pigment ink: Page Craft, *Clearsnap* (brown); *Stampabilities* (Pumpkin); VersaColor, *Tsukineko* (Green Tea, Indigo, Scarlet)

Dye ink: black, *PrintWorks*

Brown paper: *Hobby Lobby*

Cardstock: *Bazzill Basics Paper* (Tan Textured, Pumpkin)

Watercolor pencils: *Staedtler* (yellow, brown)

Alphabet tiles: *Limited Edition Rubberstamps*

Eyelet: gold, *Creative Imaginations*

Butterfly charm: *PSX*

Daisy accents: Jolee's by You, *EK Success*

Wire: gold, *Artistic Wire*

Plastic magnifying glass: *Manto Fev*

Other: paintbrush, water, raffia, twig, cotton swab, eyelet-setting tools, scissors, adhesive

Finished size: 2½" x 4¾"

WRAPPING PAPER

1 Beginning in one corner of paper, stamp Swirl Frame with brown. Stamp entire paper, one row at a time.

2 Apply brown ink to shadow background stamp. Stamp off a few times, then stamp inside each frame.

3 Stamp leaf, butterfly, and Gerbera Daisy images over blocks, using desired ink colors.

4 Color Gerbera Daisy with yellow and brown watercolor pencils. Blend with damp paintbrush.

TAG

1 Cut stamped wrapping paper into tag shape. Adhere torn cardstock strips to top and center, trimming edges.

2 Ink edges of alphabet tiles with brown. Adhere to tag to spell "NATURE."

3 Adhere daisy accents to tag; adhere magnifying glass on top.

4 Attach twig to tag with wire, securing wire ends in back.

5 Adhere butterfly charm.

6 Cut ¾" x 1" piece of pumpkin cardstock; ink edges with brown. Fold over top of tag; set eyelet. Add raffia.

Set your creativity free with altered books

Cut, tear, paint, glue, or stamp—anything goes in this hot new craft!

WHAT ARE ALTERED BOOKS?

Altered books are ordinary hardcover books that have been turned into works of art by adding almost anything imaginable to their pages. The object is to change a book into a special place to keep trinkets, photos, thoughts, mementos, or anything else that expresses your individuality. Many crafters like to give their books a nostalgic feel by aging pages or adding vintage images and ephemera—but there are no rules. Anything you can do with paper, you can do with your altered book. Let's get started!

Designer: Jennifer Mayer Fish

SUGGESTED SUPPLIES

Alter-able book: *Hot Off The Press* Cardstock

Patterned paper, corrugated paper, Textured papers, acetate sheet (transparency)

Embellishments, ephemera, alphabet tiles: *Hot Off The Press*

Eyelets, brads, pebble alphabets, tags, metal accents, skeleton leaves: *Making Memories*

Craft glue: Tacky Glue, *Aleene's*

Other: photos, trinkets, hole punch, craft knife, cutting mat, double-sided tape, glue stick, steel ruler, fibers, rubber stamps, ink, chalk, spray paint

HOW TO MAKE A COLLAGE

Here are a few guide tips for planning and creating a collage. You can also refer to p. 184 for even more ideas.

- Choose a theme for the collage based on your main accent piece.

- Select a color scheme, then choose additional embellishments, papers, and text or alphabet tiles that are compatible with your colors and theme.

- Create your collage by assembling a background, adding a focal area made of larger items, then finishing it with smaller pieces.

HOW TO AGE PAGES

Chalk or Ink: Lightly dab a cosmetic sponge in the color.

Rub on the page in a circular motion.

Spray paint: Hold the can about 12" above the book and spray lightly, moving the can in a continuous circle.

HOW TO MAKE A WINDOW

HOW TO MAKE A POCKET

Cut a hole in a page with a craft knife. Glue text or images on the following page so they show through the window.

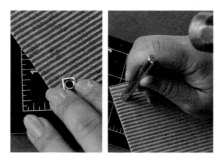

Fold a paper rectangle in half with the fold at the bottom. Trim the pocket to fit the page. Punch holes in the two upper corners. Insert eyelets. Turn over and set.

Adhere the pocket to a page.

HOW TO MAKE A TORN POCKET

First color the page directly behind the one you want to be the pocket flap.

Tear the top half of the flap page away and glue the untorn edges to the page behind.

HOW TO MAKE A NICHE

Glue together a chunk of pages (50 or more) along their edges. *Note: Your niche will be as deep as the thickness of the pages you glue together.*

Draw an opening on the page preceding the glued chunk (first page).

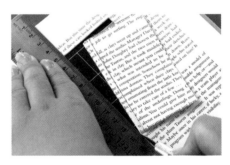

Cut the opening in the first page and through all the glued pages; adhere the chunk to the page following it.

HOW TO MAKE AN ENVELOPE POCKET

Apply glue to the edges of the niche.

Cut an acetate pane (transparency sheet) to fit the opening and glue it to the back of the first page.

Place a trinket inside the niche and glue down the first page. *Note: This will permanently seal your trinket in an enclosed compartment. If you want to be able to remove it, omit the acetate pane and the first page. Cut the opening through only the glued pages.*

Open a purchased envelope and use it as a pattern to cut a pocket. Fold and adhere it to a page, leaving the flap unsealed so items may be placed inside.

MORE ALTERED IDEAS

After you've mastered these fun techniques, here are a few more to try:

- Make your altered book from a children's board book. The heavy cardboard pages are great for making niches. You can paint over the illustrations or cover them with paper.

- Cut a vertical slash in your page and set eyelets in pairs on either side of it. Lace fiber through the eyelets and tie as you would the laces of a shoe.

- When you make a niche, try printing text on the acetate pane and placing a photo inside.

- Instead of gluing the pages together for a niche, punch holes through the corners of several pages, thread fiber or wire through the holes, and tie the pages together.

- Set evenly spaced eyelets around the edge of a page and sew with a running or overcast stitch. Or, explore the possibilities of cross-stitching your pages. You can easily punch stitching holes in paper with a piercing tool.

- For a real aged look, apply walnut ink to your pages, then tear and burn the edges, or rough them up with sandpaper.

- Try multiple pockets on a single page, or hide secret niches under tags or flaps.

- Cut windows in irregular shapes, or trim them to follow the outline of the image that will peek through the opening.

Book Review

Find more beginning altered book techniques and detailed instructions in *How to Alter Books If You Think You Can't* by Sara Naumann and Paris Dukes, Hot Off The Press, *www.craftpizazz.com.*

For some fun advanced techniques, read *Altered Books 102 Beyond the Basics* by Beth Cote, Design Originals, *www.d-originals.com.*

The Golden Dollar Game

Liven up any gathering or party with these fun golden dollar boxes, submitted by Melissa Deaken. Decorate matchboxes (available from DMD, Inc.) with patterned cardstock or paper, tuck in a mini chocolate bar, then tie them up with a ribbon. Turn these favors into a party game by hiding a golden dollar in one. The lucky recipient of that box gets to keep the dollar and receives a special treat, too!

Inside

Altered Coin Book

Designer: Erin Tenney

SUPPLIES

Olive cardstock: *Bazzill Basics Paper*

Plaid patterned paper: Small Great Plaid; Great Room Collection, *Chatterbox*

Silver dollar folder: *H.E. Harris & Co.*

Vellum envelope: *Impress Rubber Stamps*

Alphabet stamps:

Playful, Printers Type: *Hero Arts*

Uppercase and Lowercase Antique, Lowercase Buttons: *PSX*

Ink:

Distress: *Ranger Industries*

Walnut: *7gypsies*

Basic Black: *Stampin' Up!*

Accents:
Brads, charms, metal frame, metal word, page pebbles, photo holder, rub-on letters, rub-on words, safety pin, stickpin, tag, metal washer: *Making Memories*

Heart token, alphabet stickers: *Doodlebug Design*

Alphabet stickers: Mini Bubbletters, *KI Memories,*

Alphabet stickers: Domino Tiny Type & Tiny Trinkets, *Paper Fever*

Alphabet stickers: Antique ABC's; Real Life, *Pebbles Inc.*

Linen thread: *Hillcreek Designs*

Snowflake charms, tiny white bells: *Crafts Etc!*

"Celebrate" pewter word, metal frame: *K&Company*

Buttons: *Chatterbox*

"always believe" woven label: Inspirational 1; Threads, *Me & My Big Ideas*

Watch crystal: *7gypsies*

Label holder: Jo-Ann Essentials, *Jo-Ann Stores*

Slide frame, star stud: *Scrapworks*

Bubble letters: Trinkets and Treasures, *Li'l Davis Designs*

Ribbon:
Brown gingham

Brown grosgrain, narrow and wide

Red satin

Other: 1½" punch, double-sided tape

Finished size:
7½" x 6" closed,
7½" x 18½" open

COVER

1 Cut plaid paper to 7½" x 4½" and adhere to front cover.

2 Cut (or piece) cardstock to 7½" x 14" and adhere over spine and around cover. Adhere wide brown ribbon over paper seam.

Begin with a coin book.

3 Fit photo under metal frame and adhere to front cover.

INSIDE

1 Peel off top layer of cardboard with fingernail or sharp object.

2 Distress peeled surface with walnut ink.

3 To create circular pieces, punch photos, patterned paper, and cardstock. Ink edges. Embellish as desired (see photo).

4 Arrange all items, then adhere to folder.

Simple Sentiments

Add sweet messages of love to family members' holiday gifts:

You are the Christmas of my life, every day of my life.

To my Santa—
from the Mrs.

Winter is a time for frosty days and snowy nights—
a time for home.

Softly as a new snow you crept into my life.

The happiest moments of my life have been the few which I have spent in the bosom of my family.

—*Thomas Jefferson*

Love is The Reason Matchbox

Designer: Katie Hacker

SUPPLIES

Heart stamps: Small Hearts, All Night Media, *Plaid*

Alphabet stamps: Swirl, All Night Media, *Plaid*

Adhesive: Crafter's Pick The Ultimate!, *API*

5" length 24-gauge silver wire: ColourCraft, *Beadalon*

Assorted pink beads: Blue Moon Beads, *Elizabeth Ward & Co.*

Other: fuchsia and black ink; 1½" x 2" matchbox; dark pink, light pink, and white paper; pink vellum; pink chalk; cotton swab; 6" length of pink, gray, and mauve sheer ribbon; 1" silver heart frame; ½" white heart button; two ¾" clear flat glass marbles; fine-tip black pen or computer and printer; scissors

Finished size: 1½" x 2"

PREPARE

1 Cut light pink paper strip to cover outside of box.

2 Cut ⅝" vellum strip to fit around box.

3 Cut 2⅛" x 2" piece dark pink paper for inside of drawer.

4 Cut ¼" strip light pink paper to fit lengthwise in drawer.

5 Print "Love is the reason for it all" on white paper.

STAMP & EMBELLISH

1 Randomly stamp hearts on light pink paper strip with fuchsia.

2 Stamp "LOVE" on center of vellum strip with black.

3 Stamp heart on piece of light pink paper with black; apply pink chalk inside heart and trim.

4 Stamp mini heart on piece of dark pink paper with black; adhere glass marble over image and cut extra paper around marble. Repeat.

5 Stamp mini hearts on ¼" strip of light pink paper with black.

6 Stamp mini heart on piece of vellum; cut out.

ASSEMBLE

1 Adhere stamped light pink paper strip to outside of box.

2 Wrap stamped vellum strip around box with seam in back; adhere.

3 Adhere stamped, chalked heart to box.

4 Adhere marble with heart to box.

5 Adhere dark pink paper piece inside drawer and then adhere ¼" strip of light pink paper with hearts over it.

6 Adhere frame over sentiment, cut out, and adhere in drawer.

7 Adhere second marble with heart in drawer.

8 Adhere mini heart on vellum in drawer.

FINISH

1 Adhere two beads to the lower edge of the vellum to hold it in place. Glue four more beads between the vellum and the frame.

2 Adhere heart-shaped button and beads in drawer.

3 Punch two holes ½" apart on drawer's lower edge.

4 Thread ribbon through holes; wrap wire around ribbons.

5 Coil wire ends and thread bead on each end.

Bonus Ideas

■ Display the matchbox on a shelf with your favorite miniatures and collectibles.

■ Personalize the matchbox by replacing the contents of the drawer with your favorite small collectibles such as charms, beads, buttons, or glass pebbles.

■ Transform the matchbox into a gift tag with these easy steps:

  1 Punch two holes ¼" apart in the top of the drawer.

  2 Thread ribbon through the holes.

  3 Tie the ribbon to the gift.

■ Adhere the matchbox to a card, altered book, or collage for a unique miniature accent.

DESIGN CHALLENGE

THE CHALLENGE:
You are a saver and recycler who hates to throw things out! How can you give your collection of containers, boxes, and tins new life? We asked three designers to invent a new use for an everyday container. Their creative ideas will inspire you to turn something old into something bold.

JENNI'S SOLUTION
Jenni created a Christmas gift box from a familiar mint tin. She covered the outside with papers and accents, and tucked a tag booklet inside.

Inside

Hidden Treasures
Designer: Jenni Bowlin

SUPPLIES

Patterned paper:
 Christmas words, *Daisy D's*
 Brick Red Diamond, *K&Company*

Tin mint box: *Altoids*

Stamps:
 Elegant Star, *PrintWorks*
 Hidden Treasures, *Toybox Rubber Stamps*

Black solvent ink

Antique silver key, bubble numbers: *Li'l Davis Designs*

Liquid adhesive: Perfect Paper Matte, *USArtQuest*

Ivory acrylic paint: *Delta*

Other: foam brush, sandpaper

Finished size: 3¾" x 2½"

INSTRUCTIONS

1. Sand outside of tin. Paint bottom and sides and let dry.

2. Stamp star on sides with solvent ink.

3. Trace lid shape on Christmas paper and cut out. Adhere to lid.

4. Cut 2" strip red paper and adhere to lid center.

5. Brush ivory paint lightly across red paper with fingers and let dry. Stamp phrase.

6. Apply adhesive to top to seal project using foam brush; adhere key and numbers while adhesive is still wet.

MINI CHRISTMAS BOOKLET

A petite Christmas booklet tucked inside a creative gift box makes a sentimental holiday memento. Include photos accented with brads, bookplates, tags, fibers, lace, photo holders, vellum envelopes, ribbons, and letters.

'Tis The Season

Designer: Doreen McBride

DOREEN'S SOLUTION

Doreen gave a small coffee container a makeover. Her white and blue color combination expresses the cool, crisp temperatures of the holiday season. This lidded container makes great gift packaging.

SUPPLIES

All supplies from Close To My Heart unless otherwise noted.

Cardstock: Moonstruck (blue), Ultra White

Dot patterned paper: Moonstruck

Dye ink: Moonstruck; Exclusive Inks

Rubber stamps: sentiment, pine tree (from 'Tis the Season set)

Coffee container: General Foods International Coffee, *Kraft Foods*

Snowflake eyelets: *Bizzy Bee Eyelets*

Permanent adhesive tape: *Tombow*

Other: blue organdy ribbon, eyelet-setting tools

Finished size: 2½" x 4⅛" x 2½"

INSTRUCTIONS

❶ Cut paper to 2⅜" x 12" and adhere around container; place seam in back. Cut blue cardstock strip and adhere over seam.

❷ To create accent piece, cut white cardstock to 1¾" x 2½"; lightly sponge with ink. Stamp sentiment. Mat with blue cardstock. Set eyelet. Stamp two trees on white cardstock, cut out and adhere to sentiment. Adhere piece to container front.

❸ Using lid as template, cut out paper to fit lid and adhere.

❹ Wrap container with ribbon and tie bow on top. Adhere eyelet to bow.

Christmas Container

Designer: Kelly Lautenbach

SUPPLIES

Cardstock: red, sage

Chip canister: Torengos, *Procter & Gamble*

Rubber stamps: Holly, Merry Christmas (from Holly Christmas Set), *Close To My Heart*

Solvent ink: Black, Olive, Red; StazOn, *Tsukineko*

Small hole punch

Accents:

    "'Tis the Season" ribbon: Ribbon Words, *Making Memories*

    "Made by Hand" twill tape: Haberdasherie, *7gypsies*

    Gingham ribbon: green, black

    Buttons: Savory, *SEI*

    Beads: Accent Beads, *Close To My Heart*

    Thin silver wire

Wire cutters

Finished size: 8½" x 3"

CONTAINER

❶ Rub Olive ink on top and bottom container edges and let dry.

❷ Randomly stamp holly, berries, and "Merry Christmas" on sage cardstock.

❸ Cut paper to fit unpainted portion of container; adhere.

❹ Punch small holes approx. 1" apart around container top edge.

❺ Cut long length of wire. Thread wire through hole in top edge. Add beads and buttons. Loop wire loosely over top edge and insert in next hole (see Figure a). Repeat around entire top. Twist ends together to finish and tie ribbons to wire.

❻ Cut out stamped holly leaves and berries and adhere to container.

TAG

❶ Cut tag from stamped cardstock and mat with red cardstock.

❷ Make wire hanger for tag and embellish with buttons.

❸ Adhere tag to front.

a

Loop wire

DESIGN CHALLENGE

THE CHALLENGE:

You need a card, small gift, or centerpiece. But the projects you like best in your idea books aren't for the occasion you need them for. Help! What do you do now?

See what two of our designers did. Then try it yourself, and send us a photo of the results.

CHALLENGE #1: We loved the look of Alisa Bangerter's Be Mine valentine card from *Paper Crafts* Feb. 2004 issue—but we had a birthday to celebrate and wanted to catch up with an old friend.

Thinking of You Card

Designer: Nancy Church

SUPPLIES

Green cardstock

Green striped paper: *Pebbles Inc.*

Vellum

"Thinking of You" sticker: Deja Views, *C-Thru Ruler Co.*

Patterned fabric: floral, orange/yellow checked

Metal-rimmed tag: *Making Memories*

Yellow flax: Waxy Flax, *Scrapworks*

Silver butterfly charm

Green chalk

Other: white thread, sewing machine

Finished size: 4¼" x 5½"

INSTRUCTIONS

1 Make card base with cardstock; cover with striped paper.

2 Cut strip of floral fabric. Tear strip of vellum slightly wider than fabric; chalk edges. Machinestitch fabric and vellum to card. Add sticker.

3 Cut square of floral fabric to fit inside tag. Stitch to tag.

4 Tear strip of checked fabric; tie to top of tag. Tie charm around fabric knot with flax.

5 Adhere tag to card.

Happy Birthday Card

Designer: Wendy Anderson

SUPPLIES

Cardstock: brown, cream, pink

Brown patterned cardstock: *Making Memories*

Ink: Sand, Soft Sand; Memories, *Stewart Superior*

Pink round and flat eyelets: Eyelets, Dotlets, *Doodlebug Design*

"happy birthday" metal accent: *Making Memories*

Picture fasteners: *Making Memories*

Pink gingham ribbon: *Impress Rubber Stamps*

Cupcake sticker: *Debbie Mumm*

Other: white thread, sewing machine, metal adhesive

Finished size: 4¼" x 5¼"

INSTRUCTIONS

1 Make card base with cream cardstock. Ink edges with Soft Sand and Sand.

2 Cut brown patterned cardstock to fit card front.

3 Cut pink cardstock to fit bottom of patterned piece. Ink edges; adhere to brown patterned cardstock.

4 Machine-stitch around cardstock piece. Add ribbon where colors meet; adhere ends in back. Adhere "happy birthday" accent to ribbon with metal adhesive.

5 Adhere cupcake sticker to brown cardstock and trim. Mat with cream cardstock and ink edges. Add round eyelet and ribbon.

6 Attach picture fasteners to cardstock piece with flat eyelets (see photo); slide cupcake piece under fasteners. Adhere cardstock piece to card front.

CHALLENGE #2: We love Valentine's Day and Teresa Synder's Lollipop Flower Pot, from *Paper Crafts* Feb. 2004 issue—but we're coming up on fall and need something for Thanksgiving and Christmas.

Christmas Crate

Designer: Wendy Anderson

SUPPLIES

Handmade paper: green, red, *Provo Craft*

Textured cardstock: gold, green, red; Beaded Vine, Artistic Scrapper, *Creative Imaginations*

Gold vellum

Wood crate: *Wal-Mart*

Ribbon: wide gold, assorted for gifts, *Offray*

Gold wire: *Artistic Wire*

Star punch: *Emagination Crafts*

⅛" hole punch

Excelsior

Floral foam

Bamboo skewers

Other: spray adhesive or adhesive sheets, adhesive dots, pencil

Finished size: 13" x 6½" x 5¼"

TREE AND GIFTS

❶ Cut three tree pieces from green textured cardstock, using pattern on p. 280.

❷ Punch holes along edges and whipstitch tree pieces together with gold wire, leaving long wire tails at top.

❸ Punch three stars from vellum and adhere together at top of tree, with wire tails in center. Curl wire tails around pencil.

❹ Cut skewers to various lengths.

❺ Cut pieces of handmade paper twice as long as you'd like for the gifts. Fold paper pieces over top of skewers and glue in place. Add ribbon as desired.

BASE

❶ Cover sides of crate with gold and red textured cardstock, using spray adhesive or adhesive sheets. Tie wide gold ribbon around crate.

❷ Cut floral foam pieces to fit inside tree and box; adhere in place. Insert skewer into foam in tree.

❸ Adhere excelsior over foam in crate. Arrange tree and gift skewers.

WHIPSTITCH

Use a whipping motion over the edges to finish.

Bonus Idea

The Christmas Crate will come in handy when your family draws names for Christmas gift-giving this year. Write each person's name on the back of a gift skewer. Then, let everyone pull a skewer from the crate to find out whose name goes on their shopping list.

Pumpkin Planter and Tag

Designer: Nancy Church

SUPPLIES

For both:

Cardstock: brown, green (2 shades), orange (3 shades), *Bazzill Basics Paper*

Orange chalk: Chalklets, *EK Success*

Fine sandpaper

For planter:

Galvanized tin planter: *Michaels*

Leaf punches: *EK Success*

Paper crimper

Excelsior

Floral foam

Bamboo skewers

For tag:

Vellum

Black gingham ribbon: *Offray*

Rectangle punch: *Fiskars*

Font: 2Ps Chicken Shack, *www.twopeasinabucket.com*

Silver brads

THE
SOLUTIONS
Nancy and Wendy changed the containers and the hearts and candy to create these striking Christmas and Autumn centerpieces.

Finished size approx. 14" x 7" x 3"

PUMPKIN ARRANGEMENT

❶ Cut pumpkins from all three shades of orange cardstock, using patterns on p. 281. Create matching pairs so they can be adhered together.

❷ Chalk edges and distress with sandpaper. Crimp some pumpkins with paper crimper.

❸ Cut stems from brown cardstock, using pattern. Punch leaves from green cardstock. Adhere to pumpkins.

❹ Cut skewers to various lengths; adhere pumpkins in back-to-back pairs on skewers.

❺ Trim and fit floral foam tightly inside planter and adhere in place. Adhere excelsior on top and insert pumpkin skewers.

TAG

❶ Cut tag from orange cardstock. Cut strips from other shades of orange cardstock; adhere to tag. Chalk edges and distress with sandpaper.

❷ Print "I think you're the pick of the patch!" on vellum. Attach to tag with silver brads.

❸ Punch two rectangles in top and tie to planter with ribbon.

CRATE PATTERN

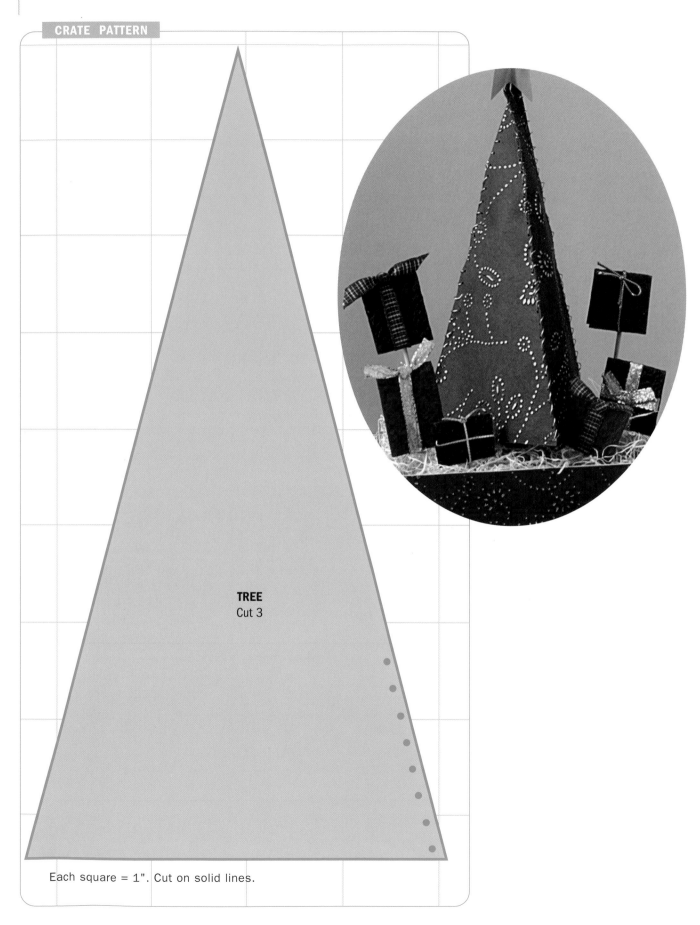

TREE
Cut 3

Each square = 1". Cut on solid lines.

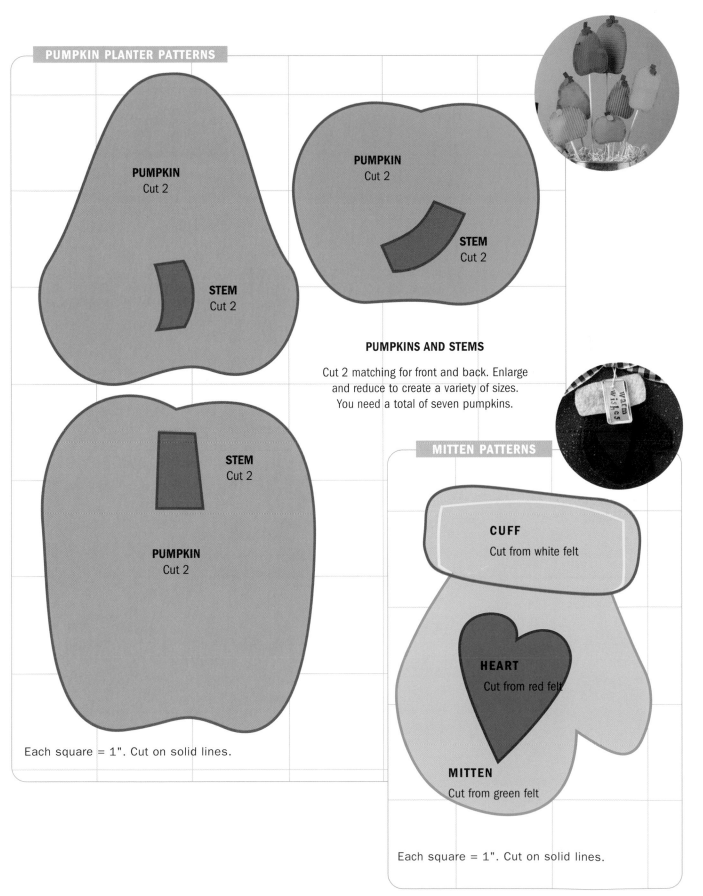

PUMPKIN PLANTER PATTERNS

PUMPKIN
Cut 2

STEM
Cut 2

PUMPKIN
Cut 2

STEM
Cut 2

PUMPKINS AND STEMS

Cut 2 matching for front and back. Enlarge
and reduce to create a variety of sizes.
You need a total of seven pumpkins.

STEM
Cut 2

PUMPKIN
Cut 2

Each square = 1". Cut on solid lines.

MITTEN PATTERNS

CUFF
Cut from white felt

HEART
Cut from red felt

MITTEN
Cut from green felt

Each square = 1". Cut on solid lines.

Kindness Treat Bag

Designer: Wendy Anderson

SUPPLIES

Yellow patterned cardstock: *O'Scrap!*

Cream cardstock

"kindness" sticker: *O'Scrap!*

Green grosgrain ribbon: *Offray*

Cream eyelets: *Doodlebug Design*

Font: P22 Garamouche, *P22 Type Foundry*

Ink: Sand, Soft Sand; Memories, *Stewart Superior*

Other: white thread, sewing machine, cellophane bag, butterscotch candy or lemon drops, hole punch

Finished size: 7½" x 4¼"

INSTRUCTIONS

1 Cut yellow cardstock into two strips and adhere together (see Figure a).

2 Fold to make bag (see Figure b).

3 Fill cellophane bag with candy; fold top over twice.

4 Place candy bag in treat bag, positioning folded top of candy bag inside top of treat bag (see Figure c). Punch two holes through front flap and front of bag. Set eyelets through flap only.

5 Print "your" and "means so much" on cream cardstock, allowing 2½" between lines. Cut out and adhere sticker to center; ink edges with Soft Sand and Sand. Machine stitch along edges. Adhere to front of bag.

6 Print "Thank you!" on cream cardstock. Cut into tag and ink edges. Add eyelet and tie tag to treat bag with ribbon.

CHALLENGE #3: We loved Linda Beeson's sweet Valentine Treat Bags from *Paper Crafts* Feb. 2004 issue—they were a perfect inspiration for creating other small gifts.

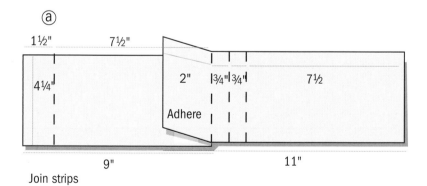

ⓐ

1½"   7½"

4¼"   2"   ¾" ¾"   7½

Adhere

9"   11"

Join strips

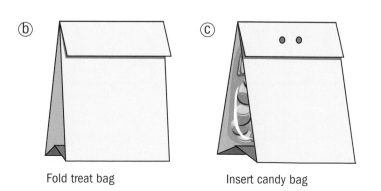

ⓑ   ⓒ

Fold treat bag   Insert candy bag

THE SOLUTIONS
Wendy and Nancy changed the papers and accents to create this sunny yellow "thank you" gift and warm holiday gift bag.

Warm Wishes Treat Bag

Designer: Nancy Church

SUPPLIES

Patterned paper: Wild Berry Splatter, *Bo-Bunny Press*

Metal-rimmed vellum tag: *Making Memories*

Felt: green, red, white

Alphabet stamps: *Hero Arts*

Black ink

Green gingham ribbon: *Offray*

Other: hole punch, string, cellophane bag, malt balls or hot cocoa mix

Finished size: 4¾" x 5"

INSTRUCTIONS

❶ Follow steps 1–4 for Kindness Treat Bag to assemble treat bag, filling it with malt balls or hot cocoa mix. *Note: Adjust measurements as desired.*

❷ Cut mitten pieces, using pattern on p. 281. Adhere to bag.

❸ Tie treat bag closed with ribbon.

❹ Stamp "warm wishes" on vellum tag. Tie to bow.

Tips & Tricks

Why wait until the New Year to get organized? Make a resolution to put everything in its place today. A recent article reported that the average person spends more than 78 hours each year trying to track down misplaced items at home. That's over three days a year that could have been spent stamping! It can be overwhelming to think about getting organized. Here's how to get started:

MAKE A LIST

Think about what you need to store and how you use each item. It's great to have everything stored away, but remember to keep your frequently used and favorite items easily accessible. Follow our checklist to make sure you have the stamping fundamentals within reach.

INKS

○ Black
○ Watermark
○ Colors I use most
○ Other: _____

STAMPS

○ Alphabets & sentiments
○ Holiday
○ Favorites
○ Other: _____

EMBOSSING POWDER

○ Clear
○ Black
○ UTEE
○ Colors I use most
○ Other: _____

TOOLS

○ Adhesives
○ Scissors
○ Embossing heat tool
○ Eyelet setter
○ Stamp cleaner
○ Other: _____

Use this as a starter list and store all of your items just like you store your fundamentals, keeping the fundamentals on top and near your work area. Trade or give away those items you no longer use. This makes more room for supplies you do use!

Keeping a list of your supplies helps to manage your organization. Keep this list handy and update it often so you can easily check if you have the basic supplies needed for a project. As supplies are used up while stamping, make a note at the bottom of your list and refer to it as your shopping list the next time you hit the craft or stamp store.

STORE SUPPLIES

If you don't already have containers and organizers for your stamping supplies, consider the following tips before you buy anything:

Out of sight means out of mind. If you can't clearly see your supplies it's easy to forget what you have on hand. Consider clear containers such as glass jars, baskets, or plastic frames turned upside down. If you don't use clear containers, carefully label other containers so you can read at a glance what is inside.

Use a system that makes sense to you. If alphabetizing isn't your thing, consider color-coding your containers. Use one color for stamps, another for inks, another for embossing supplies, etc. Color-code your labels or use colored ink when writing them.

Store supplies to make them last.

Rubber stamps: rubber-side down and out of sunlight and heat. *Note: Many people store unmounted stamps on plastic within three-ring binders.*

Ink pads: lids closed tightly and stored lid-side up. *Note: The exception for this is pigment inks. Store these upside down.*

Pens and markers: caps tightly closed and stored horizontally.

Reinkers: top tightly closed and out of sunlight and heat.

Paper: flat and within a folder or other container to protect edges from getting mangled.

BONUS STORAGE TIPS

Stamp It! readers have a wealth of helpful tips! Here are some of our favorite storage ideas.

I store my un-mounted rubber stamps in empty CD cases. I take the insides out of each case so there's just a clear empty shell. Then I line the inside of the case with a piece of cardstock, which has been stamped with the images that will be stored in that particular case. This storage method keeps me organized and reduces the amount of space I use for my stamps. The great thing is you can store these CD cases in regular CD holders.

Cindy Keery
Abbotsford, BC, Canada

I always got frustrated when using my alphabet stamps because I'd have trouble finding a particular letter, and it was difficult to keep them in order in the box that they came in. I went to a local, well-known discount store and purchased a clear "car garage," which is supposed to be used for toy cars. It has two sides with small compartments perfect for the alphabet stamps! I put one alphabet set on each side. Now the sets stay in alphabetical order all the time.

Leslie Block
Boyds, MD

I keep my stamps in a tackle box. I was going to buy a stamp storage box, but much to my surprise, I saw that tackle boxes have many of the same features and are much less expensive. It is easy to carry with me when I scrap away from home, and the see-through boxes are great!

Melissa Supan
Duluth, MN

I have tried a variety of ways to store my ever-increasing stamp collection. What I have found to be the best system for me is an old dresser! The top drawer holds all my Christmas stamps, organized by similar design styles in inexpensive clear plastic boxes. The next drawer has all my background, frame, shadow, and flower stamps. The remaining drawers hold common themed stamps. All is organized without being too rigid. I always find what I am looking for and cleanup is easy.

Another good idea: I have plastic containers with drawers. These work great, too. Each drawer holds a common theme or style of stamp. But, after six containers and my stamp collection still growing, I knew I needed something much BIGGER.

Kim Kasanic
Farmington Hills, MI

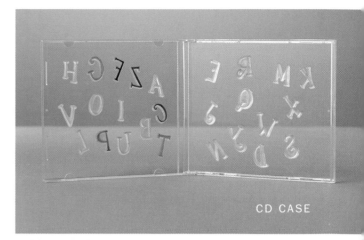

CD CASE

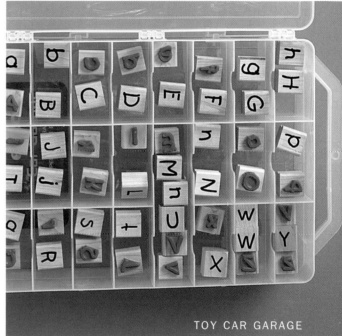

TOY CAR GARAGE

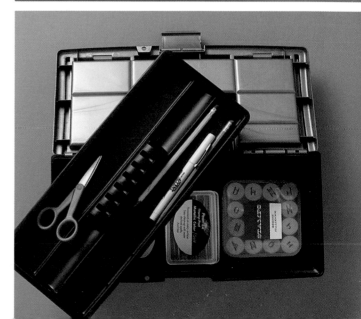

Organizers From Around The House

Don't let that old REVOLVING SPICE RACK gather dust—use it to organize your paper crafting supplies. Store buttons, brads, glue, glitter, and eyelets inside spice bottles, putting the tallest bottles on the top shelf. For ribbon, fiber, and twine, make a hole in the jar lid with a nail and thread the material out the top; then just pull and cut. Add bottles of glue and paint to fill extra spaces.

PLASTIC AMMUNITION BOXES hold the alphabet stamps that Jenn Nunley used to both love and hate. "They get all mixed up and out of order, even upside down," she wrote. But that was before she discovered that the .45 size ammo box is perfect for her PSX and small Hero Arts stamps. So now it's love, not war, in the stamp department.

Reader Cleaning Tips

We asked you to share your best tips for cleaning rubber stamps and your response gave us a wealth of information. To get rid of the toughest inks and keep your stamps in tip-top shape, try some of these ingenious ideas from our readers using products you already have on hand. Happy cleaning!

"The best cleaner I've found for rubber stamps is a nail brush and hand-sanitizing gel. The brush is great for all stamps, especially those with deep etchings. The sanitizing gel takes off all inks—including the permanent ones—and it's easy to clean off the stamp with a damp paper towel."

Kim Rayko

"An easy and fun way to remove excess ink is with a solution of equal parts rubbing alcohol and baking soda. Set just the rubber portion of the stamp in a paste for a few minutes. Then rinse with warm water."

Nancy Black,
Willseyville, NY

"Clean stains off of your stamps by inking the rubber with a clear embossing ink. Let it sit overnight and then clean as you usually would."

Lisa Lang,
Liberty Township, OH

"For tough ink stains on my stamps I use plain old vegetable oil from the kitchen. Liberally apply it to the rubber with a cotton ball. Let it sit for about 10 minutes, then rinse with dish soap and warm water. It's inexpensive, always on hand, and it works like a charm every time."

Jan Williams,
Mississauga, Ontario, Canada

Refreshing STORAGE CONTAINER

Clear mint containers make instant storage for the tiniest of paper crafting supplies. This Tic Tac container keeps brads, eyelets, and other embellishments convenient and visible while you create. Just add a label describing the contents. Flip-top mint containers make handy dispensers as well. A side bonus—your minty breath will make you a great paper crafting companion!

CLEARLY ORGANIZED

With all the useful and versatile paper crafting tools available, organization can become a challenge. Wouldn't it be great to see all of your tools at a glance? You can! This over-the-door shoe organizer, available at most department or discount stores, works for storing more than sneakers. You can tuck all kinds of paper crafting tools and supplies into the see-through pockets, including stamps, ink pads, punches, adhesives, and more. When you need something, you'll be able to find it quickly and easily.

INSTANT WORKSPACE CLEANUP— AT THE TURN OF A PAGE

Adhesives, inks, paints or markers will never mess up your workspace again! Katie Young uses old, outdated magazines (but not *Paper Crafts*) to save her tabletop. Place the magazine underneath your work and allow the glue and ink run over onto the pages. When the page is a big mess, just turn to the next page for a new, clean surface. Magazine ink won't rub off on your projects or hands as newspaper ink does. Thank you, Katie, for submitting that great idea.